The Intellectual
Construction of
America

The

University of

North Carolina

Press

Chapel Hill and

London

The Intellectual
Construction of
America

EXCEPTIONALISM AND IDENTITY

FROM 1492 TO 1800

Jack P. Greene

The paper in this book meets the

guidelines for permanence and durability

of the Committee on Production Guidelines for

Book Longevity of the Council

on Library Resources.

Library of Congress

Cataloging-in-Publication Data

Greene, Jack P.

The intellectual construction of America :

exceptionalism and identity from 1492 to 1800 /

by Jack P. Greene.

p.   cm.

Includes bibliographical references and index.

ISBN 0-8078-2097-0 (alk. paper)

1. National characteristics, American.

2. United States—Civilization—To 1783.

3. United States—Civilization—1783–1865.

I. Title.

E162.G85   1993

973—dc20   92-46707

CIP

97 96 95 94 93   5 4 3 2 1

FOR AMY

Contents

Preface, xi

Prologue, 1

1. EXPECTATIONS
The European Fabrication of America in the Sixteenth Century
8

2. ENCOUNTERS
Projection and Design in the Construction of English America,
1580–1690
34

3. EXPERIENCES
The Behavioral Articulation of British America, 1690–1760
63

4. EVALUATIONS
The Conceptual Identification of British America, 1715–1775
95

5. EXAMINATIONS
The European Response to the American Revolution, 1776–1800
130

6. EXPLANATIONS
Revolution and Redefinition, 1774–1800
162

Epilogue, 200

Index, 211

Illustrations

Renaissance Discoveries, 2

Vespucci Awakens a Sleeping America, 9

America at the End of the Sixteenth Century, 14

Invasion of America, 19

Mutiny in Jamaica, 23

Utopia, 27

A Century of Spanish Activities in America, 31

East Coast of North America in the Late Sixteenth Century, 35

America, 41

Connecticut Colony Seal, 43

New York Colony Coat of Arms, 44

Design of Philadelphia, 57

View of Savannah, 59

Sachem and Soldier, 64

Colonel Jacque, 71

Tobacco Plantation, 74

Hercules and the Waggoner, 77

Public Buildings of Williamsburg, 82

View of Philadelphia, 86

View of Boston, 88

Town and Country, 91

Community Scenes, 97

John Bartram's House and Garden, 103

New England View, 108

New York City Hall, 113

Tryon's Palace, 115

Faneuil Hall, 120

Charleston Exchange, 121

Redwood Library, 126

Nassau Hall, 127

America as Example, 133

Pennsylvania State Seal, 137

America as a Land of Freedom, 144

An American Settlement, 146

America and Fame, 153

Liberty Displaying the Arts and Sciences, 157

Maryland State Seal, 165

An American New Cleared Farm, 172

View from Bushongo Tavern, 176

Seat of Moses Gill, 181

View of Mulberry Plantation, 186

The Beckoning West, 190

A Settled Rural Landscape, 192

Seat of Colonel George Boyd, 194

Philadelphia Public Buildings, 198

Invitation from America, 203

Preface

This small volume represents a modest expansion of the Anson G. Phelps Lectures given at New York University in the fall of 1990. It uses literary evidence to explicate the changing content of the intellectual constructs produced to identify the new entity *America* between Columbus's first encounter with the New World in 1492 and 1800. According special attention to the ideas of distinctiveness that powerfully informed the identification of America throughout the early modern era, it is also a study of the origins of the concept of American exceptionalism.

I wish to thank New York University, the Department of History, the Schools of Arts and Sciences and Law and Chancellor L. Jay Oliva, Dean C. Duncan Rice, Professors Warren Dean and William Nelson, and, most of all, Professor Patricia U. Bonomi for the invitation to give the Phelps Lectures and for their splendid hospitality while I was doing so. I am also grateful to those who attended the lectures for their questions and comments. Richard and Claudia Bushman, Thelma Foote, Ned Landsman, J. R. Pole, Alden Vaughan, and many others raised questions that helped me to refine my argument. Thad W. Tate and an anonymous referee read the first draft of the manuscript for the University of North Carolina Press, and their suggestions contributed to major improvements. So also did the counsel of Amy Turner Bushnell, to whom the volume is dedicated. Both the University of California, Irvine, and The Johns Hopkins University provided time and resources for the reading on which the volume is based. Jacqueline Megan Greene prepared the index. Carla Gerona and Karin Wulf helped read proofs. J. R. Pole and Amy Turner Bushnell offered many valuable suggestions about the illustration captions.

Baltimore, Maryland   September 7, 1992   Jack P. Greene

The Intellectual
Construction of
America

Prologue

As a physical entity, the two large continents that since the beginning of the sixteenth century have been known as America were every bit as old as the Eurasian land mass from which they were separated by the world's two largest oceans. As a conceptual entity, however, America, as the Mexican historian Edmundo O'Gorman correctly informed us more than three decades ago,[1] is a relatively recent invention, an intellectual construct brought into being during what we now know as the early modern era. Divided into numerous cultural and linguistic groups of various sizes and socioeconomic and political organizations, the indigenous inhabitants of the Western Hemisphere apparently lacked any sense of the entirety of the lands in which they dwelled and so had no need for a general name for them beyond the designations they gave to their world as a whole. Thus, the idea of America as a place distinct from Europe, Africa, and Asia initially arose out of the Europeans' need to come to terms with and to incorporate into their existing cosmography a vast region previously unknown to them.

From its very beginnings, however, the concept of America has referred not only to a specific geographical space but also to the meanings, the characterizations, that were attached to that space by its many contemporary interpreters. Of course, those meanings invariably referred to the physical attributes, the distinctive geographical structures and configurations, of America. Even more importantly, however, they were the products of two other variables deriving out of efforts, starting within a decade after the contact initiated by Colum-

1. Edmundo O'Gorman, *The Invention of America: An Inquiry into the Historical Nature of the New World and the Meaning of History* (Bloomington, Ind., 1961).

Renaissance Discoveries. Entitled Nova Reperta, *this engraving illustrates the idea of America as a blank slate and the Renaissance as a new era. It presents America, illustrated by an essentially open map, as first among many Renaissance discoveries, including the lodestone, gunpowder and other military technology, the printing press, improved metal clockworks, dyewoods, and alchemy. A young woman directs attention to these new phenomena, while an elderly man representing old ways departs from the scene. From Johanes Stradanus [Jan van der Straet], a Flemish resident of Florence,* Nova Reperta *(Antwerp, 1600). Courtesy of the Folger Shakespeare Library, Title Page, Art Volume f52.*

bus and his party in the fall of 1492, of various European invaders and immigrants to establish their mastery over the region. First were the aspirations, goals, standards, and norms the immigrants and their progeny hoped to achieve and to implement in their new homes and their interpretations of indigenous resistance to their pursuit of those ends. Second were the social results of two sets of interrelated but analytically separable interactions that occurred as a result of their efforts: the interactions—the recurring clashes and subsequent integration—among the area's many indigenous societies and the various invading immigrant cultures and those between these inhabitants, both old and new, and the physical entities they occupied.

If these variables principally shaped the meanings with which America's new inhabitants and their many observers invested or endowed the new conceptual entity of America, those meanings, as they have altered over time in response to shifting circumstances, have, to an important degree, in turn been chiefly responsible for shaping the changing identities of America as a whole and of its many constituent parts, the images by which America has been known and characterized and through which it has been rendered tractable and comprehensible to both its inhabitants and the rest of the world. This book explores at a general level the early stages of this ongoing process of identification between 1492 and the establishment of the new federal union of the United States during the closing decades of the eighteenth century. Beginning with an analysis of the expectations generated by America among its earliest European interpreters, it examines how successive generations of inhabitants and observers of continental Anglo-America encountered, experienced, examined, evaluated, and explained America.

This subject is a venerable one in American historiography. Indeed, if, to a significant degree, every society's sense of collective self depends heavily upon conceptions of what it has been, historians have played a principal, though by no means an exclusive, role in the formation of American identity ever since the beginnings of the professionalization of American history with George Bancroft during the middle decades of the nineteenth century. Culminating in the work of Frederick Jackson Turner, one powerful strain of American historical scholarship has emphasized the special character of the American experience.

This interpretation stressed the extent to which the allegedly wide open spaces and extensive resources of the North American continent and the capacious opportunities they presented to the industrious and resourceful immigrant proved uncongenial to Old World institutions, habits, and mentalities and operated to produce a society—as well as a history and an identity—that, in its organization, psychology, and dynamics, was dramatically different. Altogether more open, more expansive, more equal, more democratic, and more congenial to the aspirations of ordinary free people than the societies of the Old World, the American societies created by immigrant Europeans, according to this view, were, if not sui generis, at least distinctly American.

This interpretation of the character and meaning of the American experience did not long go unchallenged. Already during the last decade of the nineteenth century and the first decades of the twentieth, some historians were examining it and condemning its uncritical underlying parochialism and chauvinism. Insisting that the colonial past should be seen in terms of the larger imperial context of which the North American colonies were a part, the imperial historians emphasized the close connection between them and the British Isles and other contemporary British colonies in the West Indies, the Atlantic, and Canada. At the same time, the Progressive historians endeavored to show that the political and economic life of the American nation could be interpreted in terms of the same categories of social and political analysis that were then being used by historians in Europe to describe the development of the Old World.

Although these efforts raised serious questions about the idea that the United States had a distinctive history that could only be written in its own terms, they never succeeded in entirely supplanting it. Kept alive through the 1920s and 1930s by the debates over why both working-class radicalism and socialism failed to develop much vigor in the United States,[2] it enjoyed an astonishing revival during the quarter century following the conclusion of World War II. Indeed, a central assumption of both the emerging American studies movement and the so-called consensus historians was that America, at least in its continental British-American variant, was and had always been fundamentally different from Europe and that any variations among localities, regions, or social groups within America were far less important than the similarities that made American culture, defined as the culture of those areas that became the United States, different from that of Europe.

Building on Tocqueville's observation that "the position of the Americans" was "quite exceptional,"[3] scholars and social and political commentators during the 1950s and 1960s articulated what came to be known as the concept of *American exceptionalism*. Seeking to

2. Seymour Martin Lipsett, "American Exceptionalism Reaffirmed," in *Is America Different?: A New Look at American Exceptionalism*, ed. Byron E. Shafer (Oxford, 1991), 2–3.

3. Alexis de Tocqueville, *Democracy in America*, 2 vols. (New York, 1960), 2:36.

identify those "elements of American life" and those "distinctively American *clusters* of characteristics" that seemed to make the United States "unique" and "different in crucial ways from most other countries,"[4] these commentators stressed the predominance of the middle class and the absence of class conflict among the free population as well as the lack of divisive debates among rival social ideologists.

As they sought to explain why the United States did not seem to conform to the Marxist "model of societal progression for the developed nations of the world," some commentators even went on to argue that the United States was an *"exemplary* nation" that either "by Providence" or by the wisdom of its founders had been exempted "from the laws of decadence or the laws of history." "As the *first new, self-conscious nation*, able to control its own fate and future," the United States began, according to this view, and as Daniel Bell has recently reaffirmed, as "a modern civil society" that explicitly rejected the old European social order and accepted "the principle[s] of toleration and diversity, and the consensus by plural communities on rules of procedure and rules for negotiation, within the frame of constitutionalism," an "open society," in other words, in which "each man was free to 'make himself' and (he hoped) to make a fortune."[5]

As two later generations of historians have sought over the past quarter century to relate the American to the broader European past, they have subjected the idea of *American exceptionalism* to closer scrutiny and found it seriously deficient. With reference to the colonial period, the emergence of a deepening interest in social history beginning in the mid-1960s produced a deluge of specialized studies that seemed to indicate that in terms of many of the basic conditions of their lives, the family, community, and social structures they created, their patterns of population movement, the cultural and religious values to which they subscribed, the economic behavior they exhibited, and even the dynamics and frames of reference of their public lives the experiences of colonial Americans did not depart radically from those of contemporary Britons in the home islands. "One by one," Joyce Appleby noted in 1984, "the props under the notion of

4. Shafer, ed., *Is America Different?*, v–vi, viii; Lipsett, "American Exceptionalism Reaffirmed," 1.

5. Daniel Bell, "The 'Hegelian Secret': Civil Society and American Exceptionalism," in Shafer, ed., *Is America Different?*, 51, 61, 70.

American exceptionalism," at least as that notion had been applied to the colonial period, "have disappeared,"[6] and John Murrin has noted that in my own effort to interpret the findings of recent social history literature on the colonies I have "destroyed American exceptionalism, or most of it, for the colonial period."[7]

Powerful as it is, however, the current effort to assimilate colonial American to early modern European history takes little account of an extraordinarily large body of contemporary testimony from the sixteenth through the eighteenth century and beyond that did indeed see America as a special, and in many ways even an exceptional, place. Contrary to what many modern scholars have implied, few, if any, contemporary interpreters envisioned America as a place without social dependents, social stratification, social conflict, or social failure. They did not tout it as an entity that would provide universal success for its inhabitants or elevate all of them to the middle class. Most of them did, however, depict it, in comparative terms, as an exceptionally promising field for the pursuit—and realization—of collective as well as individual aspirations.

Far from being the creation of later historians and social analysts, then, the concept of American exceptionalism with its positive connotations was present at the very creation of America. Rooted in the earliest efforts by Europeans to come to terms with the newfound continents on the western side of the Atlantic and the new societies they were creating there, this concept, already by the end of the sixteenth century and well before the English had succeeded in establishing permanent settlements anywhere in the Americas, had become one of the principal components in the identification of America. During the next two centuries, moreover, the English experience in North America and the eventual establishment of the independent and extended republic of the United States during the last quarter of the eighteenth century only served to enhance its explanatory authority for those many con-

6. Joyce Appleby, "Value and Society," in *Colonial British America: Essays in the New History of the Early Modern Era*, ed. Jack P. Greene and J. R. Pole (Baltimore, 1984), 304.

7. John M. Murrin, "The Irrelevance and Relevance of Colonial New England," *Reviews in American History* 18 (1990): 180. For a general critique of the concept of American exceptionalism as it has been applied to later periods and to labor history, see Sean Wilentz, "Against Exceptionalism: Class Consciousness and the American Labor Movement, 1790–1820," *International Labor and Working Class History* 26 (1984): 1–24.

temporaries who sought—through their words and their behavior—
to articulate or to realize the meaning of America. By the beginning
of the nineteenth century the idea of America as an exceptional entity
had long been an integral component in the identification of America.

Of course, at no point during the long colonial period did all contemporaries subscribe to this essentially benign and celebratory conception of America. A parallel—and every bit as ancient—counter-
tradition saw America as a nursery of malignant forces: a place of
ruthless exploitation, profound moral corruption, palpable cultural regress, and even marked physical degeneration. Yet this unflattering
tradition implicitly assumed that, in its essential character, America
was sharply distinguishable from, if patently inferior to, the Old
World. Whether positive or negative, then, contemporary conceptions
of America during the early modern era often assumed that the New
World of America was a special place that deviated sharply from the
Old World societies of Europe.

Indeed, the very pervasiveness and persistence of the assumption of American distinctiveness throughout the colonial era strongly
suggests that modern analysts are making a mistake not to take it
seriously. If the early modern inventors of America were wrong in
thinking that social conditions there differed markedly from those
in Europe, how could such an idea have enjoyed such widespread
currency for so long—and why? Unless we are prepared to dismiss
such a ubiquitous notion as little more than self-serving hyperbole or
cruel illusion, we must consider more fully precisely what it meant
to the people who articulated and used it, how it served to help them
organize, characterize, and achieve mastery over the new worlds they
were envisioning, creating, and observing in America. In particular,
we need to consider whether, if America was not exceptional in the
sense modern scholars have employed that term, it was exceptional
from the points of view of—and within the terms employed by—
contemporaries. Only by asking and tentatively trying to answer such
questions will we be able to understand what significance to attribute
to the notion of exceptionalism in the fabrication of the New World
during the early modern period.

This volume will consider two principal subjects: first, the changing
patterns of identification developed to comprehend the new conceptual
entity of America during its first three centuries, and second, the place
of the notion of exceptionalism in those patterns.

CHAPTER ONE

Expectations

THE EUROPEAN FABRICATION

OF AMERICA IN THE SIXTEENTH

CENTURY

When Columbus dropped anchor at the island he called San Salvador, he initiated the process by which a series of very different—and very old—worlds and a rich variety of places, cultures, and peoples were slowly revealed to an astonished Europe. As Europeans gradually came to grasp the immensity and complexity of some of those worlds during the sixteenth century, they both endowed them with the collective name America and began to develop verbal and graphic images of them and the peoples they contained. Throughout this process, Europeans were constantly assessing and reassessing their own roles in relationship to the new continents. This chapter will consider the expectations articulated as a result of those assessments during America's first century of existence.

Of course, America was not the first place to confront Europe with profound cultural differences. For several centuries, parts of Europe had been in more or less continuous contact with the Slavic and Islamic peoples on their eastern and southern borders. If the Crusades had

Vespucci Awakens a Sleeping America. This engraving shows the Italian explorer Amerigo Vespucci awakening the slumbering continents of America, depicted as a woman resting on a hammock, clad only in a feather cap and belt, and surrounded by strange animals. A graphic example of the European assumption of Old World cultural superiority over the New, the scene shows Vespucci arriving in a ship capable of crossing a wide ocean, finely clothed, and carrying a sword, navigation instruments, and a banner with the cross of Jesus. Vespucci brings European technology, religion, and civility to an America whose inhabitants yet live in primitive social conditions, engage in cannibalism, and have no means of transportation other than the canoe, a paddle for which rests against a tree. From Johanes Stradanus, Nova Reperta *(Antwerp, 1600). Courtesy of the Folger Shakespeare Library, Plate 1, Art Volume f81.*

operated to demystify the Levant for Europeans, the Ottoman advance during the fifteenth century had helped to define Europe as a larger cultural entity that, notwithstanding the diversity of its parts, was linked together by common social as well as religious values. Contemporaneously with the beginnings of the American encounter, "Turkish pressure during the late fifteenth and the sixteenth centuries," as Paul Coles has observed, was stimulating "a process of self-examination which led members of the [European] societies concerned increasingly

9

to identify themselves and to distinguish themselves from the Ottoman enemy by reference to" their Europeanness, including especially their Christianity.[1]

Also, at the same time, penetration into Africa and Asia provided Europe with still further cultural contrasts, with palpable evidences of alterity or "otherness" with which its inhabitants had to come to terms. Yet, if their detailed knowledge was slight, Europeans had long known about both continents and had had several centuries to assimilate the differences between their own cultures and those of the exotic East. Through the embroidered travels of Marco Polo and William of Rubruck and the fabricated travels of Sir John Mandeville, medieval Europeans had long been familiar with the worlds beyond Islam. Although they had filled those alien worlds with the strange animals and the "physically deformed and culturally repellent" wild men with which they had long "peopled the margins of the world outside the narrow confines of Christendom,"[2] the acquisition of more detailed and accurate knowledge as a result of more sustained and regular contact with both Africa and Asia beginning in the last half of the fifteenth century presented them with few difficulties. As Donald F. Lach has shown, the development of a more precise sense of the otherness of the Asian world did not prevent Europeans from acquiring a grudging appreciation for its richness and complexity or from shifting "the locales of the monstrous peoples and mythical animals of earlier times . . . from known places to those which still lay beyond the ken of most European adventurers." At least in the short run, as Lach has noted, "the revelation of Asia to pre-industrial Europe" required no substantial or rapid modification of any of the "basic tenets of Western life, faith, or institutions."[3]

For Europeans, however, the new continents across the Atlantic were never just another contrasting cultural world on a par with

1. Paul Coles, *The Ottoman Impact on Europe* (London, 1968), 145–49. See also R. W. Southern, *Western Views of Islam in the Middle Ages* (Cambridge, Mass., 1962).

2. Margaret T. Hodgen, *Early Anthropology in the Sixteenth and Seventeenth Centuries* (Philadelphia, 1964), 102. See also Mary B. Campbell, *The Witness and the Other World: Exotic European Travel Writing, 400–1600* (Ithaca, N.Y., 1988), 47–161, and John Block Friedman, *The Monstrous Races in Medieval Art and Thought* (Cambridge, Mass., 1981).

3. Donald F. Lach, *Asia in the Making of Europe*, 2 vols. (Chicago, 1965), 1:xii, xvii.

Africa and Asia. They differed from those continents in at least two important senses. First, as Europeans gradually came to realize that Columbus had happened upon a vast landmass, the very existence of which had been previously unsuspected and was therefore, in J. H. Elliott's phrase, "quite outside the range of Europe's accumulated experience and of its normal expectations," they had to reconstruct the cosmography that had served them since antiquity.[4] Second, and even more important, their position as the discoverers of America suggested a sort of proprietary relationship to the new continents. Discovery, as Michael T. Ryan has noted, "implied a certain ownership, if not legal then at least intellectual and psychological."[5] If Europeans could never be much more than sojourners in the old worlds they encountered in Africa and Asia, America, having been uncovered and, in a sense, "given to them" by their own initiative, seemed to be theirs to expropriate and to define. For that reason, again, in Elliott's words, "America was peculiarly the artifact of Europe, as Asia and Africa were not" and never could be.[6]

As they came to appreciate that America was not, as Columbus thought, the eastern rim of Asia, as the process of discovery and exploration made clear that the newly found lands were actually the " 'fourth part' of the world,"[7] Europeans could scarcely avoid recognizing their many novelties. Dramatically revealed by the hitherto unknown animals, plants, and peoples it contained and by its peculiarities of climate and terrain, the newness of the New World—in the words of the French philosopher Louis Le Roy, "new lands, new seas, new formes of men, manners, lawes, and customs; new diseases and new remedies; new waies of the Heavens, and of the Ocean never before found out"—fired the imaginations of at least some Europeans.[8] American nature demanded new words to describe its "mountainous,

---

4. J. H. Elliott, *The Old World and the New 1492–1650* (Cambridge, 1970), 8. See also Edmundo O'Gorman, *The Invention of America: An Inquiry into the Historical Nature of the New World and the Meaning of History* (Bloomington, Ind., 1961), 51–69, and W. G. L. Randles, *De la terre plate au globe terrestre* (Paris, 1980).

5. Michael T. Ryan, "Assimilating New Worlds in the Sixteenth and Seventeenth Centuries," *Comparative Studies in Society and History* 23 (1981): 536.

6. Elliott, *Old World and the New*, 5.

7. O'Gorman, *Invention of America*, 123.

8. Louis Le Roy, *Of the Interchangeable Course, or Variety of Things in the Whole World* (London, 1594), 127, as quoted by Ryan, "Assimilating New Worlds," 523.

riverine, and tempestuous" character. The literary scholar Mary B. Campbell has noted that such "vernacular English words" as *"waterfall, cataract, lagoon, whirlpool, swamp, keys, hurricane, tornado,* [and] *thunderstorm* . . . all joined the language during the first century . . . of English exploration."[9]

If, however, "the discovery of America, or of the Americans," was, as Tzvetan Todorov has declared, "certainly the most astonishing discovery" in human history,[10] and if, as Stephen Greenblatt has noted, "Columbus's voyage initiated a century of intense wonder,"[11] most recent analysts of the European reaction to that discovery agree that America "made relatively little impression on Europe" during the half century following its discovery.[12] Although "Early Modern Europe showed itself quicker to respond to the experience of the New World of America, than Medieval Europe to the experience of the world of Islam," the "apparent slowness of Europe in making the mental adjustments required to incorporate America within its field of vision," writes Elliott, was "one of the most striking features of sixteenth-century intellectual history."[13] The "new lands and new peoples abroad," agrees Ryan, "registered little impact on the values, beliefs, and traditions of the sixteenth and seventeenth centuries."[14]

Modern scholars have offered a number of explanations for this ex-

9. Campbell, *Witness and the Other World,* 226. Many such words of course came into English via Spanish.

10. Tzvetan Todorov, *The Conquest of America* (New York, 1982), 4.

11. Stephen Greenblatt, *Marvelous Possessions: The Wonder of the New World* (Chicago, 1991), 14.

12. Hodgen, *Early Anthropology,* 113.

13. Elliott, *Old World and the New,* 8, 17.

14. Ryan, "Assimilating New Worlds," 519. See also Elliott, *Old World and the New,* 2–3, 56–59, and "Renaissance Europe and America: A Blunted Impact?," in *First Images of America: The Impact of the New World on the Old,* ed. Fredi Chiapelli, 2 vols. (Berkeley and Los Angeles, 1976), 1:11–23; G. V. Scammell, "The New Worlds and Europe in the Sixteenth Century," *Historical Journal* 12 (1969): 389–412, and *The World Encompassed: The First European Maritime Empires, c. 800–1650* (Berkeley and Los Angeles, 1981). Important exceptions are William Brandon, *New Worlds for Old: Reports from the New World and Their Effect on the Development of Social Thought in Europe, 1500–1800* (Athens, Ohio, 1986); Walter Prescott Webb, *The Great Frontier* (Austin, Tex., 1964); Ernest J. Burrus, "The Impact of New World Discovery upon European Thought of Man," in *No Man Is an Alien: Essays on the Unity of Mankind,* ed. J. Robert Nelson (Leiden, 1971), 85–108; and Arthur J. Slavin, "The American Principle from More to Locke," in Chiapelli, ed., *First Images of America,* 1:139–64.

traordinary slowness. Some have emphasized the European preoccupation with a "superabundant" variety of internal problems, including the endemic anxieties and difficulties always to some degree present in a "disease and poverty-ridden" society,[15] the ongoing struggle with the Ottomans, the religious strife associated with the Protestant Reformation, and the wars arising out of conflicting national and dynastic ambitions. Others have pointed to the engrossment of early modern thinkers with other, to contemporaries at least, even more exciting developments that coincided with the first phases of the encounter with America. These included the revival of interest in antiquity associated with the Renaissance, the theological debates stimulated by the Reformation, the so-called educational and scientific revolutions, and the expansion of external trade both within Europe and between Europe and the Levant, Africa, Asia, and America.

Yet other analysts have stressed the "sheer immensity of the challenge"[16] presented by America and the problem of absorbing so much new information. As several scholars have suggested, this process was inhibited by the very orientation of European society. A "traditional culture, suspicious of change, and oriented to a mythic past, whose members" both "venerated origins as sacred" and "fulfilled themselves in relationship to a divine reality outside time,"[17] Europe during the early age of expansion, these scholars emphasize, was "a world that still sought its future in the past."[18] This traditional orientation, moreover, seems to have been intensified by the Renaissance. Believing "in the superiority and omniscience of the Ancients"[19] in virtually every category of intellectual and cultural endeavor from literature, philosophy, and art to politics, Renaissance scholars found "the ideal age" in "neither the present nor the future but [in] the past . . . of the Greeks and the Romans."[20] A society so "obsessed with the merits of antiquity"[21] and "so completely transfixed on its past"[22] unavoidably found it almost impossible to assimilate America's many novelties as novelties.

15. Scammell, "New Worlds and Europe," 390, 395.
16. Elliott, *Old World and the New*, 8.
17. Ryan, "Assimilating New Worlds," 523, 534.
18. Hodgen, *Early Anthropology*, 114.
19. Scammell, "New Worlds and Europe," 393.
20. Todorov, *Conquest of America*, 109.
21. Scammell, "New Worlds and Europe," 395.
22. Ryan, "Assimilating New Worlds," 534.

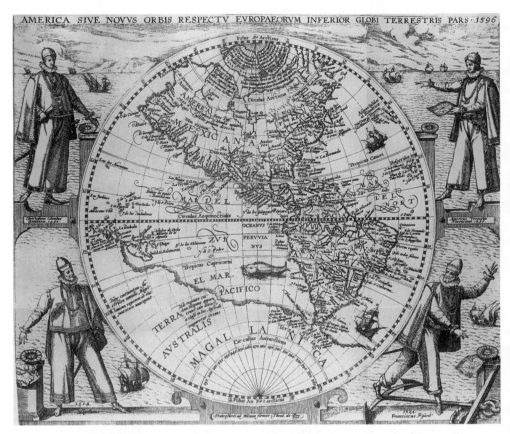

America at the End of the Sixteenth Century. This circular map shows what Europeans had learned about the two American continents during the century before 1598. The figures in each corner represent famous explorers and conquistadors who acted in the service of Spain: Columbus, Vespucci, Magellan, and Pizarro. From Theodore De Bry, a Flemish engraver, Grand et Petits Voyages, America *Series, 1598. Courtesy of the Library of Congress, neg. no. LCUSZ62-89908.*

But by far the most persuasive explanation for the failure of Europeans to develop an appreciation of the novelties of America, most recent scholars seem to agree, lies in the correlative tendency of European discoverers to perceive and interpret their findings in terms of the world whence they came. The pressures operating to produce such a result were overwhelming. Not only, as Harry Levin has stressed, did those who encountered America at first hand have to explain their

14   findings "in terms which those who" had "never been there" could

"readily comprehend,"[23] they also used analogies and comparisons with the familiar so that they could themselves "grasp the unknown by means of the known."[24]

Such behavior is scarcely peculiar to the Columbian exchange. Recent anthropologists have taught us that "knowledge of other cultures and eras" invariably "depends on the cultures and eras doing the knowing" and that cultures almost always "meet indirectly, according to conventional expectations of the cultures themselves."[25] No wonder, then, that Europeans, in their efforts "to see, portray, and impose form on the new worlds," displayed little interest either in transcending their own traditional categories of analysis or in representing whatever differences they perceived in their "own terms."[26] No less than others in similar situations throughout the long history of humankind, they saw "only what they expected to see, and ignored or rejected those features of [American] life . . . for which they were mentally unprepared."[27] If, as one of his younger contemporaries noted in 1528, Columbus was intent upon giving "those strange lands the form of our own,"[28] he set a pattern that was followed by most of his successors.

This pattern profoundly affected the ways Europeans perceived Amerindians. All but oblivious to Amerindian identities, they saw the indigenous peoples essentially as inferior or debased projections of themselves. For centuries, Europeans had employed "simile and analogy" to render people different from themselves comprehensible. Time after time, they had "converted the features of an alien territory into more or less grotesque collages of the familiar."[29] The encounter with America simply provided the occasion for another exercise in such projection. Rather than trying to understand Amerindians "as

23. Harry Levin, *The Myth of the Golden Age in the Renaissance* (New York, 1969), 59.

24. Todorov, *Conquest of America*, 128.

25. James A. Boon, "Comparative De-enlightenment: Paradox and Limits in the History of Ethnology," *Daedalus* 109, no. 2 (1980): 89, and *Other Tribes, Other Scribes: Symbolic Anthropology in the Comparative Study of Cultures, Histories, Religions, and Texts* (Cambridge, 1982), ix.

26. Ryan, "Assimilating New Worlds," 522, 536.

27. Elliott, *Old World and the New*, 17.

28. The humanist Hernán Pérez de Oliva, as quoted in ibid., 15.

29. Campbell, *Witness and the Other World*, 177.

they really were," Europeans saw them through "the veil of . . . traditional interpretation[s] of distant people[s]" as newly encountered equivalents of the wild men or savages with which, throughout the Middle Ages, their ancestors had peopled unknown areas of the non-Christian world.[30]

Hairy people who lived like wild beasts in the woods without clothes, housing, agriculture, religion, law, any apparent social and political organization, or reason to restrain their darker passions, savages had long been an established social category in European thought. Given enhanced authority by the "Renaissance rediscovery of the Classical theory that the earliest men were naked forest dwellers," the concept of the savage seemed an appropriate identification for many Amerindian groups, including the Ciboney and Caribs encountered by Columbus around the Caribbean and the Tupinamba in Brazil.[31]

There was indeed little in European traditions to support any other kind of understanding of Amerindians. The Christian and the classical traditions, "the most firmly established elements in Europe's cultural inheritance," were, as Elliott has observed, "the obvious points of departure for any evaluation of the New World and its inhabitants,"[32] and neither offered a framework for a more sympathetic interpretation of America's indigenous inhabitants. Providing "the most important basis for the distinction between 'us' and 'them' in sixteenth century Europe," contemporary European religious thought regarded all non-Christian peoples as heathens or pagans.[33] In a culture that "could still see itself as a Respublica Christiana, paganism," a concept freighted with condescension, "was the [single] most inclusive, unambiguous category of otherness" and rapidly became, in Ryan's words, "a central organizing category governing much of Europe's early relationship to the new worlds."[34] So did the classical category of barbarian. A term originally meaning non-Greek but extended by Renaissance writers to include all people who "were not Christian Europeans or ancient Greeks and Romans" and usually implying a high degree of cultural crudeness, barbarian, reports the anthropologist John H. Rowe, was

30. Hodgen, *Early Anthropology*, 102, 192. See also Todorov, *Conquest of America*, 128, 168.

31. John H. Rowe, "Ethnography and Ethnology in the Sixteenth Century," *The Kroeber Anthropological Society*, no. 30 (1964): 5, 7.

32. Elliott, *Old World and the New*, 24.

33. Rowe, "Ethnography and Ethnology," 5–6.

34. Ryan, "Assimilating New Worlds," 525.

"one of the commonest terms applied to the inhabitants of all the newly explored lands."[35]

By describing and conceiving of Amerindians in terms of these traditional categories, Europeans linked them directly to the many pagan and barbarian peoples, both past and present, with whom they were already familiar, to their own heathen and barbaric past, and even to the less culturally developed peoples on the fringes of European society. As Margaret T. Hodgen has shown, in the ethnographic literature of the sixteenth and seventeenth centuries, both "the German tribes described by Caesar and Tacitus in the first century A.D." and "the Irish, the Laplanders, the Finns, and other outlying and relatively uncivil . . . folk" still present in Europe seemed to serve as appropriate "comparisons and parallelisms" for "the newly discovered savages" in America.[36]

As Hodgen notes, such similitudes operated to draw "all savage and barbarian peoples into the same frame of reference"[37] and thereby powerfully to suggest that, in Ryan's phrase, "a real, not simply a metaphorical, relationship inhered between the exotic and the antique," that they were in fact "interchangeable." Thus did European discoverers and observers bend "the new worlds . . . to serve the cause of tradition." Rather than undermining or challenging the existing intellectual order, the New World "offered those mired in traditional pursuits another opportunity to ride their favorite hobby horse" and thereby "provided pasturage for old ideas." By at once robbing the New World of its differences and making it into a "very old" world, this process "blunt[ed] the force" of its impact and reduced its "uniqueness to similarity," with the result that, again in Ryan's words, "the *real* discovery" was "not the exoticism of the other but his ultimate similarity with peoples already assimilated into European consciousness."[38] In this emerging view, there was nothing that was exceptional about America.

This assimilation of the indigenous inhabitants of America to traditional European social categories did not entirely rule out a favorable assessment of them. Many writers, beginning with the Milanese humanist Peter Martyr, emphasized the supposed innocence, felicity,

35. Rowe, "Ethnography and Ethnology," 6.
36. Hodgen, *Early Anthropology*, 343.
37. Ibid., 128.
38. Ryan, "Assimilating New Worlds," 523, 525, 527, 529, 533–34.

and good-naturedness of Amerindians. Along with "its Biblical parallel, the Fall of Man and his expulsion from Paradise," the "Greek Legend of the Golden Age,"[39] a "well remembered myth" given renewed emphasis during the Renaissance,[40] envisioned a period "in some remote past, when life was good and simple" and people lived in a state of "pristine bliss."[41] Modified only to include the apparent masterlessness of many Amerindian groups, this myth provided a ready-made "vocabulary"[42] by which European commentators could draw an analogy between Amerindians and the inhabitants of the Golden Age. The tendency to glorify Amerindians by depicting them as strong-limbed Greeks who, though pagan and simple, lived free with little labor in a blissful state of nature without regard for private property or "lawsuits engendered by the words Thine and Mine" was widespread. Like the French poet Pierre Ronsard, many viewed Amerindians as "happy people, free of care and troubles," living contentedly in a "golden age."[43]

But this interpretation belied the implications of the very language Europeans most often employed to describe Amerindians. Of course, that language—savagery, heathenism, and barbarism—powerfully suggested "an unfavorable verdict" about the nature of Amerindians and their cultures. For all their supposed simple felicity, Amerindians were neither Christian nor, by European standards, civilized, but pagan and primitive, at most the equivalents of Europe's own early rude inhabitants before their conversion to Christianity and acquisition of civilized manners. In their nakedness and laziness, their sodomy and their lasciviousness, their cannibalism and their bellicosity, Amerindians appeared little short of bestial. "In the oft-cited words of Thomas Hobbes, who," as Hodgen points out, "summarized both a large literature and the existing state of informed opinion, the life of these supposedly society-less, stateless groups of 'noble' savages was 'solitary, poore, nasty, brutish and short.'"[44] "On the whole," Elliott writes, "the image of the innocent Indian was most

39. Hodgen, *Early Anthropology*, 281.
40. Levin, *Myth of the Golden Age*, 59.
41. Scammell, "New Worlds and Europe," 396.
42. Levin, *Myth of the Golden Age*, 65.
43. Brandon, *New Worlds for Old*, 15–16.
44. Hodgen, *Early Anthropology*, 361.

Invasion of America. This scene depicts a fight during the early sixteenth century between the Portuguese and Amerindians at Garasu in Brazil. Emblematic of the thousands of similar battles that took place in the New World, this engraving shows Portuguese soldiers defending a stockade with cannon and firearms against a much larger Amerindian force armed with bows and arrows. In two adjacent stockades and on an open-air fire, small groups of Amerindians are cooking fish and human limbs, while Amerindians on both sides of a river block the stream with trees in an effort to prevent two boatloads of Portuguese soldiers from reaching an elaborate fort on the coast. From the German edition of Theodore De Bry, Grand et Petits Voyages, America *Series, 1598. Courtesy of the Library of Congress, neg. no.* lcusz62-45101.

easily maintained by those Europeans who had never actually seen one. Europeans who had experienced any prolonged contact with him were as likely as not to swing sharply to the other extreme." "Idealists might see the Tupinambas, Aztecs or Red Indians as noble savages," notes Geoffrey Scammell, but "others knew better." To the vast majority of Europeans on the spot, the theme of "primaeval innocence" quickly gave way to an image of Amerindians as "degenerates, natural cowards, natural slaves."[45] "If human, theirs was," by the most charitable European assessments, "a degraded humanity" indeed.[46]

Few Europeans actually denied that Amerindians were human, and those who insisted upon their common humanity with Europeans, Africans, and Asians found an explanation for their cultural degeneracy in the legend of Noah. Some commentators speculated that, while Amerindians were descended from Noah, they had gradually lost in the Americas whatever knowledge of antediluvian religion, arts, and sciences they might have inherited from him. As Hodgen observes, this theory of decay accorded well with "that tormenting anxiety of the Renaissance, the theory of the world's mutability and decay."[47]

By whatever process they had degenerated so low from the standards of civilized and regenerate man, Amerindians represented, preeminently for Europeans, in Olive Patricia Dickason's words, "antistructure, man before the acquisition of culture had differentiated him from animals." As "living metaphors for antisocial forces that could be brought under control only by" bringing them into "spiritual and cultural conformity" with Europeans, Amerindians provided a challenge for Europeans that was every bit "as powerful as the lure of gold and silver." As the agents of God and civility, Europeans, it seemed to many of them at the time, had been assigned a critical role in a "providential design" through which God intended to recall Amerindians to the true faith and lead them back into civilization. Through "the process of evangelization and assimilation," Amerindians would be rescued from the darkness in which they dwelled, and European

45. Elliott, *Old World and the New*, 42; Scammell, "New Worlds and Europe," 410.

46. Hodgen, *Early Anthropology*, 363.

47. Ibid., 262–63. See also Don Cameron Allen, *The Legend of Noah: Renaissance Rationalism in Art, Science, and Letters* (Urbana, Ill., 1949), esp. 113–37, and Lee E. Huddleston, *Origins of the American Indians: European Concepts, 1492–1729* (Austin, Tex., 1967).

missionaries and colonizers would fulfill their exalted part in God's plan. In this process, the ease with which Iberians conquered one New World civilization after another could only be taken as dramatic signs both of "divine approval of their actions"[48] and "of the superiority of Christianity over all other men and civilizations."[49]

The unquestioned assumption of European superiority which underlay this view of the Amerindians and of their relationship to Europeans was present from the first encounter. Todorov has suggestively analyzed the many ways in which the "prejudice of superiority" informed Columbus's first contacts with Amerindians in the Antilles: in his superficial assessment of them, in the "mixture of authoritarianism and condescension" with which he treated them, in his "incomprehension of their language and of their signs," in his casual abduction of several of them, and in his obviously greater interest in the land and its products than in the people—in all these behaviors Columbus revealed a set of attitudes that would continue to characterize European behavior toward the indigenous inhabitants of America for the next several centuries.[50]

In an era in which revived respect for antiquity had severely "undermined the ethnocentric self-assurance which had previously characterized Europeans,"[51] the, to them, obvious superiority they enjoyed over peoples in the New World must have provided Europeans with some comfort. Along with the demonic and pejorative vision of the Amerindians that supported it, however, this apparent superiority also operated as a profound exercise in "self-deception for those who wielded it, authorizing and excusing (and, inadvertently, confessing)" a manifold variety of "what can only be termed abominations."[52] In total disregard for Amerindian rights to territory, government, or cultural integrity, it served as a justification for European occupation, colonization, and, in many cases, enslavement. As savages, Amer-

48. Olive Patricia Dickason, *The Myth of the Savage and the Beginnings of French Colonization in the Americas* (Edmonton, Alberta, 1984), 273–74. On the providential components in Columbus's relationship to the New World, see Pauline Moffitt Watts, "Prophecy and Discovery: On the Spiritual Origins of Christopher Columbus's 'Enterprise of the Indies,'" *American Historical Review* 90 (1985): 73–102.

49. Scammell, "New Worlds and Europe," 410.

50. Todorov, *Conquest of America*, 33.

51. Rowe, "Ethnography and Ethnology," 7.

52. Campbell, *Witness and the Other World*, 209.

indians, their European conquerors assumed, were entitled to no such rights. Worst of all, as it became clear that Amerindians would not always embrace Christianity willingly, Europe's presumptive superiority could be used to excuse the veritable destruction of Amerindian culture by persuading European conquerors that "all of the unhappiness, all of the persecution" which they visited upon Amerindians from Labrador to Cape Horn was nothing more than "well-merited punishment."[53]

Of course, not all Europeans accepted the view of Amerindians as inferior, cultureless natural people without reason. Beginning in the 1510s and continuing throughout the rest of the sixteenth century, an impressive group of Spanish thinkers argued for a more empirical—and more favorable—view. These included especially Francisco de Vitoria, professor of theology at the University of Salamanca; Bartolomé de Las Casas, a former colonist turned Dominican who became the principal champion for more benign treatment of Amerindians; and the Jesuit missionary José de Acosta, whose *Natural and Moral History of the Indies*, published in 1589 and translated into many languages, "was one of the most widely read and influential books of the time" and quickly became a standard work on Amerindians as well as a major source of information about the Incas and the Aztecs.[54]

By strenuously insisting upon the rationality of Amerindians, by defending their rights to self-governance and territory, and by denying the right of Europeans to enslave them, these writers and others at least challenged, if they never fully succeeded in undermining, the prevailing assumption of Amerindian inferiority. Moreover, Acosta and, to some extent, even Las Casas developed theories of cultural evolution designed to distinguish among Amerindians according to their levels of civility. Constructing a "hierarchy of excellence with the people most like Christian Europeans at the top,"[55] Acosta distinguished among three classes of barbarians. The highest category were those who, like the Chinese and Japanese, had developed letters and a high degree of civility. Following them were those who, like the

53. Hodgen, *Early Anthropology*, 363; Dickason, *Myth of the Savage*, 273–75. Urs Bitterli, *Cultures in Conflict: Encounters between European and Non-European Cultures, 1492–1800*, trans. Ritchie Robertson (Oxford, 1989), suggestively analyzes the varieties of interaction between Europeans and Amerindians.

54. Rowe, "Ethnography and Ethnology," 9.

55. Ibid., 8.

Mutiny in Jamaica. Strife and conflict among America's European invaders are revealed in this depiction of a battle on the island of Jamaica during Columbus's fourth voyage to America at the beginning of the sixteenth century, when mutineers led by Francisco Poresio unsuccessfully fought forces loyal to Columbus while Amerindians looked on. From the German edition of Theodore De Bry, Grand et Petits Voyages, America *Series, 1598. Courtesy of the Library of Congress, neg. no. LCUSZ62-33893.*

Mexicans and Peruvians, lacked writing but lived in complex societies under a stable government and with a coherent religion. At the bottom were those who, like the Caribs and the Brazilians, still, to one degree or another, lived in a savage state.[56]

56. Anthony Pagden, *The Fall of Natural Man: The American Indian and the Origins of Comparative Ethnology* (Cambridge, 1982), provides the most recent and fullest account of the debate over the character of Amerindians. See also the new general study by Robert A. Williams, Jr., *The American Indian in Western Legal Thought: The Discourses of Conquest* (New York, 1990).

By this theory, Acosta made some barbarians equivalent to Europeans except with regard to their religion. If they were all Asian, at least some Amerindians, the Mexicans and Peruvians, had been elevated above the savage state. Most important for the purposes of this book, however, Acosta's scheme presented an evolutionary sequence that implied that, just as Europe's own early forest dwellers had slowly developed into civilized societies, savages, even of the most barbarous nature, "could in due course, with care and persistence, be induced to live in an ordered polity" and, like the more developed Amerindian societies, gradually become more civilized.[57]

If the theories of Acosta and others projected a more positive assessment of the cultural potential of Amerindians and through their emphases upon the common humanity and rationality of Amerindians even posited a degree of equality between them and Europeans, it is extremely important to note that those theories displayed little concern to develop an appreciation of the unique othernesses of Amerindians and no concern at all for the preservation of that uniqueness. If "the prejudice of superiority" provided an insuperable "obstacle in the road to knowledge" about Amerindians, so also, as Todorov has argued, did "the prejudice of equality," which, as he has explained, consisted "in identifying the other purely and simply with one's own 'ego ideal' or with oneself." By exposing the barbarism of Spanish exploiters of Amerindians, Las Casas and others like him sought to achieve better treatment for America's indigenous inhabitants. The program they envisioned for those inhabitants, however, looked ahead to their eventual transformation into Europeans and to the obliteration of Amerindian cultures.[58]

Indeed, by incorporating Amerindians into an evolutionary scheme, they manifested a degree of condescension comparable to that of the most unapologetic believers in European superiority. By saying that "they (*over there*)" were then "even as we (*here*) were *once*," men like Las Casas and Acosta were merely suggesting that Amerindians were capable over time of achieving civilization, which they thought of wholly in European terms. Even those most interested in acquiring accurate knowledge about Amerindians, like the Franciscan missionary to Mexico Bernardino de Sahagún, unwittingly "impose[d] a European organization upon American knowledge" and thereby con-

57. Elliott, *Old World and the New*, 48–49.
58. Todorov, *Conquest of America*, 165–67.

tinued to provide support for the assumption of European cultural superiority.[59]

If transformation of Amerindian peoples into civilized Christians offered Europeans a wide scope for action, so also did the lands and resources over which those savage people seemed, from a European perspective, to exercise a tenuous sway. We have already mentioned Todorov's point that Columbus was far more interested in the places than in the peoples he encountered during his voyages. Everywhere he went, the first questions he asked were whether there was any gold and where it was, and he was fascinated by the lushness of the Caribbean world and attentive to all possibilities of "temporal prosperity."[60] Once his discoveries had been identified as a new world, however, no aspect of that world probably operated more powerfully upon the European imagination than did its immense space. "The discovery of so vast a country," declared Montaigne in the late 1570s, was a development that was indeed worthy "of very great consideration."[61]

As the awareness of the seeming boundlessness of America penetrated more deeply into European consciousness, America, in the words of the Dutch historian Henri Baudet, became a place "onto which all identification and interpretation, all dissatisfaction and desire, all nostalgia and idealism seeking expression could be projected."[62] "In observing America," Elliott has shrewdly noted, Europe "was in the first instance, observing itself."[63] Throughout the Middle Ages, Europeans had posited the existence of a place—for a time to the east, but mostly to the west of Europe—without the corruptions and disadvantages of the Old World. The discovery of America merely intensified this "nostalgia for the Golden Age and the Lost Paradise"

59. Ibid., 233. By incorporating them into an allegedly universal history generalized from the European or Western experience, such evolutionary schemes operated both to deprive Amerindians of their own histories and identities and to serve as a rationale for maintaining distance and separation between them and Europeans. Johannes Fabian, *Time and the Other: How Anthropology Makes Its Object* (New York, 1983), suggestively explores this theme as it relates to the development of the discipline of anthropology.

60. *Select Letters of Christopher Columbus*, ed. R. H. Major (London, 1897), 105.

61. *The Essays of Michel Eyquem de Montaigne*, trans. Charles Cotton (Chicago, 1952), 91–92.

62. Henri Baudet, *Paradise on Earth: Some Thoughts on European Images of Non-European Man* (New Haven, Conn., 1965), 55.

63. Elliott, "Renaissance Europe and America," 20.

and actually aroused new hope for their discovery somewhere on the western edge of the Atlantic.[64] Following Pierre d'Ailly's speculations in his *Imago Mundi* that the earthly paradise was situated in a temperate region on the other side of the equator, Columbus was only the first explorer to speculate, during his third voyage, that he was near the "spot of the earthly paradise."[65] As Scammell has noted, Europe's intractable problems with disease, poverty, and disorder provided a powerful stimulus for the wish to find "paradises in distant places."[66]

Remarkably soon after its discovery, in fact, America became the locus for a variety of "imaginary . . . utopian constructions."[67] Indeed, Sir Thomas More invented the very term *utopia*, literally meaning no place, in 1515–16 in his famous tract of that name. An ironic and satiric humanist critique of Europe's own political and moral failures, *Utopia*, as all students of More agree, was principally inspired by "the maladies of the European polities of the early sixteenth century."[68] Whether More's acknowledged reading of the accounts of Vespucci's voyages and his interest in his brother-in-law John Rastell's projects for the New World merely "freed More's fancy," as J. H. Hexter has noted,[69] or actually inspired the specific form he gave to Utopia, as Arthur J. Slavin has suggested,[70] it is significant for both emerging expectations about America and the subsequent development of the utopian tradition that More located Utopia in the Atlantic and used as his central literary device the experienced traveler just returned from a voyage with Vespucci from the "unknown peoples and lands" of the New World.[71]

64. Loren Baritz, "The Idea of the West," *American Historical Review* 46 (1961): 617–40; Durand Echeverria, *Mirage in the West: A History of the French Image of American Society to 1815* (Princeton, 1957), vii. See also Lewis Mumford, *The Myth of the Machine: The Pentagon of Power* (New York, 1970), 3–27.

65. *Select Letters of Columbus*, 137; Todorov, *Conquest of America*, 16–17.

66. Scammell, "New Worlds and Europe," 390.

67. Echeverria, *Mirage in the West*, vii.

68. J. H. Hexter, *More's Utopia: The Biography of an Idea* (Princeton, 1952), 95. See also Frank E. and Fritzie P. Manuel, *Utopian Thought in the Western World* (Cambridge, Mass., 1979).

69. *The Complete Works of Sir Thomas More*, ed. Edward Surtz and J. H. Hexter, 4 vols. (New Haven, Conn., 1965), 4:xxxi–xxxii.

70. Slavin, "American Principle," 142–47. Slavin plausibly speculates that Vespucci's reports on the absence of private property among Amerindians may have informed More's attack on the institution.

71. Sir Thomas More, *Utopia*, in Surtz and Hexter, ed., *Complete Works*, 4:49.

Utopia. The perfect commonwealth which some people hoped to find in the vast unexplored spaces of the New World is illustrated by this woodcut. It shows European discoverers off the coast of an idyllic island conversing with—and learning from—a local luminary. From the Rotterdam edition of Thomas More, Utopia, *1518. Courtesy of the Folger Shakespeare Library, PR2321 U82 1518 Cage, p. 12.*

By associating Utopia with the New World, More, in this extraordinarily influential work, effectively directed attention not just to Europe's own internal social, moral, and political problems but also to the as yet unknown potential of the immense New World. Made just three years before Cortez began his conquest of Mexico and provided some detailed knowledge about what America's most complex societies were really like, that association, in the first instance, suggested the heady possibility of finding a place somewhere in the vastness of America where all of the problems of a decadent Europe had either been resolved or had not yet been permitted to develop. Nor did this close association between America and the utopian tradition die with More. Through Jonathan Swift and beyond, utopian writers continued to identify the dream of a perfect society with America and to locate their fairylands, their New Atlantis, their City of the Sun in some place distant from Europe and in the vicinity of America.

Of course, these early utopias, like European perceptions of Amerindians, were all heavily shaped by older European intellectual traditions. Almost without exception, they looked backward to Europe's "own ideal past" rather than forward into some wholly novel world of the future.[72] Invariably, their authors turned their imaginary "new worlds into very old ones."[73] For this reason, it is obviously incorrect to suggest, as so many scholars have done, that the encounter with America immediately enabled the European "to picture himself as a free agent in the deep and radical sense of possessing unlimited possibilities in his own being, and as living in a world made by him in his own image and to his own measure."[74] Nevertheless, with its large unexplored areas and its many unfamiliar groups of peoples and cultures, America did provide Europeans with a powerful additional impetus for posing basic questions about their own society and its organization, values, and customs and thereby acted as a powerful stimulus to and exerted an important influence upon the emergence of the utopian tradition in early modern Europe.

That tradition consisted of several types of utopias, ranging from pastoral arcadias to perfect commonwealths to millennial kingdoms of God. Whatever their form, however, they all betrayed "deep dissat-

72. Elliott, "Renaissance Europe and America," 20.
73. Ryan, "Assimilating New Worlds," 533.
74. O'Gorman, *Invention of America*, 129.

isfaction"[75] with contemporary Europe and were intended, in More's words, as "example[s] for correction" of European "errors."[76] Having expressed this dissatisfaction, before the discovery of America, in their "longing for a return to . . . the lost Christian paradise, or to the Golden Age of the ancients," Europeans now exchanged this desire for "a world remote in time" for one distant in space.[77] Arcadia, Eden, the New Jerusalem, or the scientifically advanced and dominated Bensalem created by Francis Bacon now could be plausibly located in America. In their good order, just government, supportive society, peaceful abundance, and absence of greed, vice, private property, and lawsuits, these happy social constructions, situated by their authors in the New World, served as the antithesis of the Old.[78]

Although Europeans continued to locate their utopias in the unknown wilds of America, the dream of finding a perfect society or the terrestrial paradise somewhere in the physical spaces of America gradually diminished over the sixteenth century. As America and Amerindians came to be better known and as no such utopias were discovered, people realized that America, to the extent that it was known, was not an unalloyed paradise to be contrasted with a European hell. More and more, in fact, Europeans came to see America less as an exotic new land inhabited by innocent primitives and containing many wonders awaiting European discovery than as a vast field for exploitation and development by Europeans. Like its indigenous inhabitants, its physical spaces and social landscapes, most of which appeared to Europeans to be either inappropriately utilized or wholly unoccupied, seemed to be at an early stage of cultural evolution and in need of European knowledge and skill to bring them up to their full potential.

75. Elliott, *Old World and the New*, 26.

76. More, *Utopia*, 55.

77. Elliott, *Old World and the New*, 25.

78. Howard Mumford Jones, *O Strange New World: American Culture, The Formative Years* (New York, 1964), 14–21, 35–36; J. C. Davis, *Utopia and the Ideal Society: A Study of English Utopian Writing, 1516–1700* (Cambridge, 1981), 20–23; Francis Bacon, "New Atlantis," and Tommaso Campanella, "The City of the Sun," in *Ideal Commonwealths*, ed. Henry Morley (London, 1901); Frank E. Manuel, "Toward a Psychological History of Utopias," in *Utopias and Utopian Thought*, ed. Frank E. Manuel (Boston, 1966), 70–80; Baudet, *Paradise on Earth*, 32.

America, in short, came to be known primarily as a place to be acted upon by Europeans. If early explorers and observers turned America into an unexceptional place by assimilating it to traditional European models, its European invaders slowly identified it as a place that provided exceptional opportunities for the mass conversion of souls to Christianity or, more commonly, for the acquisition of individual wealth and fame. Beginning with the 1519–21 discovery and conquest of Mexico, with its large and, to the Spaniards, seemingly more intelligent populations, hundreds of Franciscan, Dominican, Augustinian, and eventually Jesuit missionaries were drawn to the New World to participate in the great work of evangelization.

But not even the prospects for such an abundant harvest of souls exerted as powerful a force on the imaginations of Europeans as did the vast wealth uncovered, first in Mexico and then, two decades later, in Peru. The daring conquests of Cortez and Pizarro and the consequent acquisition of the gold, silver, and other treasures after which Columbus had so assiduously inquired in 1492 and for which Spanish explorers had been searching for a quarter of a century spurred a feverish quest for glory and riches at the same time that it indelibly stamped the image of America as an arena for the pursuit of individual and national material gain. If America did not contain the earthly paradise, it did seem to offer an unusual potential for the enrichment of a vast number of European immigrants and their supporters at home, a potential that, to contemporary Europeans, seemed exceptional in every sense. As America gradually came to be better known, even, in the words of the most recent analyst of early modern European travel literature, to be "*the* place to talk about," it also became "the locus par excellence of commercial activity, [and] political expansionism," virtually "a clean slate" upon which those in search of fame and wealth could write heroic stories or those who were simply out of options or down on their luck in Europe could find "a second chance."[79]

As America was "invested with the main chance," it was, more and more, "divested of magic."[80] For the new European exploiters of America, Amerindians came to seem far less like innocent savages and far more like the devil's children. What had initially seemed to be a paradise turned out to be a desert or a wilderness, "haunted by demonic beings," infested with poisonous snakes and plants and vicious

79. Campbell, *Witness and the Other World*, 209, 224.
80. Baritz, "Idea of the West," 633.

A Century of Spanish Activities in America. This engraving provides an un-flattering panorama of Spanish activities in the Americas during the sixteenth century. In the foreground, Spanish civil and military officers confer with an ecclesiastic, while Spanish gentlemen look on. In the background, Spanish soldiers and French corsairs use Amerindian and African slaves to carry off the riches of the Spanish empire, while friars, supported by other Spanish soldiers, endeavor to erect a cross. From Theodore De Bry, Grand et Petits Voyages, America Series, 1634. Courtesy of the Library of Congress, neg. no. LCUSZ62-32091.

alligators, and subject to terrifying hurricanes and other inimical acts of nature.[81] Indeed, in conventional iconography the allegorical figure of America was usually represented with an alligator, which, as Hugh Honour has pointed out, quickly "acquire[d] a derogatory significance, especially when set beside Europe with her bull, Asia with her camel, and Africa with her lion."[82]

But it was not only the people, animals, plants, and natural phenomena native to America that gave it an ill fame but also the behavior of the Europeans who went there. In *Utopia*, More had worried whether the discovery of America, "which was thought likely to be a great benefit to" the discovers, might "by their imprudence, cause . . . great mischief."[83] That seemed to be precisely what had happened as, unable to control their lust for riches, the Spaniards had themselves turned savage in their wholesale exploitation and destruction of entire nations of Amerindians. Not all the demons infesting America were Americans. Outside the bounds of traditional restraints, Europeans in America, heedless of all civilized conventions and of all social and human costs, had permitted their most primitive instincts to triumph in their avid quest for individual gain. Instead of having improved the New World by subjecting it to the direction of a civilized Europe and bringing its inhabitants under the aegis of the true God, Europeans appeared rather, as Montaigne worried in the late 1580s, to "have greatly precipitated its declension and ruin by our contagion, and . . . we have sold it our opinions and our arts at a very dear rate. It was an infant world, and yet we have not whipped it and subjected it to our discipline, by the advantage of our natural worth and force, neither have we won it by our justice and goodness, nor subdued it by our magnanimity." "By the pattern and example of our manners," he complained, Amerindians had learned little more than "treachery, luxury, avarice, and . . . all sorts of inhumanity and cruelty."[84]

As the black legend of Spanish cruelty circulated widely through Europe during the late sixteenth century, America came more and more to be viewed as a place of cultural regress, for natives and immigrants alike, a place that was almost wholly barren of culture and

81. Mircea Eliade, "Paradise and Utopia: Mythical Geography and Eschatology," in Manuel, ed., *Utopias and Utopian Thought*, 265.

82. Hugh Honour, *The European Vision of America* (Cleveland, 1975), 8.

83. More, *Utopia*, 53.

84. *Essays of Montaigne*, 440–41.

that was important chiefly for the riches it yielded in such abundance for the benefit of a Europe that was the exclusive seat of civilized life. In the prospects it offered for material gain and in its cultural impoverishment, America during the first century that it was known to Europeans seemed, from a European perspective, to be very different from Europe, and the possibilities for gain exerted such a powerful allure as to induce people to forbear the benefits of a civilized cultural life, at least for a time. By the close of the sixteenth century, a significant number of French, Dutch, and English people were looking to the New World in the conviction that the inhabitants of nations other than Spain and Portugal should share in the rich material opportunities it offered.

CHAPTER TWO

Encounters

PROJECTION AND DESIGN IN THE

CONSTRUCTION OF ENGLISH AMERICA,

1 5 8 0 – 1 6 9 0

As the riches they were bringing into Europe and the power and resources that flowed therefrom so powerfully attested, the Spanish and Portuguese during the sixteenth century provided effective examples for conquering, exploiting, colonizing, and evangelizing the new worlds they had begun to uncover a century earlier. At the same time, the efforts of Spanish-, French-, and English-sponsored explorers yielded at least a general idea of the nature of the lands along the eastern coast of North America and the people who inhabited them. By the time English people began to exhibit a sustained interest in America during the closing decades of the sixteenth century, a few still dreamed about the discovery of yet another rich Amerindian empire like those of the Aztecs, Mayas, and Incas encountered earlier in the century, and Sir Walter Ralegh actually tried to find the mythical kingdom of El Dorado in the upper reaches of the Orinoco River basin. Far more prevalent, however, was an image of America as a place that, with very few exceptions, was as yet little removed from a

34

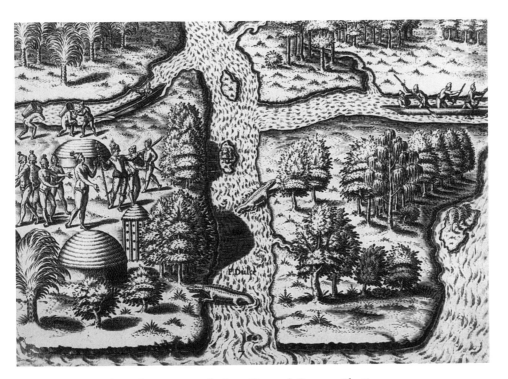

East Coast of North America in the Late Sixteenth Century. The European conception of eastern North America as a land lightly occupied by alligators and primitive people, living in insubstantial huts and supporting themselves by hunting and fishing, can be seen in this engraving of a 1564 painting by Jacques Le Moyne. It depicts Admiral Jean Ribault landing on the coast of Florida preparatory to building a fort and establishing a colony of French Protestant settlers. This was the view of North America during the last half of the sixteenth century when, despite Spanish objections and opposition, northern Europeans—French, English, Dutch, and Swedes—began to undertake projects of trade and colonization in that vast region. From the German edition of Theodore De Bry, Grand et Petits Voyages, America Series, 1591, after the painting by Jacques Le Moyne, 1564. Courtesy of the Library of Congress, neg. no. LCUSZ62-49752.

state of nature and was therefore awaiting, even inviting, Europeans to employ their superior culture, knowledge, and skills to exert mastery over and refashion it, to transform its untamed physical spaces into cultured, that is, Europeanized, landscapes, and to give Amerindians a boost up the cultural ladder.

As Englishmen assessed the situation from a Protestant perspective, the Spanish, in their greedy and bloody quest for riches, had been

35

guilty of the most sordid and treacherous acts of cruelty and barbarism toward Amerindians and had thereby at once signally failed to meet the noblest challenge presented by America and betrayed the obligations thrust upon Europeans by the Columbian discovery. Early exponents of vigorous English activities in America had few doubts that their countrymen, as representatives of the true faith, would do considerably better in this regard and bring themselves much glory in the process. If, at the same time, they also reaped some of the material benefits of America's widely heralded but unexploited riches and helped to resolve or alleviate some of the many problems of contemporary England, so much the better. No less than the Iberians, then, English (as well as French and Dutch) proponents of American ventures thus saw America as a locus for the pursuit of European ambitions. How the English envisioned and encountered America during their first century of intensive activity there and how those projections and encounters affected early notions of American exceptionalism is the subject of this chapter.

The English image of America on the eve of colonization is abundantly manifest in the prolific writings of Richard Hakluyt the younger, that indefatigable exponent of English planting in the New World. Issued in 1584 on the very eve of Ralegh's first efforts to establish a colony in Virginia, Hakluyt's "Discourse of Western Planting" provided a comprehensive summary of the arguments and justifications then circulating in England for English entry into the American arena. In it and in several other shorter pieces, Hakluyt systematically laid out the rationale for such ventures. In doing so, he revealed that the English, no less than the Spanish, had thoroughly embraced the emerging European conception of America as a place to be acted upon and within by Europeans.

In the "Discourse," Hakluyt listed as first among the "manifolde" benefits he expected to accrue to the "Realme of Englande by the Westerne discoveries" the opportunity for "inlargeing the glorious gospell of Christe, and reducinge of infinite multitudes of these simple people that are in errour into the right and perfecte way of their salvacion." That "this moste godly and Christian work" could best "be perfourmed" by the English Hakluyt had no doubt. Pointing out that the Spanish with their superstitious and false religion had already established over two hundred churches with large numbers of Amerindian communicants in America, he predicted that the English, representing the "true and syncere Relligion" and, in contrast to the

Spanish, eschewing "filthie lucre" and "vaine ostentation," could do far "greate[r] thinges" toward "gayninge . . . the soules of millions of those wretched people" and thereby bringing "them from darknes[s] to lighte, from falshoodde to truthe, from dombe Idolls to the lyvinge god, from the de[e]pe pitt of hell to the highest heaven."[1]

Hakluyt did not suggest that the work of evangelization would be either easy or safe. He knew from the Spanish experience that knowledge of Amerindian languages and military support were essential for missionary success. He knew that the Protestant missionaries who had accompanied the would-be French colonizers Nicholas Villegaignon and Jean Ribault and English maritime explorers Sir Francis Drake, Martin Frobisher, and Edward Fenton had not managed to convert a single "Infidell." He was aware as well of Amerindian resistance to Spanish efforts at conversion. But he speculated that Spanish difficulties proceeded from their "hatefull . . . usage" of Amerindians and suggested that "a gentle course without crueltie and tyrannie [such as] best answereth the profession of a Christian" would guarantee English success in planting Christianity among Amerindians and make the English "seating [al]most void of blood." As soon as "the naturall people" of America learned that the English would treat them with "all humanitie, curtesie, and freedome," he predicted, they would eagerly "revolte cleane from the Spaniarde" and "yelde themselves" to the English.[2]

Significantly, however, Hakluyt expressed no reluctance to employ force in the event that some "stubborne Savages . . . refuse[d] obedience" to the English or showed themselves "desirous to expel us, and iniuriously to offend us." If the English "proceed[ed] with extremitie," he was confident that they could "conquer, fortifie, and plant" settlements in America that would be "most firme and stable" and serve as a base from which, "in the end," Amerindians could all be brought into "subjection and to civilities." If force was necessary to attain such a noble objective, Hakluyt was quite willing to use it.[3]

Bringing light, salvation, and culture to Amerindians was not the

1. Richard Hakluyt, "Discourse of Western Planting," in *The Original Writings and Correspondence of the Two Richard Hakluyts*, ed. E. G. R. Taylor, 2 vols. (London, 1935), 2:211, 214, 216.

2. Ibid., 215, 217, 318; Hakluyt, "Inducements to the Liking of the Voyage Intended towards Virginia," 1585, in Taylor, ed., *Original Writings*, 2:334; Hakluyt, "Epistle Dedicatory to Sir Walter Ralegh," no. 2, 1587, in ibid., 377.

3. Hakluyt, "Inducements," 329–30; Hakluyt, "Epistle to Ralegh," no. 2, 377.

only challenge Hakluyt held out to stimulate interest in American enterprises. Indeed, he spent far more space touting America as an avenue for the enhancement of the wealth and power of the English nation. Just as the wool trade had earlier enabled England to raise "it selfe from meaner state to greater wealthe and moche higher honor, mighte and power then before, to the equallinge of the princes of the same to the greatest potentates of this parte of the worlde," so had the endeavors of Spain and Portugal beyond Europe wrought enormous changes in their fortunes. "Poore and barren and hardly able to susteine their inhabitaunts," both countries, wholly as a result of "their discoveries" overseas, Hakluyt emphasized to his audience, had "progressed" so rapidly and achieved such wealth and power as to give them excessive influence on the European stage.[4]

Although Hakluyt did not ignore the possibility of finding gold, silver, copper, and precious stones, his projections for enhancing England's national wealth in America primarily emphasized production and trade. Lying in similar latitudes to the broad area stretching from the Mediterranean to Scandinavia, the soils, at least as reported by Huguenot colonists for southeastern North America, had such "fertilitie and riches" as to suggest that North America, or Virginia, as the English called this vast region, might supply England with virtually every commodity it then obtained from the Levant, Muscovy, and other parts of Europe. Because the inhabitants of this area were allegedly of such "a gentle and amyable nature" and so "willingly" obedient that they would be "contented to serve those that shall with gentleness and humanities goo aboute to allure them," Hakluyt foresaw no serious problems from them. With ground so "fatt" and a labor force so compliant, he envisioned the development of many profitable plantations and a vast trade in which drugs, wine, olive oil, grains, spices, lumber, naval stores, leather, sugar, and other commodities produced in America would be exchanged for English wool and other manufactures.[5]

Such a flourishing commerce, in Hakluyt's view, was bound to be of enormous benefit to the English. Not only would it help to compensate for the nation's then "decayed trades" with the rest of the Old World, but it also promised to increase naval and military resources

4. Hakluyt, "Discourse of Western Planting," 233–34, 313.
5. Ibid., 222–33, 235; Hakluyt, "Inducements," 330–31; Hakluyt, "Epistle to Ralegh," no. 2, 378.

substantially, "inlarge the Revenewes of the Crowne very mightely and inriche all sortes of subjectes ingenerally." American plantations, in short, promised to bring "inlarged domynions, power, Revenewes, and honnor" to the nation and to be "long . . . profitable and gaine-full . . . to those of our nation there remaining." That they might also help the English to siphon off some of the vast treasures the Spanish derived from their colonies and thereby "to abate the pride of Spaine" and to pull Philip II "downe in equalitie to his neighbour princes" was also an appealing prospect.[6]

By actively taking advantage "of so great and so abundant a boon," Hakluyt thus argued, the English could at once secure two beneficial national objectives. First, they could reverse the country's trading fortunes and thereby prevent it from "returne[ing] to [its] former olde meanes[s] and basenes[s]" and enable it to continue "to stande in [its] present and late former honor glorye and force, and not neglegently and sleepingly to slyde [back] into beggery" and national insignifi-cance. Second, it could provide the strength to "cutt the combe of the frenche, of the spanishe, of the portingale, and of enemies, and of doubtfull fr[i]endes to the abatinge of their wealthe and force, and to the greater savinge of the wealthe of the Realme" of England.[7]

The recovery of English trade was not the only socioeconomic diffi-culty for which Hakluyt sought a solution through western planting; equally important, substantial emigration to American plantations seemed to offer a way out of the series of worrisome and debilitating problems contemporaries associated with overpopulation and under-employment. "For all the Statutes that hitherto can be devised, and the sharpe execution of the same in poonishinge idle and lazye persons," Hakluyt lamented, "wante of sufficient occasion of honest employ-ment" could not "deliver our common wealthe from multitudes of loyterers and idle vagabondes." So populous had England become, Hakluyt complained in a famous passage, that it was "swarming w[i]th lustie youthes that be turned to no profitable use" and "every arte and science" had "so many [practitioners], that they can hardly lyve one

6. Hakluyt, "Discourse of Western Planting," 222, 270, 315, 317–18; Hak-luyt, "Epistle to Ralegh," no. 2, 374; Richard Hakluyt, lawyer, "Pamphlet for the Virginia Enterprise," 1602, in Taylor, ed., *Original Writings*, 2:339, 374.

7. Hakluyt, "Epistle Dedicatory to Sir Walter Ralegh," no. 1, 1587, in Tay-lor, ed., *Original Writings*, 2:365; Hakluyt, "Discourse of Western Planting," 314, 317.

*America. This engraving puts forward the idea of America as an arena for Euro-
pean economic and cultural enterprise. It shows American peoples, animals, and
products displayed amidst European traders under the guns of a European fort,
while two European figures raise an Amerindian chieftainess in a giant conch
shell to a higher level of civility. With the horn of plenty in her right hand and
showering her surroundings with gold, she symbolizes the abundance associated
with America by European colonial enterprisers. From Jacob Van Meurs, in
Arnoldus Montanus, De Niewe en Onbekende Weereld (Amsterdam, 1671).
Courtesy of the Library of Congress, neg. no. LCUSZ62-32366.*

by another, nay rather they are readie to eate upp one another: yea
many thousandes are in this Realme, w[hi]ch havinge no way to be
sett on worke be either mutinous and seeke alteration in the state, or
at leaste very burdensome to the common wealthe, and often fall to
pilferinge and thevinge and other lewdnes[s], whereby all the prisons
of the land are daily pest[e]red and stuffed full of them, where either
they pitifully pyne awaye, or els[e] at lengthe are miserably hanged,
even xxti. at a clappe oute of some one Jayle."[8]

For these intractable problems, it seemed to Hakluyt, "that tremendous entity America," and more especially "all those large and
spatious countries on ye easte parte of" it, "off[e]reth the remedie."
Just as the Spanish, by establishing American plantations, had created "so many honest wayes to sett" people "on work" that there was
scarcely "one theefe" to be found in their country, so the English,
Hakluyt projected, could do away with domestic unemployment and
social unrest by removing many of the "waste people" in England
to the many "dispeopled" or lightly populated "waste Contries" and
"great waste Woods [to] be [found] there." With an extent of land
that was "greater than all Europe, and in goodness of soile nothing
inferior thereunto," eastern North America had room for large numbers of people and many plantations, every one of which would have
so many "thousandes of thinges . . . to be don[e]" that not just local
Amerindians but "infinite nombers of the english nation" could "be
sett on worke to the unburdenynge of the Realme w[i]th many that
nowe lyve chardgeable to the state at home."[9]

8. Hakluyt, "Discourse of Western Planting," 234, 249.
9. Ibid., 234, 251, 317, 319; Hakluyt, "Epistle to Ralegh," no. 1, 363; "Notes
Ascribed to Richard Hakluyt," 1598, in Taylor, ed., Original Writings, 2:423;
Hakluyt, lawyer, "Pamphlet for the Virginia Enterprise," 331.

AMERICA

T' AMSTERDAM
By Jacob van Meurs, Plaetsnyder en Boeckverkooper op de Kesers graft in de Stadt Meurs. 1671.

In new plantations, Hakluyt explained, every manner of person would be useful. "All sortes and states of men," including "all severall kindes of artificers, husbandmen, seamen, merchauntes, souldiers, captaines, phisitions, lawyers, devines, Cosmographers, hidrographers, Astronomers, [even] historiographers, yea olde folkes, lame persons, women, and yonge children," could all find work and thereby be rescued from idleness at home and "made able by their owne honest and easie labour to" support "themselves w[i]thoute syrchardginge others." People from almost every category of socially superfluous and disruptive people could be put to work. Unemployed mariners could be recalled from piracy and put to work in the carrying trade. Disbanded soldiers could be retrieved from brigandage and used to police recalcitrant savages. The "frye of the wandringe beggars" that in England grew "upp ydly and hurtefull and burdenous to this Realme" could "there be unladen, better bred upp," and made useful to themselves and the nation. Debtors, people who had taken a wrong turn, even petty thieves and criminals who "for trifles" might "otherwise [have] be[en] devoured by the gallowes" could all be transported to the plantations and there usefully employed to construct forts, houses, and other buildings; to produce lumber, naval stores, staves, casks, leather, silk, and hemp; to mine gold and other precious metals and stones; to harvest fish and other products from the sea; and to cultivate and produce a wide variety of agricultural commodities, including sugar, cotton, wine, olives, and grains.[10]

But Hakluyt did not conceive of emigration simply as a vent for social undesirables and a means of social control. He also exhibited an appreciation for its potential benefits for the individuals involved. By putting themselves in useful employments in American plantations, he suggested, the down-and-out and the dispirited, those who had no chance even for a comfortable subsistence, much less for improving their circumstances, could "finde themselves" and "be raised againe," both in their economic circumstances and their own self-esteem, "to their owne more happy state." Even younger sons of substantial people who had no prospects in England, he suggested, could find opportunities to build estates in American plantations. In what can only be described as little more than a concluding aside, Hakluyt also suggested that America might provide a religious as well as an economic

10. Hakluyt, "Discourse of Western Planting," 234–36, 319; Hakluyt, "Epistle to Ralegh," no. 2, 377.

Connecticut Colony Seal. The vision of North America as a land of abundance was evoked by this official seal of the colony of Connecticut. Probably devised during the early 1640s, it shows a vineyard, a symbol of plenty, of three vines, supported and bearing fruit. From an engraving on a two-shilling Connecticut paper note. Courtesy of the American Antiquarian Society.

refuge, not for English people but for others "from all partes of the worlde" who were "forced to flee for the truthe of god[']s worde." [11]

In this utilitarian analysis of the potential benefits of American plantations, Hakluyt was both the heir of nearly a century of European perceptions and the herald of virtually every one of the themes

11. Hakluyt, "Discourse of Western Planting," 235–36, 282, 318–19.

New York Colony Coat of Arms. This coat of arms from the colony of New York depicts America as an economic partnership between the European with his weights and measures and the Amerindian with his bow, both under the protection of the English state. New York's main early products, beaver pelts and wheat, are shown by the beavers, grain barrels, and the arms of a windmill that ground wheat. From a printer's ornament of the New York printer James Parker, 1752. Courtesy of the American Antiquarian Society.

that would dominate English thought about the colonies for the next two centuries. The basic image he conveyed to his audience depicted America as a large and fruitful country available for the taking by the enterprising and the bold. In this image, Amerindians, like the land and other resources of America, were essentially passive objects who had no integrity or selfhood of their own and whose own priorities and objectives ordinarily demanded no consideration and had to be taken into account only when they represented an obstacle to English designs.

In developing this image, Hakluyt merely subscribed to one of the classic assumptions of what the literary scholar Peter Hulme has recently referred to as "colonial discourse." By systematically "denying the substantiality of other worlds, other words, and other narratives," by effectively disavowing "all contradictory evidence," that emerging discourse, Hulme explains, simply ignored abundant evidence that most Amerindians did in fact live in "settled pattern[s]" and instead presented them as following "an aimless, nomadic wandering [life] that, by extension, left the land empty and virgin"—and thus available for the use of Europeans.[12]

Of course, Hakluyt acknowledged the obligation, imposed upon English people by their superior religious and cultural development, to bring civility and Christianity to Amerindians. As candidates for instruction and conversion, they would be given, under English tutelage, opportunity to adopt a civil life and secure salvation. In the meantime, however, Hakluyt seems to have taken for granted that their low place in the chain of human cultural evolution fitted them to be no more than adjuncts to English enterprise, at best laborers in the pursuit of the "many noble endes" involved in building plantations.[13]

Like Columbus nearly a century earlier, Hakluyt was far more interested in the economic potential than in the peoples of America, in the socioeconomic salvation of England than in the spiritual salvation of Amerindians. Most powerfully, he presented America as a capacious and mostly empty country that was admirably suited for use and exploitation by English people, an unformed and still natural space in which English enterprisers could simultaneously help to solve the social and economic problems of England, enhance its wealth and international standing, and, depending on their prior circumstances, either find the means to escape the misery, the helplessness, and the despair that had been their lot in England or to advance their individual fortunes. In the America limned by Hakluyt, individuals could find opportunities to improve their lives by pursuing many of those life objectives that had been inaccessible to them in the Old World and that were customarily associated with the attainment of individual happiness.

During the very earliest stages of English colonizing activities in the New World, the younger Richard Hakluyt had thus identified America as a genuinely exceptional place. Exceptional for both its openness and its apparent richness of resources, America was an area in which

12. Peter Hulme, *Colonial Encounters: Europe and the Native Caribbean, 1492–1797* (London, 1986), 156–57, 194.

13. Hakluyt, "Discourse of Western Planting," 282.

English people, both collectively and individually, could, to an extent that was wholly impossible anywhere in the already organized, comparatively densely filled, closed, and poverty-ridden spaces of the Old World, take charge of their own lives, make new beginnings, and pursue their own ambitions.

As old as the first voyage of Columbus to the New World, the underlying assumptions of European superiority that so evidently informed Hakluyt's writings had gained enormous additional force during the sixteenth century. After a hundred years of contact, few Europeans doubted that Europe, for all its social and political warts, was, in the phrase of Hakluyt's contemporary Samuel Purchas, "the sole home of 'Arts and Inventions' "[14] and should therefore be the cultural model for all newly encountered worlds and the primary shaper of any new societies that might be established in those worlds. If Iberian successes in asserting a high degree of dominance over significant proportions of America helped to enhance this expanding and deepening sense of superiority, so also did several developments within Europe itself.

In particular, the new science and technology associated with the scientific revolution produced extraordinary advances that could only confirm Europe's sense of its own superiority. The growing use of the experimental method, the increased use of quantification and mathematics as scientific tools, and a burgeoning interest in technology led to scientific advances and technological achievements, especially in printing, warfare, and navigation, that seemed from a European point of view to put Europe miles ahead of even the most technologically advanced peoples encountered in America. Of course, as contemporaries recognized, those very advances also served as vital instruments for extending the "cultural and political influence of . . . Europe over all other parts of the globe." Although some of its leading exponents, including Francis Bacon, Johann Valentin Andrae, and Tommaso Campanella, revealed through their utopian tracts an impatience with the rate of scientific discovery and some doubt about the uses to which the advances that had been made were being put, they believed that the new scientific and technological achievements were enabling European peoples to achieve greater control over the

14. Samuel Purchas, *Purchas His Pilgrims*, in *Hakluytus Posthumus*, 20 vols. (Glasgow, 1905–7), 1:249, as cited by G. V. Scammell, "The New Worlds and Europe in the Sixteenth Century," *Historical Journal* 12 (1969): 409.

worlds they inhabited and eventually would lead to the betterment of humankind and the improvement of society.[15]

This urge for improvement was especially manifest in a contemporary rage for what would eventually be called projects and projecting that swept England, the Netherlands, France, and Spain beginning in the middle of the sixteenth century. Projects were schemes to introduce or improve manufactures, crops, agricultural techniques, transportation, internal and external markets, and employment. Planting and colonization were themselves simply enormously ambitious projects. Exponents of most projecting schemes were chiefly concerned with enriching themselves. Over time, however, the great proliferation of such schemes, many of which were successful, cumulatively served to enrich society as a whole and, by the late seventeenth century, to contribute to a sense that the world was slowly becoming more tractable and that material conditions and the quality of peoples' lives even at the lowest rungs of society were gradually getting somewhat more ample, if not necessarily better.[16]

The simultaneous expansion of commercial activity had much the same effect. Both by stimulating and then catering to new levels of consumer demand and by encouraging increased production, commercial expansion slowly operated to raise levels of material welfare throughout much of Western Europe. Already in the seventeenth century and increasingly in the eighteenth century, those levels seemed to be considerably higher than they had been earlier in Europe or than they were then among any of the native peoples of America or most of the other peoples of the world that had come within European purview since the late sixteenth century.[17]

15. See, in this connection, Allen G. Debus, *Man and Nature in the Renaissance* (Cambridge, 1978), 1, 6–7, 116–21, 134–41, and, for a slightly later period, Charles Webster, *The Great Instauration: Science, Medicine and Reform, 1626–1660* (New York, 1976), 1–31.

16. On the rage for projects in England and its effects, see Joan Thirsk, *Economic Policy and Projects: The Development of Consumer Society in Early Modern England* (Oxford, 1978).

17. The expansion of trade and its effects may be followed in D. C. Coleman, *The Economy of England, 1450–1750* (Oxford, 1977), 48–68, 131–50, and B. A. Holderness, *Pre-Industrial England: Economy and Society, 1500–1750* (London, 1976), 116–70, 197–220. See also Ralph Davis, *The Rise of the Atlantic Economies* (Ithaca, N.Y., 1973); E. L. Jones, *The European Miracle: Environments, Economies and Geopolitics in the History of Europe and Asia* (Cambridge, 1981); and Neil

But these confidence-building achievements in science, technology, and economic life were by no means the only developments in Europe that affected Europe's contribution to the identification of America. In *The Civilizing Process*, Norbert Elias has shown how, coincidental with the discovery and early colonization of America, Europeans were exhibiting an ever greater concern for civility, a concern, he argues, that over the next three hundred years actually resulted in Europe's becoming more civilized. Elias does not consider the possibility that the encounter with America may have had a role in this process. However, by providing Europeans with concrete examples of what they were not and did not want to become, more extensive and intensive contacts with the so-called primitive peoples of America and elsewhere outside Europe doubtless required them to define more explicitly standards of what was and what was not *civilized* and thereby functioned as a powerful stimulus to this civilizing process as well as a formidable blinder to the achievements of other cultures.[18]

If, however, contact with America gave Europeans heightened incentives to cultivate their own civility and if, along with their new discoveries in science and technology, their many successful efforts at social improvement, and the spread of commerce, their many achievements in that regard functioned to enhance their sense of control over their own destiny and the destinies of others,[19] they continued throughout the early modern era to exhibit a palpable awareness of their own moral and social deficiencies as identified a century before by many early modern humanists and theologians, including Sir Thomas More. Whatever the extent of their own vaunted cultural and religious superiority over peoples in other quarters of the globe, they knew that they themselves very often displayed, even within Europe itself, many of the same base and primitive characteristics that they attributed to Amerindians and later to Europeans and their descendants living in America. To the chagrin of many learned people, the new science, as Keith Thomas has shown in the case of England, coexisted

McKendrick and John Brewer, *The Birth of Consumer Society: The Commercialization of Eighteenth-Century England* (Bloomington, Ind., 1982).

18. Norbert Elias, *The Civilizing Process: The History of Manners* (New York, 1978).

19. Stephen Greenblatt penetratingly discusses this growing sense of mastery in *Renaissance Self-Fashioning from More to Shakespeare* (Chicago, 1980) and *Shakespearean Negotiations: The Circulation of Social Energy in Renaissance England* (Berkeley and Los Angeles, 1988).

with powerful undercurrents of belief in magic, witchcraft, astrology, and other forms of superstition.[20]

Perhaps more important, the new economic and religious conditions of the sixteenth and seventeenth centuries seemed to produce many unsettling side effects. The expansion of trade, the penetration of the market, the proliferation of joint-stock companies and the projecting spirit, the emergence of new and expanding forms of consumerism, and, toward the end of the seventeenth century, the development of a money economy complete with new financial institutions like national banks and mounting national debts undermined traditional foundations of authority and stimulated new and extensively manifest forms of self-interested and egocentric economic, social, and political behavior. At the same time, the religious ferment associated with the Reformation, including especially the proliferation of a bewildering variety of sects and religious opinions, led to heightened religious discord, both civil and international war, and the shattering of the old unitary ecclesiastical order. In combination, these economic and religious developments evoked widespread and continuing anxieties that, instead of achieving ever greater mastery over itself, the Old World, for all its allegedly superior learning and civility, was rapidly degenerating into social and moral chaos.

Animated by such fears and nostalgic for the older order they thought must once have existed, a long line of social critics of radically different persuasions and orientations in England called, during the century and a half from 1575 to 1725, for a return to an older, more static, and more coherent social and religious order and to the traditional values of hierarchy, stewardship, virtue, simplicity, thrift, moderation, and piety. This pervasive yearning for order and the reassertion, even revitalization, of traditional habits of social and political thought vividly indicates just how disquieting English people found the steady pace of economic, social, and religious change that began under the Tudors and how difficult it was for them to discover or invent language and patterns of perception appropriate to the changing conditions in which they lived.

By the last years of the seventeenth and the early years of the eighteenth century, a few people, including John Locke, Bernard Mandeville, and several less well-known liberal economic writers, were endeavoring to work out a rationale for the new socioeconomic and

---

20. See Keith Thomas, *Religion and the Decline of Magic* (New York, 1971).

religious order. But the logic of that new order was by and large obscured by fear and nostalgia, and most social commentary from the Elizabethan puritans through Filmer and Harrington to Bolingbroke and Swift betrayed a profound "desire for the renewal of old values and structures, the hope of a radical *renovation*," a "great instauration," that would once again restore coherence to an increasingly incoherent world.[21]

Nor were such impulses peculiar to England. No less than during the age of initial encounter, the cultures of seventeenth-century and early-eighteenth-century Europe continued to find it extremely difficult to come to terms with novelty. All of the great seventeenth-century upheavals in the Netherlands, France, Spain, and Italy were, like the English Revolution of the 1640s and unlike the democratic revolutions at the end of the eighteenth century, "dominated by the idea, not of progress, but of a return to a golden age in the past." Still holding to a theory of history that saw the past as either a providential design or a recurring cycle of advances and declines, they aspired to renovation, not innovation.[22]

Disappointed in their efforts to recapture the world they had lost in England, some people in the seventeenth century, like More a hundred

21. In this connection, see E. M. W. Tillyard, *The Elizabethan World Picture* (New York, 1944); David Bevington, *Tudor Drama and Politics: A Critical Approach to Topical Meaning* (Cambridge, Mass., 1968); W. H. Greenleaf, *Order, Empiricism and Politics: Two Traditions of English Political Thought, 1500–1700* (Oxford, 1964); Webster, *Great Instauration*, 1–31; William M. Lamont, *Godly Rule: Politics and Religion, 1603–1660* (London, 1969); Gordon J. Schochet, *Patriarchalism in Political Thought: The Authoritarian Family and Political Speculation and Attitudes Especially in Seventeenth-Century England* (New York, 1975); James Daly, *Sir Robert Filmer and English Political Thought* (Toronto, 1979); C. B. McPherson, *The Political Theory of Possessive Individualism* (Oxford, 1962); Arthur J. Slavin, "The American Principle from More to Locke," in *First Images of America: The Impact of the New World on the Old*, ed. Fredi Chiapelli, 2 vols. (Berkeley and Los Angeles, 1976), 1:139–64; Joyce Oldham Appleby, *Economic Thought and Ideology in Seventeenth-Century England* (Princeton, 1978); Isaac Kramnick, *Bolingbroke and His Circle: The Politics of Nostalgia in the Age of Walpole* (Cambridge, Mass., 1968); Mircea Eliade, "Paradise and Utopia: Mythical Geography and Eschatology," in *Utopias and Utopian Thought*, ed. Frank E. Manuel (Boston, 1966), 261; J. C. Davis, *Utopia and the Ideal Society: A Study of English Utopian Writing, 1516–1700* (Cambridge, 1981), 86.

22. J. H. Elliott, "Revolution and Continuity in Early Modern Europe," *Past and Present*, no. 42 (1969): 69; Robert Forster and Jack P. Greene, eds., *Preconditions of Revolution in Early Modern Europe* (Baltimore, 1970).

years earlier, turned to America as a place in which their objectives might be accomplished. In contrast to More, however, they thought in terms not of *finding* an existing utopia but of *founding* one in the relatively "empty" and inviting spaces of North America. Several Spaniards had preceded them in such attempts. Some Franciscans, the principal of whom was Gerónimo de Mendieta, envisioned an Amerindian commonwealth, a millennial kingdom, in Mexico "in which the Christianity of the Old World would be perfected."[23]

More modest and more successful was the effort, beginning in the 1530s, by Vasco de Quiroga, a lawyer and recent immigrant to Mexico who subsequently became bishop of Michoacán. Quiroga actually sought to implement More's ideas by establishing two communal religious villages, one near Mexico City and the other in Michoacán. Representing an effort to produce what Silvio Zavala has called a "perfect Christian commonwealth" from what Quiroga regarded as "the unformed and tractable mass of Indian population," these villages were inhabited not by Spanish settlers but by Amerindians with a few friars; land was held in common, and the inhabitants were required to work in communal enterprises and receive religious instruction.[24] At least in part inspired by the surprising success of this effort "to civilize Indians in accord with ideals associated with Christian humanism," the Jesuits, beginning during the first decades of the seventeenth century, established theocratic *reductions* among Amerindians in Paraguay that employed some of Quiroga's operating principles.[25]

But it was North America, which had a far smaller and, in most places, considerably less settled Amerindian population than many parts of Hispanic America, that seemed to offer the unlimited and, even more important, the as yet unoccupied and unorganized space in which a new society, free from the imperfections and restraints

23. John Leddy Phelan, *The Millennial Kingdom of the Franciscans in the New World* (Berkeley and Los Angeles, 1970), 77.

24. Silvio Zavala, *New Viewpoints on the Spanish Colonization of America* (Philadelphia, 1943), 113. See also Silvio Zavala, "The American Utopia of the Sixteenth Century," *Huntington Library Quarterly* 10 (1947): 337–47, and *Sir Thomas More in New Spain* (London, 1955).

25. Peggy K. Liss, *Mexico under Spain, 1521–1556: Society and the Origins of Nationality* (Chicago, 1975), 84; Magnus Mörner, *The Political and Economic Activities of the Jesuits in the La Plata Region: The Hapsburg Era* (Stockholm, 1953); Philip Caraman, *The Lost Paradise: The Jesuit Republic in South America* (New York, 1976).

of the old, might be created. In dramatic contrast to the "civilized and filled space[s]" Europeans had encountered in the Levant and the Orient, North America presented itself as an immense, sparsely populated, and bounteous territory that was "open for experimentation." Apparently with "neither a history nor any political forms at all," it invited people to consider how, in as yet unarticulated space, Old World institutions and socioeconomic, religious, and political arrangements might be modified to produce the best possible commonwealths.[26]

John Locke succinctly captured prevailing conceptions about the plasticity of the American world in his *Second Treatise of Government*. "In the beginning," Locke wrote, "all the World was America."[27] In this passage, Locke both revealed the great impact the discovery of America had upon the revival of natural law theory during the early modern era and identified America as a natural, unformed, and "free space,"[28] a place still unblemished by the corruptions and "trammels of the Old World"[29] and waiting to be the site of Europe's new beginnings. This image of America inspired English colonial organizers with the dream of creating through conscious instrumental human planning and action a New Jerusalem or a New Eden. If an existing paradise of the kind imagined by Sir Thomas More was not to be found in America, Englishmen now seized upon the challenge offered by its wide open spaces to design and construct one there.

Shakespeare set out the formula by which this dream might be realized in 1611 in *The Tempest*, which was inspired by an actual wreck in Bermuda of an English ship bound for the new colony of Virginia. In that play, it will be recalled, Prospero, the agent, in the words of Leo Marx, of "a dynamic, literate, and purposeful civilization," finds himself and his party cast up on a remote and uncultivated island where he confronts a hellish wilderness epitomized by Caliban, a savage indigene whose name is anagrammatic of the word cannibal. Regarding the challenge posed by this wilderness as a "field for the exercise of power," for the application of superior European knowledge and skills, Prospero manages in little more than a decade to bring a civilized

26. Slavin, "American Principle," 1:139–40, 143.

27. John Locke, *Two Treatises of Government*, ed. Peter Laslett (New York, 1963), 343.

28. Slavin, "American Principle," 1:139.

29. Harry Levin, *The Myth of the Golden Age in the Renaissance* (Bloomington, Ind., 1969), 61.

order out of the "hellish darkness" and natural chaos of this virgin and only lightly occupied place. In the process, he transforms "a howling desert" in which "the profane ruled" into "a magnificent garden," an "idyllic land of ease, peace, and plenty" presided over by "a highly civilized European."[30]

In this account, as Hulme has emphasized in his superb reading of *The Tempest* as a central text in the emerging colonial discourse, Prospero and Caliban stand as "archtypes of the colonizer and the colonized." Prospero could not have achieved such results without Caliban, whose labor and knowledge of local conditions were "indispensable" to Prospero's success. That success, in fact, required not just Caliban's labor and expertise but also his enslavement, his total submission to Prospero's mastery. The great results to which it led and the assumption that slavery was a "necessary stage between savagery and civility," an assumption that, as Hulme notes, was common coin in early modern colonial discourse, were sufficient to excuse that enslavement.[31]

If, therefore, as Leo Marx has pointed out, "Prospero's behavior . . . suggests that half-formed, indistinct idea of history as a record of human improvement, or progress, that was incipient in Renaissance thought generally,"[32] the price for that progress in the prospective new colonial societies of America was at least the temporary subjection of its native peoples to European mastery, including, if necessary, their enslavement. A willingness, perhaps even an eagerness, to exact this price was implicit in all early modern English and other European colonizing projects. Not just the lands and resources but the people who inhabited those lands thus beckoned Europeans to assert their mastery over the New World. Not just the prospects for personal material advancement emphasized by Hakluyt or the possibilities for escape from debilitating socioeconomic or religious conditions but also the opportunity for domination, which was implicit in Hakluyt's

---

30. Leo Marx, *The Machine in the Garden: Technology and the Pastoral Idea in America* (New York, 1964), 34–69. The quotations are from pp. 35, 41, 43, 52, 53, 63.

31. Hulme, *Colonial Encounters*, 89–134. The quotations are from pp. 99, 125, 127. O. Mannoni, *Prospero and Caliban: The Psychology of Colonization* (New York, 1956), is the classic study of this theme. Alden T. Vaughan, "Shakespeare's Indian: The Americanization of Caliban," *Shakespeare Quarterly* 39 (1988): 137–53, provides a succinct account of the "Americanization" of *The Tempest*.

32. Marx, *Machine in the Garden*, 63–64.

schemes for evangelizing Amerindians and exploiting their labor, were among the principal allurements presented to Europeans by America.

If the designers of England's many colonizing ventures were often animated by the hope of equalling Prospero's achievement, Virginia, the first permanent English American colony, was the last in which dominion over the local Amerindian population was central to the fulfillment of its initial designs. The private joint-stock company that founded Virginia, like many similar companies previously established to trade with Europe, Africa, and India, at first proposed to set up a combination of commercial factories to trade with the natives and production centers that, under English management, would employ native labor to turn out commodities that would be readily vendible in Europe.

But these plans quickly went awry. Chesapeake Amerindians turned out to have few goods the English wanted and to be thoroughly uninterested either in providing the agricultural labor needed to produce the tobacco that soon became the economic staple of the colony or in undergoing the religious conversion that would presumably have made them tractable laborers. As a result, the Virginia Company turned to England for laborers, who as company employees worked common lands under a severe military regimen. But high mortality in Virginia created such a large demand for labor that simply in order to recruit a work force the company soon had to offer incentives, primarily in the form of promises of land at the end of a set period of labor service, that ultimately helped to transform Virginia from the tight company organization originally envisioned into a society of independent producers.[33]

With regard to most later English colonial ventures, the explicit initial focus was less upon domination over either land or people than upon the nature of the social and political constructs their proponents planned to create on the supposedly blank cultural surfaces of America. Except for the island colonies in the Atlantic and the Caribbean, each of which developed without an elaborate plan, virtually every one of the new English colonies established in America after Virginia represented an effort to create in some part of the in-

33. See Sigmund Diamond, "From Organization to Society: Virginia in the Seventeenth Century," _American Journal of Sociology_ 63 (1958): 457–75, and Edmund S. Morgan, _American Slavery, American Freedom: The Ordeal of Colonial Virginia_ (New York, 1975).

finitely pliable world of America—a world that would perforce yield to English mastery—some specific Old World vision for the recovery of an ideal past in a new and carefully constructed society. Over the succeeding century and a half, what would become English North America seemed to offer a fertile soil for an astonishing number of such attempts, each of which differed radically from the others.

Far and away the most ambitious was the surprisingly successful attempt by English puritans to establish a redemptive community of God's chosen people in the colony of Massachusetts Bay and, somewhat later, in its extensions in Connecticut and New Haven. Aspiring to nothing less than the formation of the true Christian commonwealth that would serve as a model for the rest of the Christian world, John Winthrop and other leaders of this venture endeavored not only to secure perfection in the church but also to create a society that, in contrast to the increasingly chaotic world of early modern England, would conform as closely as possible to traditional English prescriptions for the ideal well-ordered commonwealth.

In pursuit of these ends, these leaders tried to design polities that would be presided over by saints, governed by a body of laws that conformed to those of God, and organized into a series of well-ordered covenanted communities knit together by Christian love and composed only of like-minded people with a common religious ideology and a strong sense of communal responsibility. With church membership confined to the regenerate and civil rights limited to church members, these polities proposed to exclude all those who stood outside the broad religious consensus, to maintain tight control over economic life, and to use strong institutions of church, town, and family to subject the moral and social conduct of themselves and their neighbors to the strictest possible social discipline and to maintain the traditional social values of order, hierarchy, and subordination.[34]

Other colonial enterprisers sought to impose on American spaces still other sorts of social and political arrangements designed to eliminate problems that characterized old England. In Maryland, the first of several colonies started by powerful English public figures with the general objective of building a vast American landed estate, Lord Baltimore hoped, in addition to providing a refuge for his Catholic co-

34. The considerable recent literature on this subject is summarized in Jack P. Greene, *Pursuits of Happiness: The Social Development of Early Modern British Colonies and the Formation of American Culture* (Chapel Hill, N.C., 1989), 18–27.

religionists, to set up a well-ordered feudal society of a kind that had not existed in England for at least a century and a half. He envisioned a social mix of yeomen and landlords in which the latter, presiding over substantial manors worked by tenants, would enjoy all of the rights, including judicial authority, and revenues and perform all of the responsibilities traditionally associated with the medieval feudal order.[35] In New York, conquered from the Dutch in 1664, the proprietor, the future James II, refused to permit representative institutions and thereby sought to implement the sort of absolutist polity that Louis XIV was then fashioning for France and that James's brother Charles II would have preferred for England.[36]

This experimental approach to colonization continued to be manifest down through the early eighteenth century. In the late 1660s, for his patron, Sir Anthony Ashley Cooper, first earl of Shaftesbury, and other proprietors, John Locke devised a scheme of social and political organization for Carolina that incorporated many of the ideas set forth in James Harrington's semiutopian tract *Oceania*. By proposing to vest two-fifths of landed property permanently in the hands of an elaborately graded aristocracy and by building in many of the balancing institutional mechanisms advocated by Harrington, this scheme sought to erect a social polity that would be immune from upheavals of the kind that occurred in England during the Civil War.[37] In the 1680s, William Penn, also influenced by Harrington, envisioned his new colony of Pennsylvania as a holy experiment that, solidly founded on principles of religious toleration and balanced government, would be free of religious and civil embroilments.[38] Fifty years later, in the 1730s, a group of humanitarian reformers designed the new colony of Georgia as a model of social benevolence that would exclude slavery and be composed of small independent landowners and producers.[39]

Nor were the English the only European colonizers to look upon

35. See Wesley Frank Craven, *The Southern Colonies in the Seventeenth Century, 1607–1689* (Baton Rouge, 1949), 183–92.

36. See Robert C. Ritchie, *The Duke's Province: A Study of New York Politics and Society, 1664–1691* (New York, 1977).

37. M. Eugene Sirmans, *Colonial South Carolina: A Political History, 1663–1763* (Chapel Hill, N.C., 1966), 10–16.

38. Gary B. Nash, *Quakers and Politics: Pennsylvania, 1681–1726* (Princeton, 1968), 3–47.

39. Paul S. Taylor, *Georgia Plan: 1632–1752* (Berkeley, 1972).

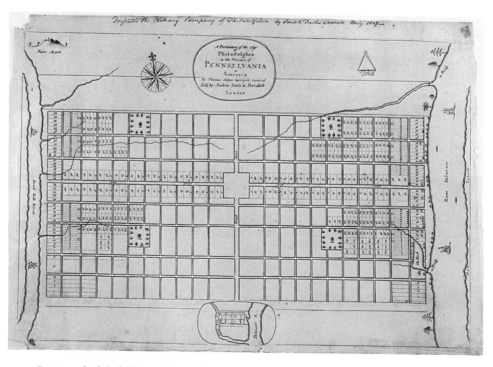

Design of Philadelphia. This early engraving by the surveyor general of the province of Pennsylvania of a plan for the new capital city of Philadelphia illustrates the conception of America as a place in which Europeans could create new societies according to their own designs. The symmetrical street plan running between the Delaware and Schuylkill rivers with numbered lots along many of the streets, a central square for the town hall and the market, and four other bounded squares at regular intervals imposes a civilized European order upon a piece of the American wilderness. From Thomas Holme, "A Portraiture of the City of Philadelphia in the Province of Pennsylvania in America," in A Letter from William Penn . . . to the Committee of the Free Society of Traders *(London, 1683), frontispiece. Courtesy of the Library Company of Philadelphia.*

North America as a venue for social experimentation. Contemporary with the founding of Virginia, William Usselinx, the Amsterdam merchant and longtime proponent of Dutch colonization in North America, proposed to establish in New Netherlands "an agrarian Christian extension of all that was best in Dutch society," a "utopian empire" that would forgo slavery and mining for "the creation of a European-style staple agriculture that could support" its "free Dutch citizens" while "simultaneously establishing the [proper] cultural milieu for the conversion of the savages."[40] Fifty years later, when the French government took over New France in the 1660s, it tried to set up a stable seigneurial regime that, "pruned of the less desirable characteristics" the seigneurial system had acquired in France, would provide the basis for "an obedient agricultural society" in which "the vast majority of persons would be firmly fixed to the land, would live peaceably in their villages, and would respond obediently to the commands of their superiors."[41]

More vividly perhaps than any other developments during the first century of English, French, and Dutch colonizing activities in America, the number and range of these experiments illustrates the extent to which America had been identified among Europeans as a site for the realization of dreams and hopes that could not be achieved in the Old World. No less than More's *Utopia*, every one of these enterprises exhibited a powerful urge on the part of their authors to reorder some aspects of the existing European world, to reverse some social, political, or economic trends they found worrisome, or to restore some imagined lost and less threatening world. In seizing upon America as the site for the pursuit of their "idealized version[s]" of the Old World,[42] the exponents of such schemes were both responding to and providing substantial reinforcement for America's emerging identification as a place that, in its exceptional openness, provided an appropriate venue in which to seek Europe's new beginnings through the assertion of European mastery in a largely uncontested field.

Of course, all of these efforts were failures. Indeed, with the exception of the puritan experiment in New England, which with strong leadership and widespread public support managed to perpetuate itself through the better part of two generations, their failures were almost immediate. In colony after colony, it was discovered, to paraphrase a familiar aphorism, that you could take Europeans out of Europe but you could not take Europe out of Europeans, who did *not* lose their vices in the new soil of America. Yet, as John Murrin has pointed out

40. Oliver A. Rink, *Holland on the Hudson: An Economic and Social History of Dutch New York* (Ithaca, N.Y., 1986), 52.

41. Sigmund Diamond, "An Experiment in 'Feudalism': French Canada in the Seventeenth Century," *William and Mary Quarterly*, 3d ser., 18 (1961): 7, 9, 14. See also Richard Colebrook Harris, *The Seigneurial System in Early Canada* (Madison, Wis., 1966).

42. Marx, *Machine in the Garden*, 62.

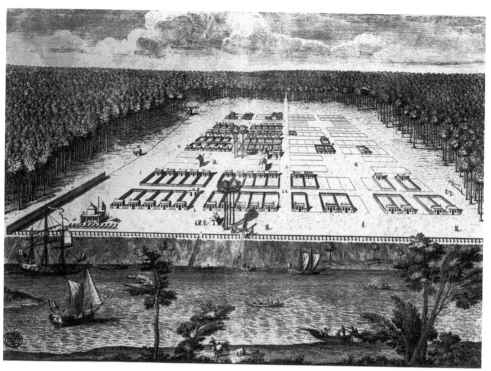

View of Savannah. Like Holme's design for Philadelphia, this engraving by Peter Fourdrinier after a drawing by Peter Gordon, an official of the trustees of the colony of Georgia, of the new town of Savannah during its construction in 1734 shows the ongoing efforts by British colonizers to order their new settlements according to a careful design. With the tent of Savannah's builder, James Ogle-thorpe, next to the town bell and the crane used to lift building materials up the steep bank of the Savannah River at the center, this illustration shows a sizable area that, in marked contrast to the dense surrounding forest, has been largely denuded of trees and already has a fort, courthouse, public mill, oven, store-house, parsonage, about eighty private houses, and the beginnings of a defensive palisade. Ships, ready for taking the produce of the colony to Britain, ride in the river, while livestock to help sustain the new colony graze across the river on Hutchinson's Island. From A View of Savannah as It Stood the 20th of March, 1734. *Courtesy of the Library of Congress, neg. no. LCUSZ62-1912.*

with regard to the English colonies, the "real significance" of these social and political experiments lies not in their predictable failures but in the fact "that they were tried at all." For over a century, the unorganized spaces of North America had encouraged some Europeans "to try out in practice" a great variety of religious, social, economic, and political ideas that could never have been attempted in the organized world of Europe itself.[43]

If they had been disappointed in their grandest visions, the English, both settlers and colonial promoters who stayed at home, had learned a lot in their first century of colonizing activities. Most of all, they had learned that plantation building was a slow process. "Planting of countries," observed Francis Bacon in reflecting on the first two decades of the Virginia colony, was "like planting . . . woods."[44] Only where the initial migration of people and capital was quite substantial, where direction and authority were reasonably clear and not open to serious contest, where the disease environment was benign and a settled family life early achieved, and where a consensus on goals was widely shared did Bacon's observation not hold true, and among the seventeenth-century English colonies only Massachusetts, Connecticut, and, later and to a lesser extent, Pennsylvania met those conditions.

Everywhere else, mortality, inadequate labor and capital, weak and uncertain authority, lack of settled family life, Amerindian resistance, natural disasters, economic false starts, and many other adverse conditions combined to make colonial development slow and to keep colonial societies simple, rude, and devoted largely to the satisfaction of only the most basic human needs. Not even the most successful of these societies managed during the seventeenth century to achieve levels of material and cultural development that marked them as anything more than crude and socially and culturally impoverished peripheries of English cultural life. Their simplicity dramatically attested to the limits imposed upon the potential for English mastery by shortages of labor, capital, expertise, and institutional supports.

If these early colonizing ventures mostly fell far short of the ex-

43. John M. Murrin, "Colonial Political Development," in _Colonial British America: Essays in the New History of the Early Modern Era_, ed. Jack P. Greene and J. R. Pole (Baltimore, 1984), 424.

44. Francis Bacon, "Of Plantations," in _Settlements to Society, 1607–1763: A Documentary History of Colonial America_, ed. Jack P. Greene (New York, 1975), 9.

pectations of their designers, they also failed during the seventeenth century to yield many of the benefits predicted by Richard Hakluyt in the 1580s. They did not solve England's many socioeconomic difficulties: poverty, unemployment, and social disorder remained persistent problems in England throughout the century. Neither, as the occurrence of the English Civil War makes clear, did they prove to be a vent for social and political discontent. They did not even significantly increase England's national wealth and power, and they certainly did not lead to the conversion of many Amerindians.

Hakluyt predicted that, among the motives that might draw people to America, the prospect of seeking "the glorie of god and the saving of the soules of the poore & blinded infidels" would attract the "fewest number," and this prediction turned out to be right on the mark.[45] Throughout the century, evangelization of Amerindians continued to receive considerable lip service but, in marked contrast to the situation in the Catholic colonies of Spain and France, very small expenditures of money and energy. Even in New England where religious concerns were most powerful, missionary activities were desultory. Clerics proved to be far more interested in ministering to the souls of their flocks and pondering the moral health of settler society than in converting Amerindians. Especially after the Virginia experience made clear that Amerindians would never be willing auxiliaries to European enterprise, colonists and their backers in England found the encounter with America's land and resources infinitely more compelling than the encounter with its peoples.

During this early period, in fact, the opportunity for individuals to achieve mastery over and wrest profits from some part of American nature rapidly came to be the principal component in the emerging identification of English America. If, as collectivities, most colonies had had disappointing beginnings, thousands of individuals who settled in them managed to acquire land, improve their personal circumstances, and build families. As English America was revealing itself to be yet another "disproving ground for utopias,"[46] as it was losing its allure as a field for social experiments, it acquired a growing reputation as an arena for the pursuit of individual betterment.

Of course, absolutely nothing was assured. That was the exhilara-

45. Hakluyt, "Epistle to Ralegh," no. 2, 375–76.
46. Daniel J. Boorstin, *The Americans: The Colonial Experience* (New York, 1958), 1.

tion of it. Very few people who migrated to English America during the seventeenth century ever acquired substantial wealth, and most of those did so in the West Indies. A far larger number of migrants were cruelly disappointed in their hopes, either dying early or never managing to get together the resources needed to make it out of servitude or dependency. In between these two extremes, however, enough people, especially those with family labor or the resources to command some bound labor, did sufficiently well to give growing force to the identification of America as a place that, in comparison with the Old World, offered exceptional scope for individual ambition.

CHAPTER THREE

Experiences

THE BEHAVIORAL ARTICULATION

OF BRITISH AMERICA,

1690–1760

Throughout much of the seventeenth century, some North Europeans had looked to North America as an unformed space onto which they could project their designs for a better, an improved European world. When they had tried to impose those designs upon the new continent during their initial encounters with it, only the New England puritans had enjoyed more than modest success. In many places, however, the first generation of immigrants did manage to establish enclaves of permanent settlement that provided a locus for thousands of men, women, and children from England, the Netherlands, France, and elsewhere in Europe to build new and, in many cases, materially and even spiritually satisfying lives for themselves and their children.

By the standards of much of the settled areas of Western Europe, however, the social results of their efforts were, in almost every case, disappointing. Efforts to imprint European cultural patterns upon the American environment were still at an early stage, but they had produced observable results. If, as late as 1700, even the most prosperous

Sachem and Soldier. This illustration of "A Sachem of the Abenakee Nation, Rescuing an English Officer from the Indians" shows both how Euroamericans had changed the landscape of America into settled farms with cultivated fields and the continued presence of Amerindians in these Europeanized areas. The particular fields depicted here are surrounded by carefully sited trees. From John Mein and John Fleming, Bickerstaff's Boston Almanac *(Boston, 1768). Courtesy of the American Antiquarian Society.*

and developed settlements were still simple, rustic, and crude, large chunks of forest and wilderness had given way to fields; houses, farm buildings, and fences formed the beginnings of a European-style rural landscape; there were several small urban seaports and inland hamlets with an expanding number of houses, stores, churches, and other public buildings and amenities; and a rough kind of socioeconomic and political order had everywhere become somewhat less tenuous.

During the next three-quarters of a century, between 1700 and the American War for Independence, the colonies experienced extraordinary growth and development. The results of the application of a degree of human physical energy that was by any measure astonishing, this experience and the behaviors that characterized it played a critical role in the formation of a colonial British American identity and in the elaboration of the conception of this broad cultural area as a collection of exceptional social entities. That experience is the subject of this chapter.

Early American historians have long appreciated the extent to which the decades on either side of 1700 were times of special difficulty for the colonies. Shifting political conditions in England, an undefined relationship between England and the colonies, fluctuating economic conditions, Amerindian resistance, wars with France and Spain, internal political and religious discord in many colonies, and rampant piracy along the seacoast were among the most obvious of the problems that, to one degree and at one time or another, confronted these new societies between 1675 and 1725. King Philip's War in New England, Bacon's Rebellion in Virginia, and Culpeper's Rebellion in North Carolina during the mid-1670s; the overthrow of the Dominion of New England in Massachusetts, the seizure of authority by the Protestant Association in Maryland, and Leisler's Rebellion in New York following the Glorious Revolution of 1688–89; more or less continuous unrest in the Carolinas from the 1690s through the revolution against the proprietors in 1719; recurrent military engagements in contested areas of New England, New York, the Carolinas, and Florida throughout the first two intercolonial wars between 1689 and 1713; and the Tuscarora and Yamassee wars in the Carolinas during the second decade of the eighteenth century—all of these difficulties had to be confronted and overcome during these years.

Whether or not such difficulties were responsible, these years also represented a low point in the exertion of the expansive energies of the settlers. Relatively few new frontier areas were opened for settlement. The French and Indian threat in the north clearly slowed settlement into Maine, New Hampshire, northern and western Massachusetts, and northern New York. Spanish St. Augustine delayed the southward expansion of Carolina, and the founding of Spanish Pensacola in 1698 and French Mobile soon thereafter further challenged English dominance in the southeast.[1] Whether from a decline in immigration, birthrate, or both, rates of population growth slowed perceptibly. Among colonists of European extraction, the growth rate dropped from about 80 percent over the two decades from 1670 to 1690 to just

1. See Douglas Edward Leach, *The Northern Colonial Frontier, 1607–1763* (New York, 1966), 109–25; Lois Matthews Rosenberry, *The Expansion of New England* (Boston, 1909), 58–63; Ruth L. Higgins, *Expansion in New York* (Columbus, Ohio, 1931), 37–41, 47–52, 56–59; Verner W. Crane, *The Southern Frontier, 1670–1732* (Ann Arbor, Mich., 1929), 47–107; and David E. Van Deventer, *The Emergence of Provincial New Hampshire, 1623–1741* (Baltimore, 1976), 62–72.

under 50 percent for the period from 1690 to 1710, the lowest percentage increase for any twenty-year period between 1670 and 1770.[2] The dearth of reliable statistics before 1697 makes it impossible to measure the impact of the first intercolonial wars on colonial trade, though the rate of increase in the volume of trade between the colonies and the British Isles, if not also in other branches of colonial commerce, may have fallen significantly.[3] A small decline in the rate of growth among the black population strongly suggests less activity in the slave trade.[4]

Nor was slowing expansion and demographic and economic growth the only unsettling development for the colonies during these years. As the founders of the colonies had been forced to abandon their initial designs and as one colony after another had managed to establish a viable demographic and economic base, settlers on the spot, like those in colonies begun without elaborate plans, substituted as their principal collective social goal the creation of some sort of recognizable version of the metropolitan society they had left behind. In new societies at the extreme peripheries of English civilization, the one certain measure of achievement was the standards of the metropolitan center, and colonists everywhere manifested a strong predisposition to reinforce their claims to an English identity by cultivating metropolitan values and imitating metropolitan cultural forms, institutions, and patterns of behavior.

The very simplicity and crudeness of their own societies during the early decades of settlement seem to have fed a residual fear of the corrosive effects of the wilderness environment. If the wilderness challenged settlers to assert their mastery over it by turning it into a cultivated landscape, it also threatened to overwhelm them. The apparent barbarism of Amerindians and the disturbing tendency of some English people on the outer fringes of settlement to "Indianize" themselves by relinquishing all concern with maintaining even the rudiments of English culture served as vivid evidence of the deleterious consequences of "the disintegrating forces which the liberty of

2. These rates were computed from "Estimated Population of the American Colonies: 1610 to 1780," in *Historical Statistics of the United States, Colonial Time to 1957* (Washington, D.C., 1960), ser. Z, tables 1–19, p. 756.

3. See Phyllis Deane and W. A. Cole, *British Economic Growth, 1688–1959: Trends and Structure* (Cambridge, 1962), 86–88.

4. See Philip D. Curtin, *The Atlantic Slave Trade: A Census* (Madison, Wis., 1969), 127–54.

a wild country unloosed."[5] Even as colonists were establishing their mastery over the physical spaces of America, they seemed to be losing control of themselves. Too many of them, one British ecclesiastic subsequently complained, seemed in the colonial wilderness to have "abandoned their native manners and religion" for "the most brutal profligacy of manners. Instead of civilizing and converting barbarous Infidels," he lamented, they had become "themselves Infidels and Barbarians."[6] Even if they managed to avoid such a dismal fate, there was always the additional, and more probable, possibility that they would become either so absorbed in the business of making a living and getting on in the world or so overcome by cultural isolation from the larger Anglophone world that their societies would "insensibly decline"[7] into what one writer later called "a State of Ignorance and Barbarism, not much superior to [those of] the native *Indians.*"[8]

Faced with such ominous possibilities, emergent elites in the colonies early began to show a powerful concern to retain and pass on to their children their English cultural inheritance. Despite the most persistent efforts, however, later generations seemed to be far "less cultivated than their elders,"[9] and from the last decades of the seventeenth century through the first decades of the eighteenth the colonies appeared to be in the trough of a cultural decline. In Virginia in the 1690s, people complained that courts were much more deficient than "in former Times, while the first Stock of Virginia Gentlemen lasted, who having had their Education in England, were a great deal better accomplish'd in the Law, and Knowledge of the World, than their Children and Grandchildren, who have been born in Virginia, and have generally no Opportunity of Improvement by good Education."[10] Similarly, Samuel Johnson, later president of King's College in New York, recalled that in the New England of his youth, during the very

5. Louis B. Wright, *Culture on the Moving Frontier* (Bloomington, Ind., 1955), 12.

6. John, Lord Bishop of Landaff, *A Sermon Preached before the Incorporated Society for the Propagation of the Gospel in Foreign Parts* (London, 1767), 6–7.

7. Louis B. Wright, *The First Gentlemen of Virginia: Intellectual Qualities of the Early Colonial Ruling Class* (San Marino, Calif., 1940), 108.

8. James Macsparran, *America Dissected* (Dublin, 1753), 10.

9. Wright, *Culture on the Moving Frontier*, 43.

10. Henry Hartwell, James Blair, and Edward Chilton, *The Present State of Virginia and the College*, ed. Hunter Dickinson Farish (Williamsburg, 1940), 45.

early eighteenth century, learning "(as well as everything else) was very low indeed[,] much lower than in earlier times while those yet lived who had their education in England."[11]

Except in the newest colonies like Pennsylvania and New Jersey, where people often expressed pride in "the mighty Improvements, Additions, and Advantages" already achieved,[12] observers fretted about the deficiencies of the colonies. While in New England Cotton Mather worried about the adverse effects of what he referred to as "creolean degeneracy,"[13] in Virginia Robert Beverley deplored the sad state of improvements after nearly a century of settlement. Lamenting the lack of towns, the failure to develop a diversified economy, and the palpable laziness of the colony's free inhabitants, Beverley even wondered whether the alterations the English had made were in any way "equivalent" to the damage they had done to Amerindians in the process.[14]

Notwithstanding all the difficulties faced by the colonies during the fifty years from 1675 to 1725 and the many negative contemporary assessments of the state of their cultural development, they retained throughout this period their images as lands of extraordinary opportunities for European immigrants and their increase. A large promotional literature associated with the new colonies established during the Restoration contributed not only to the retention but also to the magnification of those images. The most enthusiastic advocates for the colonies, the authors of this literature played a critical role in articulating a deepening conception of the English American colonies as places with exceptional opportunities for individual betterment.

This literature depicted the colonies as safe and inviting societies in which there was virtually no poverty, people could live in plenty

11. Samuel Johnson, "Autobiography," in *Samuel Johnson: His Career and Writings*, ed. Herbert and Carol Schneider, 4 vols. (New York, 1929), 1:5.

12. Gabriel Thomas, "An Historical and Geographical Account of Pensilvania and of West-New-Jersey," 1698, in *Narratives of Early Pennsylvania, West New Jersey, and Delaware, 1630–1707*, ed. Albert Cook Meyers (New York, 1912), 314.

13. Bernard Bailyn, *Education in the Forming of American Society* (Chapel Hill, N.C., 1960), 79. See also John Canup, *Out of the Wilderness: The Emergence of an American Identity in Colonial New England* (Middletown, Conn., 1990), 198–240, and "Cotton Mather and 'Creolian Degeneracy,'" *Early American Literature* 24 (1989): 20–34.

14. Robert Beverley, *The History and Present State of Virginia*, ed. Louis B. Wright (Chapel Hill, N.C., 1947), 156.

with little labor, and families, independence, and even riches could be acquired by the industrious. What made the colonies so inviting was the vast extent, ready availability, and remarkable fecundity of the land. From the by now conventional European point of view, that land was all uncultivated, unenclosed, and uninhabited. Lying "for several Ages of Time unimproved and neglected," as Daniel Defoe said of South Carolina,[15] it was before English occupation just a "Wilderness or Desart Country" that, wrote Gabriel Thomas about Pennsylvania, was entirely "void of Inhabitants . . . except [for] the Heathens"[16] and was waiting in its unoccupied state for "a good people to populate it."[17]

The great extent and unclaimed state of this land meant that immigrants could acquire as much as they could afford "for next to nothing."[18] A hundred acres in South Carolina, John Norris reported in 1712, could be purchased for less than ten acres in England, and those without money could in the population-thin and labor-poor societies of the colonies quickly find employment at such high wages that they could soon save the purchase price. Several colonies even offered land free to servants after they had finished their terms.[19] In contrast to the rest of the world, where "poor people . . . would think themselves happy, had they an Acre or two of Land," as Daniel Denton wrote about New York in 1670, the colonies had "hundreds, nay thousands of Acres" immediately and cheaply available for new immigrants, every one of whom could "furnish himself with . . . such a quantity of land, that he may weary himself with [just] walking over his fields of Corn, and all sorts of Grain."[20]

But the extraordinary thing about those acres, according to promotional writers, was that they were enormously fertile. In Pennsylvania, Gabriel Thomas wrote, farmers "commonly" got "twice the en-

15. Daniel Defoe, *Party Tyranny . . . in Carolina* (London, 1705), as reprinted in *Narratives of Early Carolina, 1650–1708*, ed. Alexander S. Salley, Jr. (New York, 1911), 227.

16. Thomas, "Historical and Geographical Account," 326.

17. Daniel Denton, *A Brief Description of New York: Formerly Called New-Netherlands* (London, 1670), 15.

18. William Penn, "Some Account of the Province of Pennsylvania," 1681, in Meyers, ed., *Narratives of Early Pennsylvania*, 210.

19. John Norris, *Profitable Advice for Rich and Poor* (London, 1712), as reprinted in *Selling a New World: Two Colonial South Carolina Promotional Pamphlets*, ed. Jack P. Greene (Columbia, S.C., 1989), 84–85, 105–6.

20. Denton, *Brief Description*, 15, 18.

Colonel Jacque. The widespread conception of colonial English America as a place where those who had failed to make it in the Old World could with enterprise and industry achieve wealth and respectability is revealed in this picture of Colonel Jacque, a fictional character from a Daniel Defoe novel. The penurious figure sitting on the right shows the colonel in his earlier state of adversity which led him into a career as a pickpocket in London, while the magnificently dressed gentleman on the left shows him after he had achieved prosperity as a tobacco planter in Virginia. In the backgound, the colonel's slaves work his plantation. From Daniel Defoe, The History of the Most Remarkable Life, and Extraordinary Adventures of the Truly Honourable Colonel Jacque, *4th ed. (London, 1748). Courtesy of the Folger Shakespeare Library, 163613, frontispiece.*

crease of Corn for every Bushel they sow" than could English farmers "from the richest Land they have." [21] In South Carolina, wrote Norris, the soil was so prolific that ten acres generated "more Profit than Twenty Acres" in England.[22] With "the Earth yielding [such] plentiful increase to all their painful labours," [23] any "Industrious Man," merely "with his own Labour," could easily, as Norris wrote of South Carolina, "maintain a Wife and Ten children, sufficient with *Corn, Pease, Rice, Flesh, Fish, and Fowl.*" [24]

By English and European standards, such widespread opportunities to acquire productive land were thoroughly exceptional. They meant, as William Penn told prospective settlers to Pennsylvania in 1681, that those who had insufficient resources ever to marry in England and could "hardly live and allow themselves Cloaths" could in the colonies marry and provide themselves and their children with abundant quantities of "all Necessaries and Conveniences." [25] The abundant opportunities also meant that those who had no resources at all in England "or such as by their utmost labors" could "scarcely procure a living" would be able, as Denton wrote, easily to procure "inheritances of land and possessions, stock themselves with all sorts of Cattel, enjoy the benefit of them whilst they live, and leave them to the benefit of their children when they die." [26] So extraordinary was the material promise of the colonies, Gabriel Thomas wrote in 1698, that even

21. Thomas, "Historical and Geographical Account," 328.
22. Norris, *Profitable Advice,* 84–85.
23. Denton, *Brief Description,* 20.
24. Norris, *Profitable Advice,* 109.
25. Penn, "Some Account," 203–4.
26. Denton, *Brief Description,* 18.

"the Idle, the Sloathful, and the Vagabonds of England, Scotland, and Ireland" had in New Jersey "a fair prospect of getting considerable Estates, at least of living very Plentifully and Happily, which Medium of Life is far better than lingering out their Days so miserably Poor and half Starved; or [risking] Whipping, Burning, and Hanging for Villanies, they" would no longer in America have any "Temptation . . . or Inclination to perpetrate."[27]

Although such possibilities were particularly attractive for people of "an inferior rank" in England, "people of all ranks," promotional writers asserted, could expect to improve their material circumstances.[28] While even men with some resources were unlikely in England ever "to be in a Capacity of otherwise Advancing their Fortune from their present State and Condition . . . to any higher Degree of Riches, Content or Repute," Norris observed, they could expect in South Carolina to "get Riches withal to Admiration." Except for "Gentlemen of Great Estates, or great Usurers," he declared, every category of independent people in England could by settling in South Carolina "advance and prefer themselves to a [vastly] more plentiful and profitable Way to Live" than they could ever do in England.[29] Even those who came with fewer resources, William Penn noted, "very often" acquired enough wealth that they could "return and empty the Riches into England; one in this capacity being able to buy out twenty of what he was when he went over."[30]

What made this process of material achievement so rapid, according to promotional writers, was the absence of expensive religious establishments and the simplicity and cheapness of government. Compared with England, the public realm in every colony was minute. Civil establishments were small. With little poverty, there were few expenses for maintaining the poor. With either weak church establishments or full religious toleration, there were "no Tithes." With no standing armies, defense costs were slight except in time of war. All of these conditions meant that taxes were indeed, as Thomas reported in regard to Pennsylvania, "inconsiderable"[31] and that the proportions of private income that went for public expenditures was "very small" in

27. Thomas, "Historical and Geographical Account," 229.
28. Denton, _Brief Description_, 18.
29. Norris, _Profitable Advice_, 134, 137, 142.
30. Penn, "Some Account," 206.
31. Thomas, "Historical and Geographical Account," 239.

comparison "with what they are in *England*." Whereas in England the "many Taxes, Rates, Assessments, and other Disbursements" to which "all Estates" were liable were so high that they took "away *one* Half, if not two Thirds, of the Value" of annual income and thereby rendered it impossible even for "an *Industrious* Man" to accumulate much profit from "his own laborious Care and Industry," in the colonies low public expenditures meant, as Norris pointed out in the case of South Carolina, that people there did not have "to straighten themselves . . . Quarterly, or oftener, to pay great Taxes, rates[,] Rents, and Assessments" and that there were "*few Occasions for*" a person "*to expend his Profits that arises from his Labour.*" As a consequence, a family in the colonies had a much better chance to obtain all "*reasonable Necessaries from their own Industry*" and "*to live very plentiful[,] . . . thrive in the World, and become Rich.*"[32]

The extreme fertility of the soil, high wages, and the powerful demand for all sorts of artisanal labor in these new societies also promised to immigrants a release from the "extreme Labour" that "Industrious Husbandmen and Day-Labourers" in England had to undergo merely "to maintain their Families." In the colonies, virtually every promotional writer agreed, only "moderate Labour" was required to produce "plenty of all things necessary for Life" as well as many of the comforts.[33] Even the work of servants and slaves in the colonies, they emphasized, was much less onerous than "that [of] many Thousand[s of] Servants and poor Laboure[r]s . . . in *England, Wales, Scotland*, and *Ireland*." In the case of South Carolina, where slavery for some Amerindians as well as for imported Africans became quickly established, writers presented the institution not as something to be condemned but as a boon to independent families. Employable "in any sort of Labour, either in Town or Country, in whatever their Masters, or Owners, have occasion to be done," slaves were a device through which free men who might once have had masters could themselves become "masters and Owners of Plantations, Stock, & Slaves, on which they [could] Live very plentifully, without being oblig'd to Labour themselves."[34]

Promotional writers did not present the attainment of material betterment with little labor as an end in itself. Rather, they offered it

32. Norris, *Profitable Advice*, 95, 108, 113–14, 129.
33. Penn, "Some Account," 209–10.
34. Norris, *Profitable Advice*, 87–88, 107–8.

Tobacco Plantation. Tobacco was the first of several staple crops that English people successfully sought to grow with slave labor on large agricultural units in the colonies. Sugar, produced only in the West Indies, was the most profitable. Rice, grown in the lower southern colonies, and tobacco, produced mostly in the Chesapeake colonies of Virginia and Maryland, also yielded substantial economic returns. All of these crops were produced on units that came to be called plantations. The large tobacco plantation worked by African slaves and depicted in this illustration became common in the Chesapeake during the half-century between 1675 and 1725, although most tobacco continued to be produced on smaller units. This picture shows two Euroamerican planters with their pipes and account books overseeing slaves packing cured tobacco into hogsheads. Tobacco plants grow in the fields behind them, while an overseer's house and the masts of ships waiting in the river to carry the hogsheads to Great Britain lie in the distance. At the top, an Amerindian face overlooks the scene. From F. W. Fairholt, Tobacco: Its History *(London, 1859). Courtesy of the Arents Collection,*

The New York Public Library, Astor, Lenox and Tilden Foundations.

as the means by which *dependent* men in Britain could become *independent*, masterless men, perhaps even with dependents of their own, in the colonies. As high as wages were, free people in the colonies, these writers reported, were uninterested in working for others because they could so easily "get Land of their own," "betake themselves to Husbandry," and "employ themselves very advantageously in their own Business."[35] "How much better for Men to improve their own Lands, for the Use of themselves, and [*their*] Posterity," than to work for others, declared Thomas Nairne in 1710 in a pamphlet extolling the virtues of South Carolina.[36] How much better for people to "live rent-free,"[37] to be "settled for" themselves and working "Advantageously to their own Benefit."[38]

In the colonies, these writers emphasized, no able-bodied man of European descent needed to live long with the "Vexation of Dependance."[39] Through the acquisition of their own independent estates, those who in England had been forced to live "in Scarcity, Poverty, and Want" could escape from dependence on the commissioners of the poor and thenceforth "scorn the Acceptance" of charity. Those who in England had labored for others could become their own masters. Those who in England had been debtors could become people of "*Credit and Honour.*"[40] Those who in England had been tenants could find a refuge from landlords. "Younger Brothers of small Inheritances" could forgo the humiliation suffered in England of watching their children forced to be "a kind of Hangers on or Retainers to the elder Brother[']s Table and Charity."[41] Those who in England had been dependent on patronage and driven into the degrading submission of clients could now make their own way and be free of the control—beyond subjection to the will—of any other man. The "difference of labouring for themselves and for others, of an Inheritance and a Rack Lease," Penn declared, was "never better understood" than among new immigrants to the colonies.[42]

35. Denton, *Brief Description*, 17; Norris, *Profitable Advice*, 105.

36. Thomas Nairne, *A Letter from South Carolina* (London, 1710), as reprinted in Greene, ed., *Selling a New World*, 35.

37. Denton, *Brief Description*, 18.

38. Norris, *Profitable Advice*, 108–9.

39. Nairne, *Letter from South Carolina*, 66.

40. Norris, *Profitable Advice*, 109, 118, 134.

41. Penn, "Some Account," 209.

42. William Penn, "A Further Account of the Province of Pennsylvania," 1685, in Meyers, ed., *Narratives of Early Pennsylvania*, 263.

Indeed, in the images limned by the late-seventeenth- and early-eighteenth-century promotional writers, these societies of independent property owners—and slaves—had few of the galling legal and social restraints that characterized old England. In the colonies, there were no monopolies of resources; no reservations of wood, water rights, fish, or game to the wealthy; no religious disabilities—for Protestants; and none of that "pride and oppression, with their miserable effects" that were endemic to all other parts of the world. Their still simple and undeveloped state even protected settlers from the corrosive effects of their own "pride and luxury."[43]

Nor were these independent people in any way "subject to the Caprice and . . . Pleasure" of their governors. Because their governments were all "founded upon the generous Principles of civil and religious Liberty," they enjoyed all "the civil Rights of _Englishmen_."[44] No laws could "be made, nor Money raised, but by the People[']s Consent,"[45] and such laws strictly prescribed "Fines, Imprisonments, Death, or other Punishments" and set such effective "Bounds to Power" that not even "the highest in Authority" could "legally oppress the meanest."[46]

In painting this alluring picture, promotional writers, not unsurprisingly, tried to minimize the unpleasant and dangerous aspects of migration and colonial life. They downplayed the dangers of the ocean crossing and the malignity of the disease environments in places like Tidewater Virginia and Lowcountry South Carolina. They denied that hotter summers and colder winters were uncongenial to English people or that there was any need to be concerned about any of the strange and terrifying creatures such as rattlesnakes and alligators that were native to America. Most of all, they minimized the military threat posed by the colonies of rival European powers and Amerindians. The latter, they insisted, either lived in amity with the English, had been subdued, or, as John Archdale was persuaded, had been thinned by "unusual Sicknesses" providentially sent by God "to make room for the English" and thereby prepare the way for his "gradual Work, . . . introducing a Civilized State" into America.[47] Whatever

43. Denton, _Brief Description_, 20.
44. Nairne, _Letter from South Carolina_, 44.
45. Penn, "Some Account," 208.
46. Nairne, _Letter from South Carolina_, 45.
47. John Archdale, _A New Description of that Fertile and Pleasant Province of Carolina_ (London, 1707), as reprinted in Salley, ed., _Narratives of Early Carolina_, 285.

Hercules and the Waggoner. This woodcut shows a waggoner in the peaceful and abundant farmlands of Pennsylvania whose safety is being threatened by demands of war, here symbolized by the mythical figure Hercules. The large houses and outbuildings, neat farm, and full wagon pulled by three horses reveal the pride taken by contemporaries in the prosperity derived from the grain economy of Pennsylvania and suggest the extent to which its inhabitants had already in just seventy years succeeded in reordering their new environment. From Benjamin Franklin, Plain Truth *(Philadelphia, 1747). Courtesy of the Library Company of Philadelphia.*

dangers lurked in the New World, none were sufficient to prevent any man, as Denton wrote in invoking a popular biblical metaphor, from sitting "under his own Vine, and . . . peaceably" enjoying "the fruits of [his] . . . own labours."[48]

Promotional writers thus summoned English people and other

48. Denton, *Brief Description*, 14.

Europeans to the colonies with the promise that they could find there the resources they needed to become masters of their own lives. In issuing this call for free people to empower themselves, these writers gave still additional emphasis to the by then well-established vision of America as a place in which the unsuccessful, the thwarted, and the discontented of the Old World could begin life anew, as a place with such extraordinary opportunities for individual material and social betterment that free people might—in the new field of action that was America—turn their repressed energies to their own ends and become active agents in their own quest for competence, substance, independence, and the capacity to shape their own lives however they wanted. That their pursuit of mastery over their own lives might involve the systematic subjugation of African or Amerindian slaves was never an explicit concern in the literature of promotion.

The experiences of the colonies during the half-century following the conclusion of the second intercolonial war strongly suggested that the promises held out by this literature were by no means illusory. The peace settlement worked out at Utrecht in 1713 marked the beginning of a quarter century of peace and prosperity for the British Empire in general. If the peace was always tenuous, it nonetheless provided the setting for the political consolidation of the Whig oligarchy within Britain and for an extraordinary commercial expansion within the empire as a whole. For the North American colonies, the effects of these developments were profound. For virtually the first time in their histories, the colonies were for a long period largely free from the anxieties and distractions of war. Even relations with Amerindians were comparatively peaceful, the Yamassee War in South Carolina in 1715–16 and the Abenaki War in northern New England in 1722–26 being the only major white-Amerindian conflicts between 1713 and 1740.

These conditions provided the foundations for an extraordinary release of expansive energies in the continental colonies. Having during the previous century already established a solid territorial, demographic, and economic base, the colonies during the years from 1713 to 1740 experienced the beginnings of a sustained period of growth that, except for a brief deceleration in the 1740s and 1750s, continued at a rapid pace through the end of the colonial period and, of course, on into the nineteenth century.

In 1713, settlers were still clustered in a series of noncontiguous nuclei up and down the Atlantic seaboard. There were two large centers of settlement, one around Chesapeake Bay and another in the coastal regions and river valleys of eastern and southern New England. Two smaller concentrations fanned out from Philadelphia and New York, and isolated nuclei were located at three widely dispersed points in Tidewater North Carolina and at Charleston and Port Royal in South Carolina. Over the next twenty-five years, settlers spread out in all directions from these nuclei, and by 1740 one long continuum of settlement stretched from Pamlico Sound in North Carolina north to southern Maine and reached inland more than a hundred miles from the New England coast and over 150 miles from the Chesapeake and Delaware into the easternmost mountain valleys of Virginia and Pennsylvania. In the South, there were larger, if still noncontiguous, centers in southern North Carolina, South Carolina, and the new colony of Georgia, founded in 1733.[49]

This extraordinary expansion of settled area was accompanied by a rapid growth of population. During the three decades from 1711 to 1740, the number of people of European extraction in Britain's continental colonies increased by over 295 percent from 189,162 to 753,621.[50] By contemporary standards in either Europe or in the colonies of other European powers in America, decennial rates of growth were remarkably high: 38.8 percent from 1711–20, 34.4 percent from 1721–30, and 39.5 percent from 1731–40.[51] Over the whole thirty-year period, the rate of increase was most impressive in the middle colonies and in the Carolinas and Georgia: 222.6 percent in Pennsylvania and Delaware, 175.1 percent in the Carolinas and Georgia, and 172.1 percent in New York and New Jersey. But the populations of

49. D. W. Meinig, *The Shaping of America: A Geographical Perspective on 500 Years of History*, vol. 1, *Atlantic America, 1492–1800* (New Haven, Conn., 1986), 91–109, 119–90, 213–54; Herman Ralph Friis, *A Series of Population Maps of the Colonies and the United States, 1625–1790* (New York, 1940).

50. These and subsequent data on population growth were derived from an adjusted version of the table on "Estimated Population of the American Colonies," 756.

51. Jim Potter, "Demographic Development and Family Structure," in *Colonial British America: Essays in the History of the Early Modern Era*, ed. Jack P. Greene and J. R. Pole (Baltimore, 1984), 123–56, and "The Growth of Population in America, 1700–1860," in *Population in History: Essays in Historical Demography*, ed. D. V. Glass and D. E. C. Eversley (Chicago, 1965), 631–46; Robert V. Wells, *Population of the British Colonies in America before 1776: A Survey of Census Data* (Princeton, 1975), 45–333.

the New England and Chesapeake colonies also grew rapidly: 149.9 percent in the former and 125.6 percent in the latter.

A substantial proportion of this population rise was the result of expanding immigration from Britain and Europe. Perhaps as much as a fourth of the increase between 1711 and 1740 can be accounted for by first generation immigrants, about three-fourths of whom came from the British Isles and the rest principally from the southwestern portions of Germany and the German-speaking cantons of Switzerland. A much higher percentage of the demographic growth, around 75 percent, was, however, the product of natural increase.[52]

As Jim Potter has pointed out, this phenomenal rate of growth was "considerably higher than that to be found in England at any time in the eighteenth and nineteenth centuries." Potter explains this extraordinary surge of white population primarily in terms of the "high productivity of American agriculture," which provided enough food to stimulate the fertility rate among women and to keep infant mortality comparatively low.[53] But it is also clear that the psychological inhibitions that acted as a brake upon reproduction in countries with less opportunity were much less powerful in the colonies, every one of which still seemed, as William Byrd of Westover remarked about Virginia in 1729, to be "an Infant country which wants nothing but people."[54]

The black population expanded even more rapidly over the same period, rising by almost 235 percent from 44,866 in 1710 to 150,024 in 1740. The decennial growth rate was high—over 54 percent—between 1711 and 1720, and, though it fell to around 32 percent during the 1720s, it rose sharply during the 1730s to nearly 65 percent, the highest growth rate for any decade between 1690 and 1770. Because the overwhelming majority of blacks, perhaps as many as 99 percent, was slave, this dramatic increase reflects a major expansion of the institution of slave labor and a significant increase in the amount of capital available for such purchases.

52. Henry A. Gemery, "European Emigration to North America, 1700–1820: Numbers and Quasi-Numbers," *Perspectives in American History*, n.s., 1 (1984): 283–342.

53. Potter, "Growth of Population," 645–46.

54. William Byrd II to Mrs. Jane Pratt Taylor, Apr. 3, 1729, in *The Correspondence of the Three William Byrds of Westover, Virginia, 1684–1776*, ed. Marion Tinling, 2 vols. (Charlottesville, Va., 1977), 1:391.

This expansion was especially rapid in the southern plantation colonies, where the number of blacks mushroomed from just over 36,000 in 1710 to over 125,000 in 1740. But the spread of slavery was by no means limited to the southern colonies. By 1740 there were still only about 24,000 blacks in the colonies north of Maryland, but this figure represented a moderately heavy increase of just over 170 percent from the 8,803 blacks in those colonies in 1710. Although New York and Massachusetts showed some leveling of growth rates after 1720, black slavery in 1740 was still an expanding, rather than a contracting, institution everywhere in the continental colonies.[55]

In contrast to the white population, a much smaller proportion of the growth of the black population can be attributed to natural increase. Average decennial natural growth rates were probably between about 17 percent and 20 percent. Although these figures were well below the 28 percent figure registered by whites, they were considerably higher than those for any other colonial society before the abolition of slavery. According to the best estimates, around 70,814 slaves, just about two-thirds of the total increase in the number of blacks, were imported between 1711 and 1740, over two-thirds of them in the 1730s.[56]

Colonial expansion also extended into the economic realm. During these years, exports to England increased sharply in every decade from an annual average value of £265,480 in 1701–10 to £667,135 in 1731–40, an overall rate of expansion of over 150 percent or just over 36 percent per decade. This rate was considerably higher than that for any other comparable time span in the eighteenth-century history of the colonies. The colonies carried on a large trade with the West Indies, southern Europe, Ireland, and, of course, Africa. Imports from England rose from an annual average of £267,302 in 1701–10 to £646,192 in 1731–40, an overall rate of growth of over 140 percent or a little more than 34 percent per decade. Along with the heavy investment in slaves, these figures reveal a significant expansion in the buying capacity of the colonies.[57]

In 1739, the long interlude of relative peace and prosperity gave way to another extended period of war and uncertainty lasting, with

55. "Estimated Population of the American Colonies," 756.

56. See Curtin, *Atlantic Slave Trade*, 89–93, 137–40.

57. "Value of Exports to and Imports from England, by American Colonies: 1697 to 1776," in *Historical Statistics of the United States*, 761.

Public Buildings of Williamsburg. Already by the early eighteenth century, colonial Americans had acquired the wherewithal to pay for some elegant buildings. Becoming the capital of Virginia early in the century, Williamsburg was never more than a small administrative center. Yet its public buildings, all constructed during the first quarter of the eighteenth century, were among the earliest, most elegant, and costliest built on the continent before 1750. Probably dating from sometime in the late 1720s or early 1730s, this engraving by an unknown artist shows all of the town's major public buildings. Viewed from the east and framed by Brafferton Hall on the left and the President's House on the right, the Wren Building of the College of William and Mary dominates the upper panel. The middle panel shows a western view of the Wren Building with the Capitol Building on the left and the Governor's Palace on the right. The lower plate depicts flora, fauna, and peoples native to Virginia. Courtesy of the Library of Congress, neg. no. LCUSZ62-2104.

only a brief respite between 1748 and 1754, until 1763. But the effects of these wars contrasted markedly with those of the earlier wars of 1689–1713. By the late 1730s, the process of growth had gained such extraordinary momentum that it proceeded with slight check throughout the last two intercolonial wars. To be sure, the movement of people into previously unsettled lands was temporarily stopped and even reversed in areas with the greatest military activity—in northern and western New England, northern and western New York, and the westernmost frontiers of Pennsylvania, Maryland, and Virginia.

But there was a great rush of population south from Philadelphia into western Maryland, Virginia, and North Carolina and west from the Carolina seacoast into the interior of both North and South Carolina. Even in the north there was a considerable expansion of settlement into interior areas away from war zones. Between 1740 and 1763, most of the unoccupied areas within 100 to 150 miles of the coast from Philadelphia to Portsmouth, New Hampshire, were filled in with new counties and towns. Following the British capture of Canada in 1759, the tempo of expansion everywhere accelerated, as settlers from the older inhabited areas and a rising tide of immigrants from Britain and Europe moved into frontier areas and into the newer colonies of Georgia and Nova Scotia.[58]

The growth of the white population also continued steadily. Between 1740 and 1770, it increased by almost 125 percent from 753,721 to 1,689,583. Though the decennial rate of increase fell somewhat from the previous three decades, temporarily stabilizing at around 30 percent, it was still remarkably high by any contemporary standards among the societies of either Western Europe or their American colonies. Moreover, the rates of increase continued to be extremely rapid in newly opened areas that were receiving heavy influxes of immigrants from older settled areas and from Europe. Thus, the white population rose by almost 228 percent in the Carolinas and Georgia, over 160 percent in Pennsylvania and Delaware, and almost 149 percent in New York and New Jersey. In the older settled New England and Chesapeake colonies, which, presumably, were losing population to newer areas, growth rates were much lower: about 98 percent in New England and 92 percent in the Chesapeake.[59]

58. See the maps for the distribution of population in 1740 and 1760 in Friis, *Series of Population Maps*, opposite p. 12.

59. "Estimated Population of the American Colonies," 756.

As in the previous thirty years, much of this increase came from immigration. Despite the fact that the wars of 1739–1763 clearly acted as at least a slight check to immigration, the total number of white immigrants during the three decades, which probably exceeded 200,000, represented almost a 40 percent increase over the previous thirty years. Non-British immigrants, mostly Germans, probably constituted about 30 percent of the total. But the highest proportions still came from the British Isles, including at least 80,000 from England and Wales, 40,000 from Ulster, and more than 20,000 from Scotland. These increasing numbers of immigrants accounted for a declining proportion of the total increase in the white population. Immigrants accounted for almost a quarter of the total growth between 1710 and 1740 but only about a fifth between 1740 and 1770. About 80 percent, or 727,822, of the total growth of 932,822 was thus the result of natural increase.[60]

The black population and the institution of slavery also continued to expand, and at a much more rapid rate than the white population. The number of blacks rose by over 200 percent from 150,024 in 1740 to 455,721 in 1770. The decennial growth rate averaged just over 45 percent, falling from a high of about 55 percent in the 1740s to just over 40 percent in the 1750s and 1760s. As in the previous thirty years, the most dramatic increases were in the colonies from Maryland south. As the institution of slavery fanned out in all directions from the Maryland and Virginia tidewaters and the South Carolina lowcountry and as large sections of both North Carolina and Georgia adopted the slave plantation system after 1750, the black population of the southern colonies leaped from just over 125,000 in 1740 to almost 403,000 by 1770, an increase of over 278,000 in just thirty years. The black population also grew steadily in the colonies to the north: Delaware, Pennsylvania, Rhode Island, Massachusetts, New York, and Connecticut all showed decennial growth rates in excess of

60. Gemery, "European Emigration," 283–342. See also Marianne Wokeck, "The Flow and Composition of German Immigration to Philadelphia, 1727–1775," *Pennsylvania Magazine of History and Biography* 105 (1981): 249–78; R. J. Dickson, *Ulster Emigration to Colonial America, 1718–1775* (London, 1966); Ian C. C. Graham, *Colonists from Scotland: Emigration to North America, 1707–1783* (Ithaca, N.Y., 1956); Audrey Lockhart, *Some Aspects of Emigration from Ireland to the North American Colonies between 1660 and 1775* (New York, 1976); Bernard Bailyn, *Voyagers to the West: A Passage in the Peopling of America on the Eve of the Revolution* (New York, 1986).

Experiences

84

30 percent for at least one of the three decades. In absolute numbers, however, the black population in the northern colonies was small, and the proportion of blacks living north of Maryland was declining continuously. The southern colonies contained just over 80 percent of the black population in 1710, just over 83 percent in 1740, and more than 88 percent in 1770.[61]

As was the case in 1711–40, a very large proportion of the increase in the black population resulted from heavy importations of new slaves from Africa and the West Indies. Approximately 177,000 slaves were imported between 1741 and 1770, with the 1740s and the 1760s exhibiting importations that were nearly as high as those for the entire period between 1711 and 1740. As these figures suggest, the rate of natural increase among blacks probably continued to be substantially lower than that for whites. Whereas slave importations accounted for around 57 percent of the total increase in the black population of the colonies between 1741 and 1770, immigrants constituted only about 20 percent of the growth of the white population. The average natural decennial rate of growth for blacks again appears to have been only around 17 percent to 20 percent, about the same as it had been for the previous three decades.[62]

Such heavy importations of slaves clearly point to a massive expansion in colonial capital formation during the period 1741–70, and the figures for imports from Britain point in the same direction. The average annual value of such imports rose very sharply from £646,192 in 1731–40 to £1,797,922 in 1761–70, an overall rate of increase of over 178 percent and an almost 40 percent rise over the rate for the previous thirty years. The decennial rate of growth showed a significant increase of almost 10 percent over the earlier period to 43.5 percent, a growth rate that far exceeded that for either the white population or the population as a whole.

By contrast, the growth rate in the volume of colonial exports decelerated sharply between 1741 and 1770. The amount of exports continued to increase, of course, but at a vastly slower pace. Whereas between 1711 and 1740 they grew by over 150 percent or just over 36 percent per decade, between 1741 and 1770 they increased by only 64 percent overall or at an average decennial rate of just 18.5 percent.

61. "Estimated Population of the American Colonies," 756.
62. Curtin, *Atlantic Slave Trade*, 133–45; "Estimated Population of the American Colonies," 756.

View of Philadelphia. The rapid growth of Philadelphia in people, wealth, and buildings provided powerful evidence of the robustness of the economies of early America. This painting of "The South East Prospect of the City of Philadelphia" from the Delaware River was the work of the artist Peter Cooper and dates from about 1720. In contrast to Williamsburg, Philadelphia had few public buildings, most of the large number of structures displayed in the painting and all but three

The wars of 1739–63 doubtless had an adverse effect upon the whole export sector of the economy, yet real figures reveal a substantial increase in the volume of total exports in every decade, from an annual average value of £1,270,717 in 1731–40 to £1,350,333 in 1741–50, £1,543,137 in 1751–60, and £2,085,238 in 1761–70.[63]

Because most people in these colonies tended to seat themselves on the land and engage in agricultural production, the spread of settlement and the growth of population and trade were not accompanied by similarly dramatic growth in urban areas. Nevertheless, significant urbanization occurred in all of the older settled areas. In 1710, no town had as many as ten thousand people, and only Boston, Philadelphia, and New York had over five thousand. By 1740, Boston contained fifteen thousand inhabitants, Philadelphia and New York had more than ten thousand, and Charleston and Newport had over five thousand.[64]

---

63. "Value of Exports to and Imports from England, by American Colonies," 757.

64. Carl Bridenbaugh, *Cities in the Wilderness: The First Century of Urban Life in America, 1625–1742* (New York, 1938), 303.

*of those identified in the key being private houses. The large number of ships in
the river attests to a thriving trade. The coats of arms in either corner are those of
William Penn and the colony of Pennsylvania. The painting hangs in the main
reading room of the Library Company of Philadelphia and is here reproduced by
courtesy of the Library Company.*

Over the next thirty years, Boston's population leveled off at about
sixteen thousand, but that of other towns continued to grow. By
1770, Philadelphia was around thirty thousand, New York, twenty-
five thousand, and Charleston and Newport, from nine to twelve thousand. Baltimore and Norfolk, towns that had developed mostly after
1750, had around six thousand, while ten towns—New Haven, Nor-
wich, New London, Salem, Lancaster, Hartford, Middletown, Portsmouth, Marblehead, and Providence—had around four thousand, and
three others—Albany, Annapolis, and Savannah—had nearly three
thousand. Perhaps as many as fifty other places had between five
hundred and three thousand inhabitants.[65]

65. Carl Bridenbaugh, *Cities in Revolt: Urban Life in America, 1743–1776* (New
York, 1955), 5, 216–17; Sam Bass Warner, *The Private City: Philadelphia in Three
Periods of Its Growth* (Philadelphia, 1968); James T. Lemon, "Urbanization and the
Development of Eighteenth-Century Southeastern Pennsylvania and Adjacent
Delaware," *William and Mary Quarterly*, 3d ser., 24 (1967): 501–42; Joseph A.
Ernst and H. Roy Merrens, " 'Camden's turrets pierce the skies!': The Urban Pro-
cess in the Southern Colonies during the Eighteenth Century," ibid. 30 (1973):

View of Boston. For a much longer time than Philadelphia, Boston had been a prosperous port and bustling urban center. This engraving by James Turner shows its dense housing, its many churches, and its shipping facilities in 1744, just about the time that it reached its colonial apex. In stark contrast to this urban scene, the lower panel offers two views of Amerindians in a wilderness setting. This juxtaposition captured two of the principal cultural worlds that de-fined colonial British America at the midpoint of the eighteenth century. From the title page of the American Magazine and Historical Chronicle *(Boston, 1743–44). Courtesy of the Library of Congress, neg. no.* LCUSZ62-2152.

The results of countless individual decisions and behaviors, these tedious growth figures provide the best available indices for the most important developments in the history of the settler societies of colonial British America during the half-century before the American War for Independence. Promotional writers had beckoned Europeans to America with the promise that they would find in the colonies all the conditions—the exceptional conditions—necessary for them

549–74; Jacob M. Price, "Economic Function and the Growth of American Port Towns in the Eighteenth Century," *Perspectives in American History* 8 (1974): 123–86.

to establish control over their own lives, the conditions required to enable them not simply to survive but to pursue their own individual happinesses, their own personal dreams for themselves and their families. The behavioral patterns implicit in this dramatic territorial, demographic, and economic expansion provide overwhelming evidence that many thousands of immigrants and their descendants had indeed found in the colonies the lives promised by promotional writers.

By no means, of course, was everyone so fortunate. Very many did not survive the ocean passage or their initial confrontation with the unfamiliar disease environments in the colonies. Others lost their lives in accidents, to enemies among the Amerindians and the agents of other European powers, or to competitors among their fellow settlers. Still others were ruined by natural disasters or by the sorts of misfortunes that were common to early modern agricultural and commercial societies. Yet others fell victim to the malice of masters and magistrates or to their own passions; the empowering conditions immigrants sought and found in the colonies did not invariably transform their characters.

Notwithstanding all of those who were disappointed in their hopes, far and away the single most impressive conclusion to be drawn from the patterns of growth exhibited by the colonies after 1713 is that thousands upon thousands of people did succeed in realizing some significant part of the promise held out by promotional writers. Thousands did survive the passage. Thousands did acquire their own land. Thousands did marry and establish their own families, for whom they provided a comfortable subsistence and to whom they passed along whatever estates they managed to accumulate. Thousands did clear lands and build homes, farm or other work buildings, and fences. Increasingly, some significant proportion did manage without farming to build comfortable lives for themselves in countryside and towns through mercantile, artisanal, and professional pursuits. As collectivities, these people had pushed back the wilderness, built communities, roads, and bridges, established churches and other social institutions and amenities, and in general made themselves masters of large chunks of eastern North America and turned them into European-style cultivated landscapes.

When they stepped back to look at them, these achievements, exceptional by any measure, astounded the colonists and their contemporaries. In just a few decades, Benjamin Franklin noted with pride in

Town and Country. The increasingly symbiotic relationship between town and country in eighteenth-century colonial British America is illustrated by this almanac cover. Showing both an urban and a rural scene, the engraving appeared as the cover for John Tobler's The Pennsylvania Town and Country-Man's Almanack *for several different years. Published by the German printer Christopher Sower in Germantown, this one was for the year 1758. Courtesy of the Library Company of Philadelphia.*

reference to Pennsylvania in 1741, the colonists had managed to make "a Garden of a Wilderness," and an extraordinarily prolific garden at that.[66] Such rapid and visible "Improvements," another writer declared a year earlier, seemed to have "no Precedence or Example."[67] Britain's American colonies, said George Grenville's confidant Thomas Whately in 1766, had "flourished . . . beyond all Example in History."[68]

Adam Smith agreed. "The progress of all the European colonies in wealth, population, and improvement," he observed in his extended commentary on the phenomenon of modern colonization in the *Wealth of Nations* in 1776, has "been very great," but there were "no colonies of which the progress has been more rapid than that of the English in North America." Just a little more than a century before, in the 1660s and 1670s, Smith pointed out, all of the English American colonies except Barbados were "inconsiderable."

> The island of Jamaica was an unwholesome desert, little inhabited, and less cultivated. New York and New Jersey were in the possession of the Dutch; the half of St. Christopher's in that of the French. The island of Antigua, the two Carolinas, Pen[n]sylvania, Georgia, and Nova Scotia, were not planted. Virginia, Maryland, and New England were planted; and, though they were very thriving colonies, yet there was not, perhaps, at that time either in Europe or America a single person who foresaw or even suspected the rapid progress which they have since made in wealth, population, and im-

66. "An Account of the Export of Provisions from Philadelphia," Feb. 16, 1741, in *The Papers of Benjamin Franklin*, ed. Leonard W. Labaree et al., 27 vols. to date (New Haven, Conn., 1959–), 2:303.

67. Sir William Keith, *A Collection of Papers and Other Tracts* (London, 1740), 212.

68. Thomas Whately, *Considerations on the Trade and Finance of the Kingdom* (London, 1766), 81.

The *Pennsylvania*
Town and Country-Man's
ALMANACK,
For the Year of our LORD 1758.
Being the *second after* Leap-Year.
Containing almoſt every Thing uſual in Almanacks.
By *JOHN TOBLER* Eſq;

Germantown : printed and ſold by *C. Sower* jun. And
to be had in *Philadelphia* of *Solomon Fuſſel*, at the Sign of the
Hand-Saw over againſt the Church in *Second-Street*, and alſo
of *Chriſtopher Marshall* and *Thomas Say*.

provement. The island of Barbadoes, in short, was the only British colony of any consequence of which the condition at the time bore any resemblance to what it is at present.[69]

In celebrating the colonies' rise to such "height[s] of populousness, power, and wealth,"[70] in extolling their achievements in seemingly already having laid the foundations for what Jonathan Mayhew in 1754 foresaw as "another Great Britain arising in America,"[71] relatively few people of European descent thought much about the high human price those achievements had cost two large categories of "others" whose lives had been profoundly affected by them. British people had no difficulty in recognizing and condemning the Spaniards' "cruel destruction of the natives which followed the [initial] conquest."[72] Some acknowledged that the wealth of British settlers had been wrested from "Lands which were, [just] a few Years ago, the Property of the *Indians*."[73] Many even deplored the failure of the English to deliver on the early promise to rescue Amerindians from religious and cultural darkness. "Whilst we have been at so much pains to enlarge our colonies, and multiply settlements," an anonymous contributor to the *American Magazine* objected in 1757, "little has been done to spread and propagate the glad tidings of" the gospel among Amerindians. "In all our laboured improvements in arts and manufactures," this writer decried, "almost nothing has been attempted, to cultivate and civilize the untutored barbarians, whom providence by making them dependent on us, seems to have recommended to our special care."[74]

But two of the underlying assumptions of the colonizing process prevented most people of European descent from comprehending, much less regretting, just how high a price Amerindians had had to pay for these achievements. First was the long-standing conception of

69. Adam Smith, *The Nature and Causes of the Wealth of Nations*, in *The Glasgow Edition of the Works and Correspondence of Adam Smith*, ed. R. H. Campbell and A. S. Skinner, 6 vols. (Oxford, 1976–83), 2:567, 571, 597–98.

70. Harry J. Carman, ed., *American Husbandry* (New York, 1939), 529.

71. Jonathan Mayhew, *A Sermon Preach'd in the Audience of His Excellency William Shirley, Esq.* (Boston, 1754), 39.

72. Smith, *Wealth of Nations*, 568.

73. Samuel Hopkins, *An Address to the People of New-England* (Philadelphia, 1757), 27.

74. "The Planter No. II," *American Magazine* 1 (1757): 84.

aboriginal America as a "waste" and "thinly inhabited" country "quite covered with wood, uncultivated, and inhabited only by some tribes of naked and miserable savages."[75] "Subsist[ing] mostly by hunting," Amerindians, Europeans thought, had plenty of territory to convey to the "new Comers," who, in Franklin's words, "did not much interfere with the Natives."[76]

Second was the continuing presumption of cultural superiority implicit in the concept of savagery. As morally reprehensible and avaricious as he thought the Spanish were, Adam Smith had no doubt that the "Spanish creoles" were "superior to the antient Indians."[77] If Amerindians could be praised for their original innocence and generosity and pitied for the agonies visited upon them by European diseases and alcohol, they could also be scorned for their "wild and savage . . . manners," their continued preference for "their different way of living," and their sometimes ferocious resistance to white encroachments upon their lands and lives. Indifferent to European values, Amerindians, it appeared to settlers, "continued in their former indigence" by preference, notwithstanding the fact that all around them the English were acquiring property.[78] Indeed, their very failure to imitate the English seemed by itself to provide sufficient justification for taking their lands and remodeling their landscapes.

When Robert Beverley published his *History of Virginia* during the first decade of the eighteenth century, Amerindians were still, a century after the first settlement at Jamestown, a far more visible presence than black slaves. As many Amerindians retired before the white advance and as the population of blacks burgeoned through the first seventy years of the eighteenth century, however, blacks replaced Amerindians as the most conspicuous of the "insignificant others" in the lives of the settlers. Even in parts of the northern colonies, in cities and in the richer agricultural areas, settlers were more likely as the century went on to encounter blacks than Amerindians in their daily lives. Moreover, many settlers, especially but not exclusively in the colonies south of Pennsylvania, depended heavily upon black slaves for labor and other services, an incalculable but very large proportion

75. Smith, *Wealth of Nations*, 559.

76. Benjamin Franklin, "Observations Concerning the Increase of Mankind, Peopling of Countries, &c.," in *Papers of Benjamin Franklin*, 4:228.

77. Smith, *Wealth of Nations*, 568–69.

78. "The Planter No. VI," *American Magazine* 1 (1757): 274–75.

of the growing wealth and improvements exhibited by the colonies deriving directly from their efforts.

Notwithstanding their contributions, despite all the "Gain [whites received] by their Labour,"[79] blacks probably commanded even less respect from whites than Amerindians. Like Amerindians, blacks appeared to whites to be "naturally of a barbarous . . . nature."[80] Unlike very many Amerindians, however, they were condemned to heavy labor. Except for the rice swamps in the Lower South, which one observer thought required slaves to work in conditions "not far short of digging in Potosi," North American slaves, as the same writer argued, may have been only rarely subjected to the "excessive work and bad usage" that was routinely the lot of slaves on West Indian sugar plantations.[81] Regarded as wholly subservient to the designs of their white owners, however, they everywhere shared very few of the benefits that derived out of the colonies' exceptional growth, benefits to which they themselves contributed so heavily. Even as late as the 1760s, relatively few whites in the colonies saw anything wrong with that situation.

79. Anthony Benezet, *Observations on the Inslaving, Importing and Purchasing of Negroes* (Germantown, Pa., 1759), 7.

80. Hugh Jones, *The Present State of Virginia*, ed. Richard L. Morton (Chapel Hill, N.C., 1956), 75.

81. Carman, *American Husbandry*, 277, 426.

CHAPTER FOUR

Evaluations

THE CONCEPTUAL IDENTIFICATION

OF BRITISH AMERICA,

1715–1775

For Britain's North American colonies, the years between the Utrecht peace settlement in 1713 and the outbreak of the War for Independence in 1775 were years of extraordinary expansion—in settled territory, population, wealth, and social and cultural institutions and infrastructures. The costs for that expansion were excessively high for the two principal categories of "others" who were intimately and, in most cases, unwillingly involved in it: Amerindians, who lost their lands, some of their culture, and often their lives or freedom in the process, and enslaved blacks, who supplied much of the physical energy and productive labor that generated colonial growth but few of whom had any chance to share in its benefits. For thousands of white people, however, both men and women, immigrants and creoles, the dizzying expansion of these years was emblematic of their successful achievement of many of the promises held out by colonial promotional literature. How contemporaries evaluated this growth by examining and analyzing it, how they interpreted its social and cultural effects, and

*Community Scenes. At the center of her magnificent appliquéd quilt, an uniden-
tified quilt maker portrayed the settled and prosperous life of free white colonists
in a small town during the late colonial or early national period. The middle
scene shows a group of townspeople assembled on a Sunday for religious services
in a small urban community with a church, a tavern, a courthouse, and some
outbuildings. The lower panel illustrates two houses with several men, women,
and children promenading in their neighborhood, probably also on a Sunday.
One family has a buggy. The top panel presents a rural scene with sheep, cows,
a windmill, and two farmsteads with wells. Horses figure prominently in all
of these scenes of quiet activity. Courtesy of The Edison Institute, Henry Ford
Museum and Greenfield Village, Dearborn, Michican, neg. no. B33042.*

how those interpretations operated to reinforce the identity of colonial British America as an exceptional place will be analyzed in this
chapter.

   In trying to explain and to evaluate this phenomenal expansion,
contemporaries focused on four main questions: why it occurred; how
it operated; how it affected the shape and character of the societies and
cultures of the colonies; and how it influenced the free people who
participated in it. With regard to the first of these questions, Adam
Smith provided the most thorough and systematic analysis in his long
discussion "Of Colonies" in *The Wealth of Nations*, published in 1776.
Although Smith paid some attention to the colonies of other nations,
including those of classical Greece and Rome, as well as to the British
colonies in the West Indies, his extended consideration of the "Causes
and Prosperity of New Colonies" was largely an exploration of the
reasons for the rapid development of Britain's colonies on the North
American continent.[1]

   In this consideration, which repeated most of the central conclusions
of a half-century of speculation by various analysts, Smith identified
six principal causes for the colonies' rapid rise "to wealth and greatness."[2] First, and singled out by Smith as one of "two great causes of
the prosperity of all new colonies," was the cheapness and "Plenty of
good land."[3] Second was the high wages commanded by labor, which
provided a spur to individual industry and a vehicle for the expansion

   1. Adam Smith, *The Nature and Causes of the Wealth of Nations,* in *The Glasgow Edition of the Works and Correspondence of Adam Smith,* ed. R. H. Campbell
and A. S. Skinner, 6 vols. (Oxford, 1976–83), 2 : 564.
   2. Ibid.
   3. Ibid., 564–65, 572, 582.

of the population of independent producers.[4] Third was the extensiveness and openness of markets for colonial produce, the result of both a comparatively liberal trade policy by Britain and the "great internal market" the colonies were themselves creating "for the produce of one another."[5] Fourth was the low level of public expenditures and taxation.[6] Fifth, which Smith considered as the second of the two great causes of colonial growth, was the colonists' "liberty to manage their own affairs their own way."[7] Sixth and last was the superior agricultural and commercial expertise the technologically advanced colonists applied to the new lands and what Smith referred to as their "habit of subordination," by which he meant their previous socialization to a system of law and regular government.[8] To these factors, the anonymous author of *American Husbandry*, a systematic survey of the conditions and potentialities of agriculture in all of Britain's American colonies published in 1775, added a seventh cause, the "healthiness of the climate" in all but the lowest-lying areas near the coast in the colonies south of Pennsylvania.[9]

In combination, contemporary observers thought, these causes operated to produce societies for which, as Benjamin Franklin remarked in his famous essay "Observations Concerning the Increase of Mankind" in 1751, none of the "Observations made on full settled old Countries, as Europe, [would] suit."[10] The abundance and cheapness of land was, in significant part, Smith and other observers agreed, responsible for the "liberal reward of labor,"[11] which in turn made it still easier for able-bodied people to acquire land. "Land being . . . Plenty in America, and so cheap as that a labouring Man, who understands Husbandry, can in a short Time save Money enough to purchase a Piece of new Land sufficient for a Plantation," Franklin explained, "no Man continues long a Labourer for others."[12] Because they could so

4. Ibid., 575, 582.
5. Ibid., 575, 580.
6. Ibid., 565, 573–74.
7. Ibid., 572.
8. Ibid., 564–65.
9. Harry J. Carman, ed., *American Husbandry* (New York, 1939), 530.
10. Benjamin Franklin, "Observations Concerning the Increase of Mankind, Peopling of Countries, &c.," 1751, in *The Papers of Benjamin Franklin*, ed. Leonard W. Labaree et al., 27 vols. to date (New Haven, Conn., 1959–), 4:227.
11. Smith, *Wealth of Nations*, 565.
12. Franklin, "Observations," 228.

readily "become landlords themselves,"[13] hired men were "continually leaving their Master[s] . . . and setting up for themselves."[14]

The same circumstances also contributed to a degree of rustication of colonial societies that exceeded that anywhere in the Old World. With so much inexpensive land available, "no Man," Franklin reported, continued "long a Journeyman to a Trade,"[15] and few wanted to live in urban settlements. "In America," wrote the author of *American Husbandry*, "all sorts of people turn[ed] farmers." There was "no mechanic or artizan—sailor—soldier—servant, &c.," he noted, "but what, if they get money, take land, and turn farmers."[16]

Contemporary observers agreed as well that abundant land and high wages also, in the words of the author of *American Husbandry*, virtually banished "every thing that has the least appearance of begging, or that wandering, destitute state of poverty, which we see so common in England."[17] In the colonies, where, as Franklin remarked, there was "Room and Business for Millions yet unborn" and where the demand for labor seemed to be insatiable, there was bound to be "full employ." Moreover, as Franklin early and frequently contended, the same conditions strongly encouraged family formation and population growth. "In old settled Countries, as England," Franklin observed, where the population was larger than the opportunities for people to support themselves, many, facing lives of "Poverty, Diseases, and want of Necessaries," declined to marry because they could not see any way "to maintain a family."[18] In the colonies, by contrast, men and women, seeing that they could easily provide for a family, were "not," as Franklin put it, "afraid to marry."[19] As Smith noted, free British Americans also understood that their children would supply valuable labor while they remained at home and, once they were grown, would be able "to establish themselves in the same manner as their fathers did before them."[20] "Where a family, instead of being a burden, is an advantage," the author of *American Husbandry* remarked in second-

13. Smith, *Wealth of Nations*, 565.
14. Franklin, "Observations," 230.
15. Ibid., 228.
16. Carman, *American Husbandry*, 124.
17. Ibid., 52–53.
18. Franklin, "Poor Richard," in *Papers of Benjamin Franklin*, 3:440–41.
19. Franklin, "Observations," 227–28.
20. Smith, *Wealth of Nations*, 565.

ing these opinions, "marriages must abound" and population increase must be "amazing."[21]

Contemporary observers also thought that low public expenditures helped to accelerate this broad expansion in the extent of independent property holding, numbers of families, and population. As promotional writers had promised, settlers were comparatively free "from heavy taxes—from tythes—from poor rates."[22] "Generally confined to what was necessary for paying competent salaries to the governor, to the judges, and to some [few] other officers of police, and for maintaining a few of the most useful publick works," government costs, as Smith emphasized, had "always been very moderate," amounting to less than £65,000 annually for *all* of Britain's North American colonies. In contrast to the Spanish and Portuguese colonies, where the settlers, in Smith's view, were "oppressed with a numerous race of mendicant friars, whose beggary being not only licensed, but consecrated by religion, is a most grievous tax upon" the public, the British colonists paid no tithes and maintained only modest numbers of clergymen through a moderate tax or voluntary contributions. Along with the absence of rent, low public expenses, Smith emphasized, meant that independent people could retain a far "greater proportion" of their earnings than such people ever could in Britain itself.[23]

According to Smith and others, the operation of political institutions had much the same effect. Government in the colonies, they believed, was not only cheap but mild. "Derived from the original genius and strong desire of the people ratified and confirmed by the crown,"[24] colonial political institutions, Smith thought, were considerably "more favourable to the improvement and cultivation of . . . land" and the spread of property holding and individual economic competence than those of the colonies of either Spain, Portugal, or France. Extremely sensitive to "the inclinations of their constituents," those institutions had contrived a system of equitable laws primarily designed to secure to families the products of their labor. For that reason, colonial governments both commanded broad public respect

21. Carman, *American Husbandry*, 53.
22. Ibid., 65.
23. Smith, *Wealth of Nations*, 573–74.
24. J. Hector St. John de Crèvecoeur, *Letters from an American Farmer* (New York, 1957), 38.

and nourished the ambitions of all independent property holders.[25] With only such "silken bands of . . . government"[26] to hold them and "no oppressions to enslave the planter and rob him of the fruits of his industry," liberty, declared the author of *American Husbandry* in commenting on the free population of South Carolina—and pointedly not pausing to consider the situation of that colony's vast slave population—reigned "in perfection,"[27] dread of power was almost unknown, and "Bad Government and insecure Property" did not operate, as they evidently did in much of Europe, to discourage labor and population increase.[28]

As contemporaries examined them, the societies that developed out of these conditions appeared, especially in comparison with those in Europe, to be in most ways highly exceptional. With apparently no social or economic limits to demographic growth, their populations were both comparatively young and extraordinarily dynamic. Still "in the gristle, and not yet hardened into the bone of manhood," in Edmund Burke's powerful metaphor, colonial populations, Burke observed, "spread from families and communities, and from villages and nations" even "faster" than children grew "from infancy to manhood."[29] With so much unsettled land and, as the author of *American Husbandry* remarked in the case of Virginia, with "the profit[s] of agriculture [still] exceeding that of any other profession,"[30] these societies were becoming ever more rural. Because farmers and planters chose homesites largely according to the quality of the land, rural settlements were often widely scattered, particularly during the early years of settler occupation. "To people of a sociable disposition in Europe," the same writer observed in reference to New England, where close settlement had long been a cultural ideal, this lack of "regard [for] the near neighbourhood of other farmers" could only in its seeming randomness and disorder "appear very strange."[31] Observers had the same reaction to the small size and paucity of urban settlements.

25. Smith, *Wealth of Nations*, 572, 585.

26. Crèvecoeur, *Letters from an American Farmer*, 36.

27. Carman, *American Husbandry*, 305.

28. Franklin, "Observations," 230.

29. Edmund Burke, *Speech on Conciliation with America*, ed. Daniel V. Thompson (New York, 1907), 9, 17.

30. Carman, *American Husbandry*, 530.

31. Ibid., 36.

John Bartram's House and Garden. The Pennsylvania botanist John Bartram made this ink drawing of his house and garden on the banks of the Schuylkill River near Philadelphia in 1758. At the top a substantial house with Bartram's study overlooks a series of gardens connected by steps, separated by walls or walks stretching down to the riverbank, and enclosed by fences and hedges. Adjacent to the vast lower garden, which includes a spring connected by an underground conduit to a milk house at the edge of a pasture, are two long walks demarcated by rows of trees. The strolling figure may be Bartram's representation of himself. This ordered ambience was typical of the efforts of eighteenth-century American estate owners to bring their properties under control. Courtesy of the Library of the Earl of Derby, Knowsley, Prescot, Lancashire, United Kingdom.

Again in contrast to those of Europe, colonial societies also seemed to most observers to be exceptionally fluid and mobile. As they sought to describe and identify those societies, writers invariably pointed to the thousands of cases in which individuals had been able to improve their material lives. The promise of such mobility was one of the principal themes articulated in *American Husbandry*. Its author described a process by which people with no "substance" beyond that required to pay land fees "maintain[ed] themselves the first year, like the Indians, with their guns and nets, and afterwards by the same means with the assistance of their lands," providing their own labor and within "a few years" creating a situation in which they were able "to maintain themselves and families comfortably."[32] Throughout the century, commentators recounted instances in which new immigrants and young people had "in five or six Years['] Time . . . made such Farms as afford[ed] them [not only] all the Necessaries of Life in plenty" but also many of the "Conveniencies," including "clean Houses, neat, though homely, Furniture, commodious Barns, and a sufficient stock of Horses, Cows, Hogs, Poultry, &c."[33]

Indeed, in not a few instances, according to many observers, families were able to build "very considerable Estates," sometimes in a single generation, but more often in two or three.[34] Especially in places with rich agricultural lands and ready access to markets, places like Pennsylvania, Virginia, or South Carolina, families could in time readily turn industry or modest capital into "a small fortune." Persuaded that

32. Ibid., 90.

33. Roscommon, *To the Author of Those Intelligencers Printed at Dublin* (New York, 1733), 5.

34. *Money, the Sinews of Trade* (Boston, 1731), 2–3.

A Draught of John Bartram's House and Garden as it appears from the River 1758 — Seal to P Collenson

1. my Study
2. Common Flower Garden
3. upper Kitchen Garden
4. the Lower Kitchen Garden
5.6. Walks 150 yards long of a moderate descent

A new flower Garden 25 yards long & 10 Broad

The County of the River is Northwest & south east

A Pond or inving hold conveyd under ground to the Spring or milk House

Schuilkeln a River 400 Yards wide

the agriculture of South Carolina was more profitable than any in Europe or elsewhere in the continental colonies, the author of *American Husbandry* repeated "a story current in Carolina" about "a new settler, [who] not having a better habitation, took his abode for some time in a decayed tulip tree, in which he had his bed and other furniture; yet this man, poor as he may seem from hence, lived to become a considerable and wealthy planter." In the words of the same writer, the "daily instances of" such successes gave "an emulation to all the lower classes." [35] As new immigrants and young people looked around and saw "many a prosperous person, who but a few years before was as poor as" themselves,[36] they began "to point their endeavours with peculiar industry to gain an end which they all esteem[ed] so particularly flattering." [37] The end this author referred to was, of course, not merely material betterment but also social respect—and self-respect.

No serious contemporary student of the character of colonial British American societies suggested that all people succeeded in this process of social emulation. On the contrary, they pointed to many instances in which misfortune, bad planning, ignorance, inexperience, or inappropriate character traits such as laziness, extravagance, inactivity, drunkenness, and lack of dedication led to disappointment and ruin. America, they emphasized, provided no guarantees. To a far greater extent than Europe, however, it did offer a chance that, with hard work, activity, perseverance, and sobriety, they stressed, could be turned to a person's advantage.

Through the many examples they cited of those who had taken advantage of the opportunities offered by America, eighteenth-century observers contributed powerfully to reinforcing a growing identification of colonial British America as a place that, in actuality as well as in promise, had indeed provided exceptional opportunities for social mobility, a country that offered the conditions in which, in the much quoted words of the French immigrant Hector St. John de Crèvecoeur, "the idle may be employed, the useless become useful, and the poor become rich," rich at least in the sense of possessing "cleared lands, cattle, good houses, good clothes, and an increase of people to enjoy them." [38]

35. Carman, *American Husbandry*, 52, 140, 267.
36. Crèvecoeur, *Letters from an American Farmer*, 55.
37. Carman, *American Husbandry*, 52.
38. Crèvecoeur, *Letters from an American Farmer*, 42, 52, 57.

In marked contrast to Britain, where during the whole eighteenth century widespread poverty coexisted with rising living standards among most of the possessing classes, social commentators in the colonies, in fact, worried far less about material deprivation than about the adverse social and moral effects of prosperity. By no means did they regard the wealth and opportunities generated by the rapid economic and demographic growth of the colonies as an unmixed blessing. From the 1720s onward, more and more people complained that ease of life in the colonies had produced a decline in diligence and moral standards and a rise in worldliness. They lamented that current generations seemed to be inferior in industry, enterprise, frugality, and virtue to the generations who had performed the herculean tasks of wresting plantations out of the wilderness. If the industry of earlier generations and the rich soils of North America had yielded plenty, that plenty, as Dr. William Smith, provost at the College of Philadelphia, observed in 1759, seemed to have "begat Ease; and Ease begat Luxury; and Luxury introduced a fatal corruption of every good and virtuous principle."[39]

Rooted in an inherited Christian suspicion of wealth, such complaints were not new among the colonists. They had long been a standard feature of the jeremiads of the New England clergy. But their range and volume seem to have increased steadily throughout the middle decades of the eighteenth century. Not just from puritan New England but from all over the colonies came reports about the alarming effects of wealth and luxury as manifest in growing contentiousness in many areas of public life, disrespect for authority, neglect of public duty, avarice, extravagance, and pursuit of pleasure. In Virginia, Commissary James Blair chided his Anglican parishioners for addiction to "all manner of Gratifications of their Luxury, stately houses, Furniture, Equipage, plentiful Tables, Mirth, Musick, and Drinking."[40] In New England, clergymen and laymen alike deplored the "great Extravagance that People . . . are fallen into beyond their Circumstances, in their Purchases, Buildings, Expenses, Apparel, and generally whole way of Living."[41] In Pennsylvania, Chief Jus-

39. William Smith, *Discourses on Several Public Occasions during the War in America* (London, 1759), 77.

40. James Blair, *Our Saviour's Divine Sermon on the Mount*, 2d ed., 2 vols. (London, 1740), 1:127, 132.

41. Paul Dudley, *Objections to the Bank of Credit Lately Projected* (Boston, 1714), 14.

tice James Logan questioned "whether the Attractions of Pleasure and Ease" had not come to be far "Stronger than those of Business."[42] Benjamin Whitaker, Logan's counterpart in South Carolina, called upon the people "to abstain from that Luxury and Excess, which within a few Years last past, has pour'd in upon us like a Torrent" and "so greatly contributed to enervate and soften our Minds, and to sink us, into Indolence and Inactivity."[43]

To counteract such ominous developments, many people called for what Erik H. Erikson has referred to as "a reactionary return to the content and to the form of historically earlier principles of behavior,"[44] specifically to the standards of the early founders. To an important degree, the many spiritual awakenings that occurred in several colonies between 1720 and 1770 exhibited a yearning for just such a return. Although they produced a few examples of millenarian thinking that looked forward to the eventual achievement of the kingdom of God in America,[45] the primary appeal of those awakenings seems to have been for a renunciation of contemporary worldliness and a return to the simple, uncorrupted, pious, and virtuous standards of earlier generations. But much of the spiritual energy and moral fervor spawned by these awakenings quickly dissipated in the face of the continuing acceleration of the economy in the decades after 1745.[46]

If, notwithstanding their difficulties in handling it, colonial societies were known for their remarkable and widespread prosperity, they were also, contemporary observers thought, exceptional for the equality they exhibited among their free inhabitants. "There is more equality . . . among the English colonists than among the inhabitants of the mother country," Adam Smith noted in repeating a common observa-

42. James Logan, *The Charge Delivered from the Bench to the Grand Jury* (Philadelphia, 1723), 9.

43. [Benjamin Whitaker], *The Chief Justice's Charge to the Grand Jury* (Charleston, S.C., 1741), 10–11.

44. Erik H. Erikson, "Identity and the Life Cycle," *Psychological Issues* 1 (1959): 28–29.

45. See Alan Heimert, *Religion and the American Mind from the Great Awakening to the Revolution* (Cambridge, Mass., 1966), 61–67; James West Davidson, *The Logic of Millennial Thought: Eighteenth-Century New England* (New Haven, Conn., 1977), 122–29; Ruth H. Bloch, *Visionary Republic: Millennial Themes in American Thought, 1756–1800* (Cambridge, 1985), 10–21.

46. For a fuller discussion of this theme, see Jack P. Greene, "Search for Identity: An Interpretation of Selected Patterns of Social Response in Eighteenth-Century America," *Journal of Social History* 3 (1970): 189–220.

tion.[47] Despite the fact that some West Indian sugar planters had developed large estates and that, as Franklin put it, "favourites of governors" had in several mainland colonies "obtained enormous tracts,"[48] the North American colonies, where few people had yet amassed the capital or labor to operate large holdings, had, as Franklin contended in 1760, "as yet few large estates." As a result, those colonies were characterized by "a more equal division of landed property" than could be found in Europe and a comparative "mediocrity of fortune among the inhabitants."[49] In societies in which wages and the demand for labor were high enough so that even the poor, as the Boston merchant John Colman put it in 1721, could "always live like men,"[50] the "rich and poor," in Crèvecoeur's words, simply were "not so far removed from each other as they" were "in Europe."[51]

What impressed observers most about the societies of colonial British America, however, what seemed most exceptional about them in comparison with those of Europe, was the fact that the entire top of the European status order was missing. If, by the middle of the eighteenth century, colonial societies all had "many considerable land[ed] estates, upon which the owners live[d] much in the style of country gentlemen in England,"[52] they were yet, most analysts agreed, too simple and too undifferentiated to "afford that variety of tinges and gradations which may be observed in Europe."[53] They clearly did not, as the author of *American Husbandry* remarked, contain "that distinction of the ranks and classes . . . which we see in Britain, but which is infinitely more apparent in France and other arbitrary countries." Indeed, according to the same author, wealthy landed gentlemen in the colonies bore but "a minute resemblance to the gentlemen in England who live[d] upon their own estates." In contrast to their English counterparts, he wrote, American gentlemen were "quite exempt from the overbearing influence of any neighbouring nobleman, which in England is very mischievous to many

47. Smith, *Wealth of Nations*, 585.

48. Franklin to the Printer of the *London Chronicle*, May 9, 1759, in *Papers of Benjamin Franklin*, 8:341.

49. Franklin, *The Interest of Great Britain with Regard to Her Colonies* (London, 1760), in ibid., 9:86.

50. John Colman, *The Distressed State of the Town of Boston* (Boston, 1720), 14.

51. Crèvecoeur, *Letters from an American Farmer*, 36.

52. Carman, *American Husbandry*, 46.

53. Crèvecoeur, *Letters from an American Farmer*, 40.

New England View. This primitive painting by an unknown artist on the over-mantel of the Perez Walker House in Sturbridge, Massachusetts, dates from the last quarter of the eighteenth century. It shows a manicured rural landscape against the background of a substantial port town of the kind that was develop-ing throughout the northern colonies during the middle decades of the eighteenth century. The painting depicts at least four churches and numerous houses and barns against a background of many ships in the harbor, with oversized human figures indulging in leisurely walks in the still bucolic but obviously porous and moving boundary between town and country. This view conveys the contempo-rary conception of an "improved" landscape. Courtesy of Old Sturbridge Village, Massachusetts.

gentlemen of small[er] fortunes."[54] "In none of the English colonies," Adam Smith emphasized, was "there any hereditary nobility." If, "as in all other free countries," he explained, "the descendant of an old colony family" was "more respected than an upstart of equal merit and fortune," he was "only more respected" and had "no privileges by which he can be troublesome to his neighbours."[55]

Indeed, in the view of Smith and many others, the extensive independence even among the least wealthy members of American society prevented either the establishment of a European-style patronage society or that oppression of the lower orders that was so common in "old countries." Because most of them had their own means of support and because even laborers were independent, few free people "in new colonies" had much need of patronage. What Smith referred to as the "superior orders" had therefore no foundations on which to build a system of social "oppress[ion]." Instead, they were obliged "to treat" their inferiors with "generosity and humanity; at least where" those inferiors were "not in a state of slavery."[56] By this simple aside, Smith revealed once again the extraordinary extent to which the intellectual construction of America as it took further shape during the first three-quarters of the eighteenth century continued to depend upon a systematic inattention or blindness to the significant roles played by slaves in the creation of the societies of colonial British America.

The truncated nature of colonial social structures, the absence of a legally privileged elite with a vastly disproportionate share of the resources of production, meant, in the view of most observers, that colonial British American societies differed profoundly from those of Europe. Whereas the principal social categories in Europe were "lords and tenants," the title of independent freeholder applied to the vast majority of free adults in colonial societies.[57] In Crèvecoeur's eloquent and familiar words, those societies were "not composed, as in Europe, of great lords who possess everything, and a herd of people who have nothing." They had "no aristocratical families, no courts, no kings, no bishops, no ecclesiastical dominion, no invisible power giving to the few a very visible one." Instead of a landscape dominated by "the hostile castle, and the haughty mansion, contrasted with the clay-built

54. Carman, *American Husbandry*, 46–47.
55. Smith, *Wealth of Nations*, 585.
56. Ibid., 565.
57. Crèvecoeur, *Letters from an American Farmer*, 51.

huts and miserable cabins, where cattle and men help to keep each other warm, and dwell in meanness, smoke, and indigence," the colonies presented a "pleasing uniformity of decent . . . habitations" and a social lexicon that was "but short in words of dignity, and names of honour," a lexicon in which "Lawyer or merchant" were "the fairest titles" afforded by towns and "that of a farmer . . . the only appellation of the rural inhabitants." [58]

Perhaps the most exceptional result of the expansive conditions in eighteenth-century colonial British America, according to most observers, was the broad empowering of the free adult male population. As historians now appreciate, the process of early modern colonization throughout the Americas necessarily involved an extraordinary devolution of authority outward from metropolitan centers to the new colonial peripheries and, within the colonies, downward from provincial capitals to localities. [59] As Adam Smith pointed out, simply to get people in such distant peripheries to acknowledge their authority, metropolitan officials had to exercise it "with very great gentleness." [60] In the British case, the metropolitan government had to be content with what Smith described as little more than a "nominal dominion" [61] in which the colonists enjoyed "complete" liberty "to manage their own affairs their own way" in "every thing, except their foreign trade." [62]

But the point made by many contemporary interpreters was that this devolution process had extended much deeper into colonial British American societies, down to the very individuals who composed them. Widespread possession of landed property, those interpreters noted, turned the colonies into societies in which virtually "every [free] Male Inhabitant became a Freeholder, and by consequence entitled to a share in the Government of the Province." [63] By becoming freehold-

58. Ibid., 35–36.

59. See Jack P. Greene, *Peripheries and Center: Constitutional Development in the Extended Polities of the British Empire and the United States, 1607–1788* (Athens, Ga., 1986).

60. Smith, *Wealth of Nations*, 571.

61. Adam Smith, "Thoughts on America," February 1778, in G. H. Guttridge, ed., "Adam Smith on the American Revolution: An Unpublished Memorial," *American Historical Review* 38 (1953): 718.

62. Smith, *Wealth of Nations*, 585.

63. Jack P. Greene, ed., "William Knox's Explanation for the American Revolution," *William and Mary Quarterly*, 3d ser., 30 (1973): 299.

ers, every man acquired both a private and a public space. They were not only, as Crèvecoeur wrote, "the possessors of the soil they cultivate[d]" but also "members of the government they obey[ed], and the framers of their own laws, by means of their representatives,"[64] who, as Smith emphasized, "approach[ed much] more nearly" to "an equal representation of the people" than did the British House of Commons and were "in general more influenced by the inclinations of their constituents."[65]

Contemporary observers also suggested that this empowering process reached beyond the public realm. Colonial freeholders, they noted, enjoyed not only broad political privileges but also virtually complete control over their own lives and fortunes. Real power, in their view, had gradually been drawn downward from local units of government through individual freeholds and estates to the thousands of individual possessors of those properties. With "No Lords over them" and "their Estates . . . absolutely their own," each such possessor, "like *Gideon's* Brethren," resembled *"the Children of a King."*[66] No societies, wrote the author of *American Husbandry*, offered "a greater degree of independence and liberty" than Britain's North American colonies.[67]

If the broad achievement of independence as a result of the wide dispersion of property among free people was primarily responsible for this extensive devolution of authority among the free population of the colonies, the widespread diffusion of dependence through the proliferating institution of chattel slavery also had an important contributing role. As Smith noted, in societies in which slaves were property, magistrates were reluctant to intervene on behalf of slaves because such intervention necessarily interfered "in some measure in the management of the private property of the master[s]."[68] Hence, the legal system placed few restraints upon masters in the governance of their slaves. In slave societies, unrestricted authority over slaves was a necessary emblem of the masters' freedom.

Along with the relatively undifferentiated social system in which there were no legally sanctioned distinctions of rank and degree,

64. Crèvecoeur, *Letters from an American Farmer*, 38, 51.
65. Smith, *Wealth of Nations*, 585.
66. *A Plea for the Poor and Distressed* (Boston, 1754), 5.
67. Carman, *American Husbandry*, 46.
68. Smith, *Wealth of Nations*, 587.

this sweeping empowering process among free people, various observers noted, produced societies of militantly independent men. By also inhibiting the development in the colonies of those feelings "of subordination that property, ancestry or dignity of station . . . naturally excited" among Britons in the home islands, this process also, in the words of William Knox, a crown official in Georgia who in 1770 became an undersecretary of state for the colonies in London, effectively excluded "all ideas of . . . dependence." Traditional Old World–style "relation[ships] between Landlord and Tenant could have no existence," explained Knox, "where every Man held by the same tenure" and where tenants themselves acquired an interest in the improvements they made to the properties they rented. If the "Superior industry or better fortune of some enabled them to extend their possessions by purchases" while "others became wealthy thro' successful trade, . . . their riches brought them little [public] influence." Such influence, he observed, could only be obtained "by following the humor or disposition of the People." No wonder that the societies of colonial British America appeared to Knox and other contemporary observers to be deeply "tinctured with republicanism."[69] Both their governments and "their manners," Adam Smith thought, were infinitely "more republican" than those of metropolitan Britons.[70]

As the small size of their public realms attests, however, the incipient republicanism of the societies of colonial British America did not, as many contemporary observers noted, translate into wide and extended involvement in public life. Members of these societies did not shrink from expressing their opinions on public measures and were by no means overawed by authority, but the vast majority seem to have been too consumed by their own private family concerns to seek an active role in public life. As long as government made no effort to deprive them, in the words of a New York official in 1750, "of making Use of those Means which Providence has been pleased to put into our Hands, for the Ease and Comfort of Life, from what we raise and manufacture from our own Produce and Labour,"[71] most seem to have preferred to "glide through the World in a private Sta-

69. Greene, "Knox's Explanation," 299–300.

70. Smith, *Wealth of Nations*, 585.

71. [Archibald Kennedy], *Observations on the Importance of the Northern Colonies under Proper Regulations* (New York, 1750), 31.

NEW YORK · 1765

New York City Hall. The many elegant new public buildings that were built in the colonies through the middle decades of the eighteenth century testify to the accumulating wealth and expanding cultural aspirations of the colonists. This view of the New York City Hall, now Federal Hall, the meeting place of one of the earliest intercolonial congresses in 1765, is the work of Alyn Cox and is taken from a mural on the ceiling of the first-floor corridor of the House of Representatives wing in the United States Capitol in Washington. Courtesy of the Library of Congress, neg. no. LCUSA7-38846.

tion," content with "the serene and quiet Pleasures of Retirement,"[72] unencumbered with public concerns, and contributing to the public good solely by following "some honest Occupation" and living within the law.[73] People did not participate in public life because they were excluded from doing so, as were all but a few Europeans, but because they had other business to which they preferred to attend.

The right of an individual in ordinary times *not* to venture beyond his private space into the public realm was yet another powerful symbol of the liberty—the empowerment—of free men in colonial British

72. Samuel Davies, *Religion and Public Spirit* (Portsmouth, N.H., 1762), 6.

73. Samuel Whittelsey, *A Public Spirit* (New London, Conn., 1731), 12. See also Joseph Morgan, *The Nature of Riches* (Philadelphia, 1732), 21; [William Gooch], *A Dialogue between Thomas Sweet-Scented . . . and Justice Love-Country* (Williamsburg, 1732), 17.

Tryon's Palace. This architectural drawing is for the most elegant and expensive public building in colonial British America, the governor's palace built in 1767–71 in New Bern, North Carolina, during the administration of Governor William Tryon. The work of the architect John Hawke, this building provided rooms of state and quarters for the royal governor. Accustomed, like inhabitants of all the colonies, to low taxes and living in a cash-poor society, North Carolinians objected to the high taxes required to pay for this complex. In protest, some of them joined in the civil uprising known as the North Carolina Regulator Movement. Courtesy of the Public Record Office, London, United Kingdom, Colonial Office Papers, Class 700/Carolina 10.

America. In these profoundly private societies, the most popular cultural ideal was contained in the widely quoted biblical image of the independent farmer dwelling with his family *"safely under his own Vine, and securely enjoy[ing] the fruits of his labour."*[74]

According to Crèvecoeur, the same private orientation also helped to make the increasingly plural societies of the colonies work and to make them more secular. Despite cultural and religious differences, what Crèvecoeur referred to as a "promiscuous . . . mixture of English, Scotch, Irish, French, Dutch, Germans, and Swedes"[75] could live together, he thought, because they shared a common dedication to securing their families "from the apprehension of want and poverty" and, if possible, to providing them with "the enjoyment of plenty and affluence."[76] Moreover, because that same dedication mostly made people "think more of the affairs of this world than of those of the next," Crèvecoeur thought, sectarian zeal quickly gave way to "religious indifference," which, he contended, had been so widely "disseminated from one end of the continent to the other" that it had become "one of the strongest characteristics of the Americans."[77]

Contemporary analysts also argued that the conditions that operated to produce these exceptional societies in the colonies had a profound effect upon the character of the people who lived in them. In contrast to the Old World, where "involuntary idleness, servile de-

74. See, among hundreds of uses of this image, Archibald Cummings, *The Character of a Righteous Ruler* (Philadelpia, 1736), 5.

75. Crèvecoeur, *Letters from an American Farmer*, 37.

76. Thomas Warrington, *The Love of God, Benevolence, and Self-Love, Considered Together* (Williamsburg, 1753), 22.

77. Crèvecoeur, *Letters from an American Farmer*, 44, 46–47.

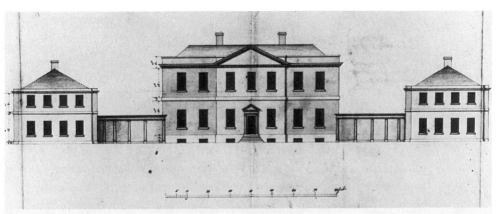

References

A Hall
B Library
C Council Chamber
D Drawing Room
E Parlour
F House keepers Room
G Servants Hall
H Great Stair Case
I Lesser Stair Case
K Secretary's Office
L Kitchen
M Scullery
N Larder
O Wash House
PP Stables
QQ Coach House
R Harness Room

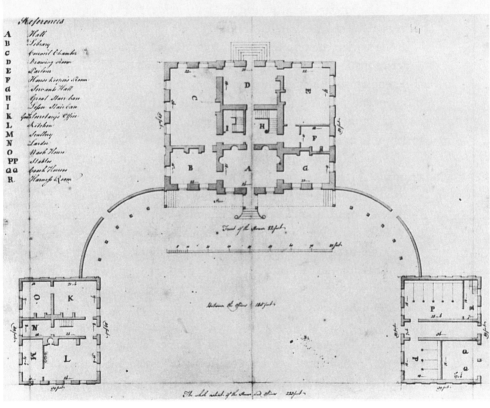

Front of the House 82 feet

Between the Offices 165 feet

The whole extent of the House and Wings 222 feet

pendence, penury, and useless labour"[78] combined to render much of the population passively dependent, ample prospects for material betterment turned people in the colonies into "free active Being[s]." By offering such abundant possibilities for "Self-Determination," for what the New England moral philosopher Samuel Johnson referred to as "Deliberation, Choice, and Design" in their lives, social conditions in the colonies, according to many observers, excited "the Powers of Self-Exertion"[79] and made people "dare to think for themselves."[80] Greater industry was one of the principal expressions of that activity. In societies in which individuals and families reaped such a high proportion of the rewards for their labor, that labor, as Crèvecoeur suggested, was effectively grounded in *"self-interest"*[81] and people were thereby rendered "very industrious."[82]

If the social conditions enjoyed and created in colonial British America made the free inhabitants more active and industrious, they also reportedly enhanced their ambitions and made them militantly independent. By presenting free people with such a sense of openness and opportunity, those conditions allegedly both encouraged parents to aspire to more for their children and raised their own expectations for themselves. Not content *"to Spend their Days in Rolling the Stone of Sisyphous,"* free people in the colonies, wrote one anonymous author, were invariably disappointed if they did not *"make a clear Gain."*[83] By freeing them from dependence upon the will of other people, indeed, in many cases, by making them masters of others themselves, those conditions reportedly fostered what Edmund Burke called "a love of freedom," a "fierce spirit of liberty," that, he posited, was "the predominating feature" in the colonial character and "stronger . . . probably than in any other people of the earth." Especially "high and haughty," according to Burke, in colonies where slavery was widespread and freedom, as a result, had become "a kind of rank and privilege,"[84] that spirit, various commentators noted, made the colo-

78. Ibid., 40.

79. Samuel Johnson, *Ethices Elementa; or, The First Principles of Moral Philosophy* (Boston, 1746), 23–24.

80. William Smith, *A General Idea of the College of Mirania* (New York, 1753), 3.

81. Crèvecoeur, *Letters from an American Farmer*, 40.

82. Carman, *American Husbandry*, 52–53.

83. *A Word of Comfort to a Melancholy Country* (Boston, 1721), 33.

84. Burke, *Speech on Conciliation*, 19–26.

nists proud, suspicious of authority, litigious, and contemptuous of servility, dependence, and failure.

Notwithstanding all of the ways that the societies of colonial British America appeared to be exceptional in comparison with those of the Old World, there was a widespread consensus among contemporary observers that they were gradually, and happily, becoming more like Europe. In the social realm, the counterpart to the concept of social mobility was the theory of social improvement or development. From his observations on early Spanish encounters with Amerindians, José de Acosta developed an explicit theory of cultural evolution during the late sixteenth century. Along with the emergence of a new interest in "natural" man among natural law theorists such as Grotius, Hobbes, Pufendorf, and Locke, the continuing perception of Amerindians and other supposedly savage peoples encountered by Europeans as living examples of a primitive state of society stimulated eighteenth-century French and Scottish thinkers to formulate a still more refined theory of the progressive development of society from rudeness to refinement "through four more or less distinct and consecutive stages, each corresponding to a different mode of subsistence, these stages being defined as hunting, pasturage, agriculture, and commerce."[85]

This four-stage theory, which came to be widely known as conjectural history and held "that societies of the European type had normally *started out as and developed from* societies of the American type,"[86] was widely used as an explanatory device by social analysts throughout the Western world during the eighteenth century. From the earliest days of English colonization in America, the conception of colonization as articulated by exponents and promoters like Richard Hakluyt the younger had presumed a similar stadial theory of sociocultural development for the new societies being established in America. If they had learned from Scottish conjectural historians, among whom Adam Smith was one of the most prominent, that even "savage and barbarous nations" exhibited what Smith called a "natural progress of law and government [and] . . . arts" toward ever greater refinement,[87] most contemporary interpreters of the societies of colonial British America had no doubt that the first century and a half of

85. Ronald L. Meek, *Social Science and the Ignoble Savage* (Cambridge, 1976), 2.

86. Ibid., 40.

87. Smith, *Wealth of Nations*, 565.

British colonial experience had amply confirmed that theory, at least in regard to those societies. Not surprisingly, therefore, it was that theory which informed their examinations and infused their analyses of those societies.

The theory was, for instance, implicit in Crèvecoeur's dark portrait of "the last inhabited districts" of America, districts still "near the great woods." During the early years of settlement in these "remote districts," according to Crèvecoeur, people lived in a kind of Hobbesian state of nature and supplied their needs almost entirely through hunting, which he regarded as "a licentious idle life." Characterized by "contention, inactivity, and wretchedness" and presided over by men who were "little better than the rest," such areas, Crèvecoeur wrote, were "often in a perfect state of war; that of man against man, sometimes decided by blows, sometimes by means of the law." In such conditions people often regressed to the primitive manners of the "wild inhabitant[s]" they had "come to dispossess" and "appear[ed] no better than carnivorous animals of a superior rank, living on the flesh of wild animals." "The manners of the Indian natives," Crèvecoeur contended, were "respectable, compared with this European medley."[88]

Exhibiting "the most hideous parts of our society," these frontier settlements, Crèvecoeur suggested, were not unique to themselves. Rather, by providing "a true idea" of America's "feeble beginnings and barbarous rudiments," they were emblematic of the first stages of colonization throughout colonial British America. Routinely, almost inexorably, this primitive stage was followed by the "progress[ive]," if gradual, improvement of these societies. As some of their earliest inhabitants were "polish[ed] by prosperity" and "more industrious people" replaced those whom law and failure had driven on to still newer areas, these "hitherto barbarous" countries were, in just a few years, Crèvecoeur wrote, "purged" of "off-casts" and transformed "into . . . fine fertile, well regulated district[s]," whose inhabitants exhibited "a general decency of manners . . . throughout."[89]

For nearly a quarter of a century before Crèvecoeur wrote, Franklin had been employing a similar conceptual scheme in writing about the changing character of "new Colonies." Specifically, he distinguished between two stages of sociocultural evolution. In the earliest stage,

88. Crèvecoeur, *Letters from an American Farmer*, 42–43, 48–49.
89. Ibid., 43.

"the first care of the planters," which engrossed virtually all of "their attention," was "to provide and secure the necessaries of life." Insofar as they had any "time to think of any thing farther," according to Franklin, they devoted their attention to "*Agriculture* and *mechanic arts*," which were "of the most immediate importance." Once the "Drudgery of Settling" was "pretty well over," however, these societies entered a second, more cultivated stage "of more wealth and leisure." By this stage the societies had enough resources to provide children with "polite and learned education[s]," and at least some individuals had sufficient "Leisure to cultivate the finer Arts and improve the common Stock of Knowledge."[90]

Against the broad background of Scottish conjectural history, the concept of improvement as employed by Crèvecoeur, Franklin, and many other observers of colonial development provided Euroamericans with the comforting vision that, notwithstanding their remoteness from the center of history in Europe, they were also incorporated into the historical process as that process had been formulated and sanctioned by Europeans in Europe, and both colonial and metropolitan analysts took pride in the rapidity with which colonial societies had moved along the trajectory from simplicity to improvement. Whereas "an hundred years ago" the whole of the colonies was "wild, woody, and uncultivated," by the third quarter of the eighteenth century it already had, in Crèvecoeur's words, many "fair cities, substantial villages, extensive fields, an immense country filled with decent houses, good roads, orchards, meadows, and bridges."[91] Whereas, as Burke declared, the colonies were initially filled only with "savage men and uncouth manners,"[92] they now had many men of learning and a few "virtuosi or ingenius Men,"[93] and every colonial society contained at least "the embryos of all the arts, sciences, and ingenuity which flourish[ed] in Europe."[94]

So improved were the "most ancient settled parts," wrote the author of *American Husbandry*, that they bore at least "some resemblance of old England." "The face of the country," he reported, "has in general

90. Franklin, "A Proposal for Promoting Useful Knowledge among the British Plantations in America," May 14, 1743, in *Papers of Benjamin Franklin*, 2:380–81; Franklin to *Pennsylvania Gazette*, Aug. 24, 1749, in ibid., 3:385–86.

91. Crèvecoeur, *Letters from an American Farmer*, 35.

92. Burke, *Speech on Conciliation*, 14.

93. Franklin, "Proposal for Promoting Useful Knowledge," 380–82.

94. Crèvecoeur, *Letters from an American Farmer*, 35, 52.

Faneuil Hall. Given by the merchant Peter Faneuil to the town of Boston for use as a public market and meeting place, this large brick structure, built in 1742, was among the first of several elaborate public buildings constructed in the colonies for civic and commercial uses through the middle decades of the eighteenth century. In the eyes of contemporaries, such buildings further improved the urban landscapes that they adorned. In this engraving, which appeared in the Massachusetts Magazine *(March 1789), the later buildings to the right of Faneuil Hall are out of perspective. Courtesy of the Library of Congress, neg. no.* LCUSZ62-2178.

a cultivated, inclosed, and chearful prospect; the farmhouses are well and substantially built, and stand thick," and there were "many considerable landed estates, upon which the owners live much in the style of country gentlemen in England."[95] Such astonishing development, Burke predicted in 1775, suggested that in just one more generation, through "a progressive increase of improvement, brought in by varieties of people, by succession of civilizing conquests and civilizing settlements,"[96] the colonies would be able to achieve what England had developed only after many centuries.

The central theme that emerged from contemporary commentary

95. Carman, *American Husbandry*, 35, 46.
96. Burke, *Speech on Conciliation*, 14.

Charleston Exchange. Built in 1771–72, the exchange in the thriving port of Charleston, South Carolina, served as both a place for commercial transactions and a customs house. Costing over £40,000, this elegant Palladian structure, like Faneuil Hall in Boston, expressed the mercantile wealth and orientation of Charleston, and residents and observers heralded it as an especially magnificent example of the sort of civic improvement taking place in urban America in the decades just before the American Revolution. From Thomas Leitch's View of Charles-Town, 1773. *Courtesy of the Museum of Early Southern Decorative Arts, Winston-Salem, North Carolina.*

on the societies of colonial British America was that, after a century and a half of existence, they had, to an exceptional degree, fulfilled the promises presented by America through the agency of early advocates of colonization. If, as Adam Smith remarked, America had been principally "peopled and cultivated" by "the disorder and injustice" of European societies[97] and, more specifically, by the inability of emi-

97. Smith, *Wealth of Nations*, 589.

grants to "find subsistence at home,"[98] many others, less desperate in their circumstances, were attracted by the promise of land and material betterment. "Hearing every day of poor people having in a few years got great estates there," "Multitudes of people," Wills Hill, Viscount Hillsborough, complained in Parliament in May 1753, "go thither yearly, who might live very well at home, and for no other reason but because they hope to live better, or to earn more money in those countries than they can do at home."[99]

Indeed, when they pondered the relative social situations of Europe and the British colonies, many commentators wondered, like the author of *American Husbandry*, that even larger numbers were not "flying from misery and oppression [in the Old World] to wealth and freedom"[100] in what Crèvecoeur, with his usual hyperbole, characterized as "the great American asylum" from want.[101] For colonists who toured the Old World, the contrast in social conditions was often powerful. Throughout the British Isles, in Ireland, Scotland, and even "many parts of England," Benjamin Franklin noted in 1772, society was composed of a very small number of "Landlords, great Noblemen and Gentlemen, extreamly opulent, [and] living in the highest Affluence and Magnificence" and a very large underclass of "Working Poor" and tenants who were impoverished, "tattered, dirty, and abject in Spirit" and lived "in the most sordid Wretchedness in dirty Hovels of Mud and Straw . . . cloathed only in Rags."[102]

In comparison, the British colonies seemed to have "the most perfect society now existing in the world."[103] "Had I never been in the American colonies, but was to form my Judgment of Civil Society" from the conditions he saw in the British Isles, Franklin declared, "I should never advise a Nation of Savages to admit of Civilisation." The principal effects of the sort of "Civil Society" he found in the Old World, he acidly remarked, was "the depressing Multitudes below the Savage State [so] that a few may be rais'd above it." Insofar as

98. Speech of William Thornton, May 8, 1753, in *Proceedings and Debates of the British Parliament Respecting North America*, ed. Leo F. Stock, 5 vols. (Washington, D.C., 1924–41), 5:567–68.

99. Speech of Wills Hill, May 8, 1753, in ibid.

100. Carman, *American Husbandry*, 305.

101. Crèvecoeur, *Letters from an American Farmer*, 42.

102. Franklin to Joshua Babcock, Jan. 13, 1772, in *Papers of Benjamin Franklin*, 19:7.

103. Crèvecoeur, *Letters from an American Farmer*, 36.

"the Possession and Enjoyment of the various Comforts of Life" were concerned, Franklin believed, "every Indian" was "a Gentleman" in comparison to the Old World poor.[104] In his estimation, there was "no Country in Europe where there" was "so much general Comfort and Happiness as in America, Holland perhaps excepted."[105]

Indeed, the exceptional character of colonial societies, their astonishing growth, and the extensive spaces of the North American continent produced, among many observers, widespread visions of future grandeur. Since the early 1750s, Benjamin Franklin had been pointing out that the rapidity of population growth meant both that within a century North America would be the home of more English people than lived in Britain itself and that, for that reason, "the Foundations of the future Grandeur and Stability of the British Empire" lay "in America."[106] "An immense Territory, favour'd by Nature with all Advantages of Climate, Soil, great navigable Rivers and Lakes, &c.," America, Franklin was persuaded, had to "become a great Country, populous and mighty."[107] Within two centuries, he predicted, "the British Colonies would overspread this immense territory . . . carrying with them the religion of Protestants, the laws, customs, manners, and language of the country from whence they sprung."[108] At that point, both Franklin and Adam Smith agreed, "the seat of the empire would . . . naturally remove itself to" America.[109]

Those who held such views found further inspiration for them in the ancient literary convention that saw *"Empire, Liberty* and *Arts, / With their resplendant Train,"* moving from east to west.[110] "The Progress of Humane Literature (like the Sun) is from east to West," wrote the New England almanac maker Nathaniel Ames in the late 1750s in a familiar passage: having earlier "travelled thro' *Asia* and *Europe,"* it had already "arrived at the Eastern Shore of *America,"* and Ames looked forward to the not very distant day when European

104. Franklin to Babcock, Jan. 13, 1772.

105. Franklin to Joseph Galloway, Feb. 6, 1772, in *Papers of Benjamin Franklin,* 19:71–72.

106. Franklin, "Observations," 233; Franklin to Lord Kames, Jan. 3, 1760, in *Papers of Benjamin Franklin,* 9:6–7; Franklin, *The Interest of Great Britain with Regard to Her Colonies* (London, 1760), in ibid., 9:77.

107. Franklin to Lord Kames, Feb. 25, 1767, in ibid., 14:69.

108. Charles Thomson to Franklin, Nov. 26, 1769, in ibid., 16:239.

109. Smith, *Wealth of Nations,* 625–26.

110. William Smith, *Some Thoughts on Education* (New York, 1752), 23.

civility and Christianity would "finally drive the long! long! Night of Heathenish Darkness from *America*" and "Arts and Sciences" would "change the Face of Nature in their Tour from Hence over the Appalachian Mountains to the Western Ocean . . . as they march[ed] thro' the vast Desert," breaking up "the Residence[s] of Wild Beasts" and Amerindians and silencing "their obscene Howl[s] . . . for ever."[111] In view of the rapid expansion already experienced by the colonies, it was no wonder, as the author of *American Husbandry* noted, that "an idea of their future independency starts into the mind of almost every man on the very mention of them in conversation,"[112] or that, after 1765, "the expectation of a rupture with the colonies," as Adam Smith reported, "struck the people of Great Britain with more terror than they ever felt for a Spanish armada, or a French invasion."[113]

In evaluating colonial British America, most contemporary observers decidedly did not define it in terms of its callous treatment of the many "others" who were systematically excluded from its largess. They did not stress the settlers' expropriation of lands from Amerindians and their expropriation of the freedom and the fruits of the labors of African Americans. Indeed, few observers ever doubted that by substituting European- for Amerindian-style patterns of land occupation and resource utilization, the settlers were engaged in a series of what Burke called "civilizing conquests" that successively contributed to the "progressive . . . improvement" of America.[114] Before the third quarter of the eighteenth century, even fewer found much wrong in enslaving and using blacks as significant but badly served contributors to that improvement. To those engaged in the process of examining and identifying colonial British American societies, the exceptional social conditions they offered to free people of European descent seemed far more salient than the plight of the "others." Such selective vision insured that among contemporaries colonial British America would be defined in terms of the benefits it provided for its dominant population and not in terms of the cost of those benefits to others.

111. Nathaniel Ames, "A Thought upon the Past, Present, and Future State of North America," 1757, in *The Essays, Humor, and Poems of Nathaniel Ames*, ed. Samuel Briggs (Cleveland, 1891), 284–86.

112. Carman, *American Husbandry*, 529.

113. Smith, *Wealth of Nations*, 605.

114. Burke, *Speech on Conciliation*, 14.

Despite this favorable image, however, the societies of colonial British America continued right down to the American War for Independence to represent something of a disappointment in terms of their failure fully to achieve the standards of civilized development represented by Europe itself. Created in the image of their creators, those societies ultimately judged themselves and were judged in terms of how thoroughly they met those standards. For Europeans as well as for their descendants in America, those standards, as I have emphasized throughout this volume, were the only legitimate standards. European culture, Edmundo O'Gorman has observed, was never conceived of as one among many cultures but as "the only truly significant culture; European history was universal history. Europe became history's paradigm, and the European way of life[, whatever its defects,] came to be regarded [again, by Europeans and Euroamericans,] as the supreme" measure by which the European societies in America were to be judged.[115] The ubiquity of the concept of improvement in the British American colonies made it clear that by removing to America the settler population had not escaped what one scholar has referred to as "the presumptive conceit of European civilization that in itself was realized the [highest development of] the nature of man."[116]

No less than the original native cultures, the new European colonies "could not be recognized and respected" in their own terms but could expect to be considered complete only when they had succeeded in transforming themselves into "a replica of the 'old' world."[117] In colonies and metropolis alike, the primary hope, the central aspiration, was not that colonial societies would come to terms with their environments but that, in the manner of Prospero and, a century later, Robinson Crusoe, they would master and reorder those environments along European lines until, as a result of a series of incremental improvements, they had slowly moved from primitive simplicity to higher—and more European—levels of cultural development.[118] In-

115. Edmundo O'Gorman, *The Invention of America: An Inquiry into the Historical Nature of the New World and the Meaning of Its History* (Bloomington, Ind., 1961), 137.

116. Fulvio Papi, *Antropologiae civita nel pensiero de Giordano Bruno* (Firenze, 1968), 200, as quoted by William Brandon, *New Worlds for Old: Reports from the New World and Their Effect on the Development of Social Thought in Europe, 1500–1800* (Athens, Ohio, 1986), 153.

117. O'Gorman, *Invention of America*, 139–40.

118. Leo Marx, *The Machine in the Garden: Technology and the Pastoral Ideal in*

Redwood Library. Impressive buildings devoted not just to civic and economic purposes but also to cultural uses increasingly began to appear in the colonies through the middle decades of the eighteenth century as part of the broader movement toward cultural improvement. The civic library was one such institution. Designed by the local architect Peter Harrison and named for its principal benefactor, the merchant Abraham Redwood, the Redwood Library in Newport, Rhode Island, was one of the earliest of such libraries and the first to have its own special building. Following the Palladian style, it was completed in 1750. From a watercolor drawing by Pierre Eugène du Simitière, 1767. Courtesy of the Library Company of Philadelphia.

deed, in this colonial context, the term *improvement* was virtually interchangeable with *European, English,* or *metropolitan.*

However powerful their expanding image as places of exceptional opportunity without many of the less desirable features of Old World societies, the societies of colonial British America fell considerably short of this exalted standard. As contemporary observers assessed

America (New York, 1964), 43–69; Octave Mannoni, *Prospero and Caliban: The Psychology of Colonization* (New York, 1956); James Sutherland, "The Author of *Robinson Crusoe,*" and Ian Watt, "*Robinson Crusoe,* Individualism and the Novel," in *Twentieth Century Interpretations of Robinson Crusoe: A Collection of Critical Essays,* ed. Frank H. Ellis (Englewood Cliffs, N.J., 1969), 25–54.

Nassau Hall. A second kind of institution built during the wave of cultural improvement that swept the colonies during the middle of the eighteenth century was the college. The College of New Jersey was among several new institutions of higher learning established during this period. Founded in 1746 and soon located in Princeton, the college initially had only a house for the president and one large three-story building for classes and student and faculty residences. Designed by the Philadelphia architect Robert Smith, this last building was named Nassau Hall after William III, the English monarch and prince of Orange and Nassau. It was the largest building in the British North American colonies in 1776. From an engraving by Henry Dawkins after a drawing by William Tennent, about 1764. Courtesy of the Firestone Library, Princeton University.

the social conditions that obtained in the colonies, they saw that in comparison with Britain and Europe the authority of traditional European social institutions such as the family, church, and community had not yet acquired much vigor as agencies of social control; that the lines between social spheres were yet indistinct and evanescent; that deference was a quality that was usually honored in the breach; that the professions were unregulated and filled with people of doubtful competence; that husbandry was carelessly practiced and agricultural experimentation infrequently undertaken; that education, reading, arts, and sciences were "shameful[ly] neglect[ed]"; that "common speech" was, by the standards of learned metropolitans, "extremely corrupt[ed]" and manners unrefined; and that concern for the public good often seemed to be subordinated to the pursuit of individual happiness.[119]

All these deficiencies, all these and many other evidences of continuing colonial provinciality and crudeness, seemed particularly discouraging to the rising generation of wealthy and educated colonists. Having learned from their parents, from travel or reading, or from the curriculum of colonial colleges or metropolitan universities what the attributes of an established British or European social order should be, many colonists of second- and third-generation wealth in the years after 1750 were strident advocates of measures designed to hasten the process of social consolidation and improvement that had been going on since the establishment of the colonies and to bring more coherence, order, and civility to colonial life.[120]

Many contemporary observers on the continent and in Britain agreed with this assessment. If they admired the colonies for their broad diffusion of property, their prosperity, their freedom, and their absence of constraining social distinctions among the free white population, they decried the comparatively crude, simple, undifferentiated, rustic, and provincial nature of those societies, many of which were in large part built on the cruel exploitation of black people through an unremitting system of racial slavery, and the impoverished and derivative character of their artistic and intellectual life. Indeed, the many social and cultural defects exhibited by the colonies persuaded some commentators, the most prominent among whom were the Comte de Buffon and the Abbé Corneille de Pauw, that conditions in America were so unfavorable to life as to cause a marked physical, mental, and moral degeneration among the creole descendants of the original European immigrants. The same unfavorable comparison of colonial societies with metropolitan European cultures underlay both a strong popular prejudice against and condescension toward the colonies in the Old World and a palpable sense of inferiority and dependence in the New.[121]

---

119. The quotations are from William Smith, Jr., *The History of the Province of New York*, ed. Michael Kammen, 2 vols. (Cambridge, Mass., 1972), 2:226–28.

120. For fuller discussions of this line of evaluation, see Greene, "Search for Identity," 205–21; John Clive and Bernard Bailyn, "England's Cultural Provinces: Scotland and America," *William and Mary Quarterly*, 3d ser., 11 (1954): 200–213.

121. Durand Echeverria, *Mirage in the West: A History of the French Image of American Society to 1815* (Princeton, 1957), 3, 6, 14–19; Henry Steele Com-

In both America and England, then, the continuing authority of European culture operated powerfully to prevent observers from developing a fully positive identification of the societies of colonial British America during the first three-quarters of the eighteenth century. The sense of openness and opportunity that had excited the founders of the colonies and even yet seemed to be the most salient positive characteristic of the societies that had emerged out of their efforts was to a considerable extent counteracted by a strong countervailing force: an inability—common to Europeans and Euroamericans alike—to evaluate these new societies except in terms of the standards of metropolitan Europe. In terms of those standards, the societies of the colonies seemed to be commendable primarily because of the exceptional opportunities they had provided for so many people of European descent to pursue their ambitions as individuals, for the peculiarly fluid and undifferentiated societies they contained, and for the enormous contributions their inhabitants had made to the enhancement of the economic and strategic power of Britain.

mager, *The Empire of Reason: How Europe Imagined and America Realized the Enlightenment* (New York, 1977), 126–27; Donald H. Meyer, *The Democratic Enlightenment* (New York, 1976), xx–xxi.

CHAPTER FIVE

Examinations

THE EUROPEAN RESPONSE

TO THE AMERICAN REVOLUTION,

1776–1800

For Britain's thriving colonies on the eastern seaboard of North America, the quarter century after 1765 was a period of extraordinary ferment. Following a long, drawn-out, and intense quarrel with Britain over their status within the British Empire during the decade before 1776, they fought a successful war for political independence, transformed themselves into republics, and endeavored to join together in an extensive federal union. These events attracted an unprecedented degree of attention from European social thinkers. This chapter considers how their examinations of these developments contributed to the ongoing process of the intellectual construction of America and how they functioned to enhance the conception of America as an exceptional entity.

Throughout much of the earlier eighteenth century, the societies of colonial British America had experienced vigorous territorial, demographic, and economic growth. As social entities, they had come to

exhibit many positive and sharply etched features, including extraordinary material abundance, wide scope for free individuals to pursue meaningful private lives, relative social equality, broad individual empowerment among the free population, and weak restrictive institutions. Although many contemporary observers praised these and other social characteristics, distance from Europe and continuing cultural provincialism functioned during the first three-quarters of the eighteenth century to prevent those societies from providing much immediate inspiration for the mounting program for social reform now known as the European Enlightenment. Indeed, when Enlightenment philosophers wished to point to an example of an enlightened society, they turned to Britain itself, specifically to England, and not to Britain's American colonies or to any other part of America, which remained, as always, largely "peripheral to Europe's experience of itself."[1]

But this situation changed radically after 1765. The American Revolution and its attendant developments made the societies and free inhabitants of the United States objects of great curiosity and considerable admiration among European social thinkers, both British and continental. Examining the nature of these new American social polities more thoroughly than any Europeans had ever previously done, they found them to be a close approximation—in many ways, an almost perfect demonstration—of their dream of a new order "in which men would escape from poverty, injustice, and corruption and dwell together in universal" prosperity, virtue, "liberty, equality, and fraternity."[2]

As European writers tried to explain how the amazing contemporary developments in the New World modified, confirmed, or extended existing conceptions of America and its meaning for humanity, those conceptions underwent a major reassessment. That reconsideration helped enormously to strengthen and to expand the by then well-established notion of America, now epitomized by the thirteen republican polities that had participated in the American Revolution, as a distinctive—an exceptional—social and political entity.

In this development, no figure played a more important role than Thomas Paine, the radical English immigrant who came to America

1. Michael T. Ryan, "Assimilating New Worlds in the Sixteenth and Seventeenth Centuries," *Comparative Studies in Society and History* 23 (1981): 537.

2. Durand Echeverria, *Mirage in the West: A History of the French Image of American Society to 1815* (Princeton, 1957), 38.

America as Example. During and after the American Revolution, European commentators heralded America as an example for the Old World. Dating from 1790, the year after the beginning of the French Revolution, this engraving shows a young woman clothed in the rich trappings of liberty and holding a staff with a liberty cap on top of it and a shield with the names of the continents inscribed upon it. She instructs a second young woman, standing for a new Europe awakening to the rights of man. Both figures radiate light and strength. At their feet, alongside an open copy of Thomas Paine's Rights of Man, *lie keys, shackles, a mask, and other discarded instruments of oppression, while two shadowy figures representing war and want retreat in the background. The image of America as clothed and Europe as naked represents a startling reversal of traditional iconography. From* Massachusetts Magazine *(1790), frontispiece. Courtesy of the Library of Congress, neg. no. LCUSZ62-45522.*

in 1774 and quickly added his powerful voice to those of the long line of observers who had emphasized the exceptional character of America. Published on January 10, 1776, his pamphlet, *Common Sense*, represented a militant brief in behalf of American independence. The society Paine encountered in America, he told readers of that pamphlet, struck him as in every way superior to the one he had left behind. Immediately upon his arrival in the New World, he had been forcefully struck by its almost total dissimilarity from the Old. "The case and circumstances of America," he observed, "present[ed] themselves as in the beginning of the world" before it had been engrossed and corrupted by the monopolizers of resources and power. Just a few months after his arrival in America, he noted that those who were "conversant with Europe" would "be tempted to believe that even the air of the Atlantic disagrees with the constitution of foreign vices; if they survive the voyage, they either expire on their arrival, or linger away in an incurable consumption. There is a happy something in the climate of America, which disarms them of all their power both of infection and attraction." [3]

Like so many earlier contributors to the intellectual construction of

3. Thomas Paine, *Rights of Man*, and "The Magazine in America," Jan. 24, 1775, in *The Complete Writings of Thomas Paine*, ed. Philip S. Foner, 2 vols., (New York, 1945), 1:376, 2:1110. For an elaboration of this and other themes developed here, see Jack P. Greene, "Paine, America, and the 'Modernization' of Political Consciousness," *Political Science Quarterly* 93 (1978): 73–92. See also Eric Foner, *Tom Paine and Revolutionary America* (New York, 1974).

MASSACHUSE

AMERICA.

EUROPE

THE
Rights
of
MEN.

C. Gullager, Del.

Engrav'd by S. Hill

America, Paine found that happy something in the extensive space and opportunity that America offered. No "country in the world," it seemed to him, provided "so many openings to happiness." "The vastness of its extent, the variety of its climate, the fertility of its soil, the yet unexplored treasures of its bowels, the multitude of its rivers, lakes, bays, inlets and other conveniences of navigation" all combined, Paine thought, to make America "one of the richest [and most inviting] subjects of cultivation ever presented to any people upon earth" and to produce societies that varied fundamentally from those of the Old World. Whereas Europe had a numerous "class of poor and wretched people," America did not. Whereas Europe was a world "wrapt up in the most absurd species of slavery," in America all free people enjoyed "all their natural and civil rights" and quickly learned that there was "no such thing . . . as power of any kind, independent of the people" and "no other race of men . . . but the people."[4]

The new and welcoming world that immigrants encountered in America, according to Paine, radically reshaped both their aspirations and their characters. "While men remained in Europe as subjects of some hereditary potentate [and in an unjust and evil society] they had ideas conformable to that condition," Paine wrote, "but when they arrived in America they" encountered circumstances that generated and encouraged "great ideas" and soon found themselves in possession of an entirely new character. The result was that the "spring, the progress, the object, the consequences, nay, the men, their habits of thinking, and all the circumstances of the country" diverged sharply from those of the Old World. "Mutual prejudices" were "worn off, a humane and philosophical spirit . . . cherished, and youth . . . stimulated to a laudable diligence and emulation in the pursuit of wisdom." Political consciousness was awakened and reshaped. "Elevated above their former rank," immigrants soon learned to consider "government and public affairs as part of their own concern," and "the theory of government" became "well known by almost every farmer in America."[5]

4. Paine, "Six Letters to Rhode Island," Jan. 1783; "An Act for Incorporating the American Philosophical Society," 1780; To Secretary Dundas, in Foner, ed., *Complete Writings*, 2:39, 337, 344, 347, 451–52.

5. Paine, *Rights of Man*; "Act Incorporating Am. Phil. Soc."; *Letter to the Abbé Raynal*; "Six Letters to Rhode Island"; To the "People of England," in ibid., 1:354, 2:39, 220–21, 258, 336, 676.

The vision Paine set forth in *Common Sense* assigned America a place of the first importance in the unfolding course of human history. Discovered just before the Reformation, as "if the Almighty graciously meant to open a sanctuary to the persecuted in future years," America had long served as a refuge from want for the impoverished and an "asylum for the persecuted lovers of civil and religious liberty from *every part* of Europe." But, Paine contended, it was now destined for an even greater role. "Every spot of the old world is overrun with oppression," he wrote in a famous passage in *Common Sense*: "Freedom hath been hunted round the globe. Asia and Africa have long expelled her. Europe regards her like a stranger, and England hath given her warning to depart." "Had it not been for America," he would later write in *The American Crisis*, "there had been no such thing as freedom left throughout the whole universe."[6]

As the last bastion of freedom, America, Paine predicted in 1776, was poised to play a much grander role. A "people who" had "virtue enough to defend themselves against the most powerful nation in the world," he thought, would certainly have the "wisdom to contrive a perfect and free form of government." With "a blank sheet to write upon," Americans had it in their "power to begin the world over again. A situation, similar to the present," he noted, "hath not happened since the days of Noah until now. The birthday of a new world," he predicted, was "at hand, and a race of men, perhaps as numerous as all Europe contains," would each enjoy "their portion of freedom." America thus had the opportunity to become "the theater where human nature" would "*soon* receive its greatest military, civil, and literary honors." "Not a place upon earth might be so happy as America," he declared, and America's happiness seemed to him to represent the best chance for recovering the world from its misery. "In a great measure," he succinctly declared in *Common Sense*, the "cause of America" was "the cause of all mankind."[7]

During the two decades following publication of *Common Sense*, Paine, acting as a vigorous and effective advocate for the "American principle of government" in Europe, frequently reiterated and elaborated upon these themes. In a series of occasional writings culminating in 1791–92 with the publication of *The Rights of Man*, he

6. Paine, *Common Sense*; *The American Crisis*, in ibid., 1:19, 21, 30–31, 123.

7. Paine, *Common Sense*; *American Crisis*; "The Forester's Letters," 1776; "A Dialogue," 1776, in ibid., 1:3, 45, 54, 2:82–83, 90–93.

called upon the people of the Old World to learn from the experiences of the American Revolution and to regenerate their governments by founding them upon "the principles of the new."[8]

For the American Revolution, Paine believed, had created the possibility of a vast political awakening of a magnitude undreamt of and unparalleled in the history of the world. By relieving Americans of the "shackles" of their former prejudices in favor of the social and political forms of the Old World, the Revolution, Paine reported, had enabled Americans to "see with other eyes; . . . hear with other ears; and think with other thoughts than those formerly used." This transformation in turn gave them "a freedom of mind" that was appropriate to the freedom of circumstances they had so long possessed. Stimulating a revolution in the "style and manner of thinking . . . more extraordinary than the political revolution of the country," this new intellectual freedom enabled Americans to make the first "improvement[s] . . . in . . . principle and . . . practise" in "the science of government" since antiquity.[9]

The "system of government" contrived by the Americans, Paine often told his European audience, was in every respect superior to any that existed in Europe. Entirely "free from corruption," it was "administered over an extent of territory ten times as large as England, *for less expense than the pensions alone in England amount to*; and under which more freedom is enjoyed, and a more happy state of society is preserved, and a more general prosperity is promoted, than under any other system of government now existing in the world." In America, Paine wrote, "the poor are not oppressed, the rich are not privileged. Industry is not mortified by the splendid extravagance of a court rioting at its expense. Their taxes are few, because their government is just; and as there is nothing to render them wretched, there is nothing to engender riots and tumults." The American system, he predicted, would wind "its progress from nation to nation" until even the European acquired "a knowledge of his rights by attending justly to . . . [his] interests" and discovered "in the event that the strength and powers of despotism" consisted "wholly in the fear of resisting it, and that in order *'to be free, it is sufficient that he wills it.'* "[10]

8. Paine, "Address to the People of France," Sept. 25, 1792, in ibid., 2:539.

9. Paine, *Letter to Abbé Raynal; Dissertation on First Principles*, 1795; *Rights of Man*, in ibid., 1:320, 447, 2:242–44, 571.

10. Paine, *Rights of Man*; To Secretary Dundas, June 6, 1792; To the Sheriff

Pennsylvania State Seal. At the beginning of the American Revolution, most of the new state governments adopted new seals in which they sought to symbolize the strengths and aspirations of their states. To emphasize the economic basis of the state, the Pennsylvania seal, adopted in 1776, showed a ship in full sail, a plough, and three sheaves of wheat on a shield supported by two rearing horses. An eagle ready to take flight is at the top, and the motto "Virtue, Liberty, and Independence," expressing three of the central principles of the Revolution, is at the bottom. From the Columbian Magazine *(June 1787). Courtesy of the Library Company of Philadelphia.*

The American Revolution, Paine told Europeans, had thus "contributed more to enlighten the world, and diffuse a spirit of freedom and liberality among mankind, than any human event . . . that ever preceded it." "So deeply rooted were all the governments of the old world, and so effectively had the tyranny and the antiquity of habit established itself over the mind," Paine declared in *The Rights of Man,*

---

of Sussex, 1792; To Thomas Jefferson, Jan. 1, 1805, in ibid., 1:353–54, 360–61, 398, 2:449, 464–65, 1454.

"that no beginning could be made in Asia, Africa, or Europe, to reform the political condition of man." By providing reason and liberty
a place to stand upon," by throwing "a beam of light over the world,
which reaches into man" in ways that could never be reversed, the
American Revolution, Paine confidently expected, was the first step in
a movement that would necessarily produce "a general revolution in
governments" all over Europe and open "a new system of extended
civilization" that would bring America new recognition as "the Parent
of the . . . world." Alone among all countries, he boasted, America
did not need to "be ashamed to tell her birth, nor to relate the stages
by which she rose to empire." America, he predicted, would "be in
magnitude" what "Athens was [only] in miniature. . . . The one was
the wonder of the ancient world; the other is becoming the admiration
and model of the present." [11]

Paine's central message as a political writer was that the world could
be changed for the better and people liberated from the tyranny of
their ancient prejudices, and the primary model that gave shape—
and credibility—to that message was America. Inspired by the openness of American society and impressed by the liberating and energiz-
ing character of its Revolution, Paine, through his militant and persistent advocacy of using the experience of the New World to transform
the Old, also became the self-appointed interpreter for that experience
for the rest of the world. In this way, Paine played a significant role
in extending the concept of America as an exceptional sociopolitical
entity and in elaborating the idea that America represented the future,
a model for emulation by not just the old European world but the
entire globe.

Paine may have been the most prolific and strident exponent of this
expanding and optimistic conception of America in Europe during the
era of the American Revolution, but he was certainly not the only
one. As Arthur Sheps has shown, British social radicals were quick
to seize upon "America as a standard of reform." [12] Richard Price, the
philosopher, and Thomas Pownall, member of Parliament and former
governor of Massachusetts, were only two of the most prominent and
most prolific of those in Britain who, both before and after the United

11. Paine, *American Crisis; Rights of Man; Letter to the Abbé Raynal,* in ibid.,
1:230–32, 239–40, 256, 320, 353–54, 371–72, 396–97, 447.

12. Arthur Sheps, "The American Revolution and the Transformation of
American Republicanism," *Historical Reflections* 2 (1975): 4–28.

States had achieved its independence, heralded the republican societies and polities of America as possible models for the rest of the world. Nor was interest in this subject limited to Britain. French social philosophers, including the Abbés Raynal and Mably, the Marquis de Condorcet, and the economist M. Turgot, and the Tuscan humanist Philip Mazzei speculated at length on the nature of republican America and its meaning for the rest of human society.

At the very beginning of the American Revolution, Price raised the heady possibility that it might "begin a new era in the annals of mankind and produce a revolution more important, perhaps, than any that has yet happened in human affairs."[13] By setting themselves up as the champions of liberty and enemies of oppression, Americans, added Turgot in 1778, had made themselves "the hope of the world."[14] By first exposing "themselves to the most dreadful calamities in order to be free" and then succeeding in their "generous efforts" in behalf of liberty, echoed Raynal in 1781, Americans had effectively made their "cause . . . that of the whole human race."[15] "Among the events in modern times tending to the elevation of mankind," Price affirmed at the conclusion of the war, "none [was] probably of so much consequence as the" American Revolution. "Next to the introduction of Christianity among mankind," he observed, that "revolution may prove to be the most important step in the progressive course of human development."[16] During the same year, Condorcet similarly rhapsodized about "the noble and moving spectacle which this new nation has given to the world."[17]

In celebrating the remarkable achievements of the new United States, British and continental writers depicted Americans almost wholly in positive terms as "heroes who" had "put their oppressors to flight, a simple People, as yet untouched by corruption, wise, upright,

13. Richard Price, *Additional Observations on the Nature and Value of Civil Liberty and the War with America* (London, 1777), in Bernard Peach, *Richard Price and the Ethical Foundations of the American Revolution* (Durham, N.C., 1979), 173.

14. M. Turgot to Richard Price, Mar. 22, 1778, in Richard Price, *Observations on the Importance of the American Revolution*, 2d ed. (London, 1785), in ibid., 222.

15. Abbé Guillaume Thomas François Raynal, *The Revolution of America* (London, 1781), 172–73.

16. Price, *Observations on the Importance of the American Revolution*, 183.

17. Durand Echeverria, ed., "Condorcet's *The Influence of the American Revolution on Europe*," *William and Mary Quarterly*, 3d ser., 25 (1968): 108.

enjoying excellent laws, the fruits of the liberty they had purchased with their blood."[18] Taking up "the flame of virtuous liberty," Americans, declared Price, had at once disseminated "just sentiments of the rights of mankind and the nature of legitimate government," excited "a spirit of resistance to tyranny" throughout Europe, and occasioned "the establishment in America of forms of government more equitable and more liberal than any that the world has yet known."[19] As a consequence of the American Revolution, announced Condorcet, people no longer had to rely on the writings of philosophers to learn about the rights of man. Now they could be "read . . . in the example of a great people." The Declaration of Independence, he wrote, provides "a simple and sublime statement of these sacred and long forgotten rights. No nation has recognized them so clearly and preserved them in such perfect integrity."[20] With such extraordinary accomplishments to their credit, Americans, as one anonymous writer observed in 1781, had indeed "rendered themselves conspicuous all over Europe."[21]

In analyzing the ways in which the American Revolution was, in Price's words, a "revolution in favour of universal liberty,"[22] these writers contributed to the expanding conception of America, championed by Paine, as a refuge from oppression. Pownall congratulated Americans upon establishing "an Asylum to which Men of all Nations who wish for and deserve Freedom may fly, and under which they may find Refuge."[23] Thenceforth, agreed Price, the United States would provide, "in a sequestered continent possessed of many singular advantages, a place of refuge for oppressed men in every region of the world."[24] "The asylum they open to the oppressed of all nations," wrote Turgot, "should console the earth."[25] The American regard for

18. Edwin G. Burrows, ed., " 'Notes on Settling America': Albert Gallatin, New England, and the American Revolution," *New England Quarterly* 58 (1985): 448.

19. Price, *Observations on the Importance of the American Revolution*, 182.

20. Condorcet, *Influence of the American Revolution*, 91.

21. *A View of North America, in Its Former Happy, and Its Present Belligerant State* (Glasgow, 1781), viii.

22. Price, *Observations on the Importance of the American Revolution*, 182.

23. Thomas Pownall, *A Memorial Addressed to the Sovereigns of America* (London, 1783), 8–9.

24. Price, *Observations on the Importance of the American Revolution*, 182.

25. Turgot to Price, Mar. 22, 1778, 222.

natural rights, said Condorcet, had the happy effect of making it possible for "any man, whatever may be his religion, his opinions, or his principles, . . . to find refuge."[26]

Also like Paine, British and continental observers heralded the United States as a model for the rest of the world. If they could succeed by their achievements in proving that people could "be free and yet tranquil and that it" was "in their power to rescue themselves from the chains in which tyrants and knaves of all descriptions have presumed to bind them under the pretence of the public good," Turgot predicted in 1778, Americans could "exhibit an example of political liberty, of religious liberty, of commercial liberty, and of industry" that would "gradually" encourage people everywhere to "open their eyes upon the empty illusions with which they have been hitherto cheated by politicians" and "compel princes to become just and cautious."[27] Simply "by laying the foundation" in America "of an empire which may be the seat of liberty, science[,] and virtue," wrote Price, Americans had given humanity every "reason to hope [that] those sacred blessings" would "spread till they become universal and the time arrives when kings and priests shall have no more power to oppress, and that ignominious slavery which has hitherto debased the world is exterminated."[28] From the perspective of the American Revolution, it seemed entirely plausible to suggest, as did the Swiss immigrant Albert Gallatin in the early 1780s, that the United States would "one day rival Europe in almost every Respect & being superior in some others . . . enlighten her, serve her as a model, & perhaps contribute to the happiness of mankind in general."[29]

In their ruminations about the broader implications of the American Revolution for the Old World and for the future of humanity, British and continental social and political commentators had to confront, like Paine, several questions. Why had an event of such far-reaching importance occurred in British North America? What kinds of societies and polities and what sorts of people could have successfully undertaken such a magnificent achievement? In the answers they gave to those questions, these writers contributed substantially to enhance the

26. Condorcet, *Influence of the American Revolution*, 93.

27. Turgot to Price, Mar. 22, 1778, 222.

28. Price, *Observations on the Importance of the American Revolution*, 182.

29. Burrows, " 'Notes on Settling America,' " 453.

by now widespread conception of America as an exceptional place that in almost every significant particular differed fundamentally from any place extant in the Old World.

In limning the distinctive character of America, these writers emphasized the same features that Old World observers had always found most impressive: its widespread economic opportunity and prosperity, the absence of a legally privileged social order, the sociopolitical equality and extent of political empowerment among the free population, and the peculiar behavioral and psychological effects produced by those conditions. Some of them traced these features of American society in part to the character and goals of the early settlers, most of whom, lured by the promise of cheap land and envisioning America "as a sanctuary for liberty," had, as Mazzei observed, left the Old World "to seek the liberty and happiness they despaired of enjoying in their homeland[s]." Thinking "solely of liberty," these "simple adventurers" purchased land from Amerindians, whom they mostly treated "with justice and consideration," established their own local representative institutions in each colony, and proceeded to build prosperous societies under the protective aegis of the English Crown.[30]

Like Franklin, Adam Smith, Crèvecoeur, and Paine before them, these writers attributed the fortunate state of colonial American society primarily to the physical circumstances and economic and political conditions the settlers had found and created in America. In a country with so much available land and such a high demand for labor, opportunity seemed to be limitless. For "any man willing to work," Condorcet noted in reiterating a by then hackneyed observation, America offered "the brightest hopes; the poor man finds it easy to earn a living, and he can be sure of finding land sufficient for his needs if he is willing to work for it."[31]

At the same time, liberty seemed almost endemic to the continent. "History does not describe any people which has ever preserved so much individual freedom in its social fabric," Mazzei wrote of the aboriginal inhabitants, and the same seemed to be true of the European settlers and their creole descendants. Throughout the century and three-quarters of the colonial period, Mazzei noted, the "abundance of land and its low price" drew large numbers of immigrants, encouraged

30. Philip Mazzei, *Researches on the United States*, trans. Constance D. Sherman (Charlottesville, Va., 1976), 5, 10–11, 55–57, 117, 214.
31. Condorcet, *Influence of the American Revolution*, 93.

a high rate of natural population growth, and enabled the inhabitants to build "a praiseworthy economy" with a relatively high standard of living that permitted virtually all free families to enjoy considerable prosperity and enabled every "hardworking man" to "obtain enough money to enjoy every privilege" available in the society.[32]

With the means of subsistence procured so easily and with no "hereditary honours and titles of nobility,"[33] the British colonies, these postrevolutionary British and continental writers emphasized, echoing earlier analysts and anticipating Tocqueville, produced a society that was "totally different from" that of the "old world."[34] Most conspicuously, as Mazzei observed, "the distinction between classes was much smaller."[35] Whereas "Old countries consist[ed], generally, of three classes of people, a gentry, a yeomanry, and a peasantry," Price pointed out, the societies of the new American states "consist[ed] only of a body of yeomanry supported by agriculture, and all independent and nearly upon a level."[36] "In this Land of Liberty," declared Pownall, there were "not . . . any Baronial or Manerial [*sic*] Dominations" or any "Feudal, any Personal services, which may be claimed by a Landlord from the Landholder, whether Prince, Baron, Clergy, or Body Corporate," "no Fee-farm Rents or Tythes to be paid," and no restrictions on the free flow of population and labor—nothing, in short, either to repress the industry and the ambitions of ordinary inhabitants or to enable the wealthy to aggrandize resources and authority.[37] In such a society, Price noted, "the rich and the poor, the haughty grandee and the creeping sycophant, [were] equally unknown."[38]

Such social conditions at once radically challenged traditional views of social organization as well as the assumptions that underlay them. Without an "unequal distribution of riches," wrote Raynal, the societies of the American states lacked the social foundations to generate and sustain either the psychology of "insolence" that so often charac-

32. Mazzei, *Researches*, 58, 122n, 220, 280, 348.

33. Price, *Observations on the Importance of the American Revolution*, 208–9.

34. Thomas Pownall, *A Memorial Most Humbly Addressed to the Sovereigns of Europe* (London, 1780), 44–45.

35. Mazzei, *Researches*, 125–26.

36. Richard Price, *Observations on the Nature of Civil Liberty, the Principles of Government, and the Justice and Policy of the War with America*, 5th ed. (London, 1776), in Peach, *Price and the Ethical Foundations of the Revolution*, 102.

37. Pownall, *Memorial to the Sovereigns of America*, 54–56.

38. Price, *Observations on the Importance of the American Revolution*, 208–9.

America as a Land of Freedom. The notion of America as a land to which freedom was natural gained an astonishing revival among European commentators during the era of the American Revolution. This notion was implicit in the depiction of America as a free Amerindian woman wearing only a skirt of feathers and carrying only a bow and arrow for her support and defense. She stands beside an alligator, one of the traditional icons for America. From John Andrews, A Collection of Plans of the Capital Cities, 2 vols. (London, 1771), 1:title page. *Courtesy of the Library of Congress, neg. no.* LCUSZ62-46091.

terized the possessing classes in Europe or "the debasement of" spirit that usually marked the condition of the propertyless.[39] "The spectacle of equality which reigns in the United States," asserted Condorcet in a passage that obviously took no account of the racial distinctions that obtained in America, made it impossible for people any longer to be-

39. Raynal, *Revolution of America*, 180.

lieve in the ideas that nature had "divided the human race into three or four orders," that one of those orders was "condemned to heavy labour and undernourishment," that "a sense of honor" could "truly exist only in certain social classes," or "that it was necessary to degrade the majority of people in order to give the remainder a little pride."[40]

As such remarks suggest, several of these postrevolutionary interpreters of America, like Crèvecoeur and Paine, were persuaded not only that the Americans lived in a distinctive society but also that the peculiar circumstances of that society had operated to give them a profoundly different character from Britons and continental Europeans. Among the Old World writers of the late 1770s and 1780s, Thomas Pownall explored this subject most fully and most perceptively, and in terms that were strongly redolent of those earlier employed by Crèvecoeur.

Pownall gave particular emphasis to the contrasting conditions of labor on opposite sides of the Atlantic. For centuries in the Old World, he wrote, agriculture had been conducted by "wretches annexed to, but not owners of the soil; degraded animals that were, as the cattle of the field, property, not proprietors. They had no interest in their own persons, none in their own labour, none in the produce, either of the earth or of their labour." Even "if they had been inspired (for they were not taught) with knowledge," he observed, "they could have no . . . motive to make one effort at improvement." Even in more modern times, the few people who had freeholds were often "so depressed by various tolls, taillages, and taxes; by being liable to military impresses; and to the civil drudgery, which took them from their own proper work and employed them in that of" various "Lords and Sovereigns," that they could hope for nothing better out of life than mere "sustenance and rest."[41]

In the New World of Anglo-America, Pownall explained, the situation of labor was exactly the reverse. With plenty of land easily available, with high wages for labor, and with none of "those oppressing, obstructing, deaddoing laws," customs, and privileges that had so long "been the bane to Industry, and blasted the fruits of labour in Europe," neither "Landworker[s n]or Mechanic[s]" had anything to hold them back. Enjoying "an uncontrulled liberty of using any mode of life they choose, or any means of getting a livelihood that their talents

40. Condorcet, *Influence of the American Revolution*, 95–96.
41. Pownall, *Memorial to the Sovereigns of Europe*, 31–32.

An American Settlement. Old World residents were interested in the process by which American settlers wrested farms out of the wilderness. During his sojourn in America in the 1750s, Thomas Pownall, one of the principal British analysts of America, sought to capture this process in "A Design to Represent the Beginning and Completion of an American Settlement and Farm." Pownall's design showed a new settlement with a log house and a sawmill producing lumber for a more refined habitation on the left bank of a river and a completed farm with a substantial house and surrounding buildings, cleared fields, and working farmers and domestic animals on the right bank. James Peake subsequently engraved this drawing. From Scenographica Americana *(London, 1768). Courtesy of the Library of Congress, neg. no. LCUSZ62-31185.*

lead them to," "Every Inhabitant of America," Pownall continued, was "his own master both in his reasoning and acting; so far as respects the individual, he is at perfect liberty to apply his power as he likes, to labour in any line, and to possess and use his property as his own. His property is free from any tenure or condition that may clog, obstruct, or divert the fruits of that labour which he hath mixt with it." [42]

"In a country like this," Pownall declared, "where every man" had "the full and free exertion of his powers, where every man" could

42. Ibid., 42–43, 48–49; Pownall, *Memorial to the Sovereigns of America,* 54–56.

"acquire any share of the good things thereof, or of interest and power which his spirit can work him up to," and where every free man labored only for himself and his family and kept most of what he produced, every man could rise "to that natural importance in the Community, which his ingenuity in his manual labour, or his improvements in his landed Property, must of course, unobstructed, give him." Moreover, because the "power which derives from property in America" increased "in proportion to the activity" that was "mixt with it by the possessor," every "active Proprietor" had it wholly within his power "every day" to enhance his "weight, and relative place" in society and to become "a more important Citizen."[43] In societies with so many easy openings to betterment, individuals had indeed, as early promotional writers had predicted, been able to take charge of their own lives and hence had "no need of the patronage of great men."[44]

That societies thus founded so completely upon the practice of "self-direction" should, long before the Revolution, have established polities based on the principle of "self-government" seemed to most British and European commentators on America entirely natural.[45] In such societies, effective power flowed not, as in the Old World, downward from a hereditary prince or some legally privileged and superior social order but upward from the vast population of independent inhabitants, whose power—the power that gave energy and direction to the polity—derived from "the landed Property" they had acquired and improved and the marketable skills they had mastered.[46] People who were so accustomed to being "their own masters" in their private lives could never permit anyone to "assume the power of directing them" in their public affairs.[47] The *genuine spirit of Government* in America, wrote Pownall, powerfully expressed "the true *spirit of liberty*,"[48] defined, in Price's words, as the capacity of every free man "to be governed by" his "own will" and not, by contrast, "to be guided by the will of another," which was the chief "characteristic of a state of servitude."[49]

43. Pownall, *Memorial to the Sovereigns of Europe*, 42–43; Pownall, *Memorial to the Sovereigns of America*, 54–56.

44. Mazzei, *Researches*, 327.

45. Price, *Observations on the Nature of Civil Liberty*, 68.

46. Pownall, *Memorial to the Sovereigns of America*, 67.

47. Pownall, *Memorial to the Sovereigns of Europe*, 42–45.

48. Pownall, *Memorial to the Sovereigns of America*, 40.

49. Price, *Observations on the Nature of Civil Liberty*, 72.

In polities so constituted, the principal goals of government were not, as in the Old World, the protection of the property of a few and the maintenance of a privileged and highly inequitable social order. In total contrast to the "false police of the Old World," the "Spirit of Police in America," according to Pownall, sought the safety of the persons and the security of the property of the many, the preservation of an equality of rights among all free men, and a system of laws that in every way possible encouraged "the activity of the Human Being."[50] "*Peculiarly a poor man's country*,"[51] America thus exhibited governments in which every free inhabitant was, "*de facto* as well as *de jure*, equal, in his essential inseparable rights . . . to any other Individual" and was, in those rights, "independent of any power that any other can assume over him, over his labour or his property." Undertaking nothing that interfered "with the free course of Labour" or "the free employment of Stock," those governments, Pownall asserted, sanctioned no monopolies, no "local or personal privileges," and no private reservations of public resources.[52]

The remarkable personal freedom enjoyed by Americans, Pownall reported, extended as well to matters of faith and the heart. Considering "Religion as an internal act of the Mind towards God" and regarding the "Right of private conscience in matters of Religion" as "one of those rights which" were "essential to the individual," Americans eschewed any "Ecclesiastical *Imperium*." Because "every Wife" in these societies was "herself a fortune" and children were "riches to the parents," both sexes, according to Pownall, prized the liberty to form "those connexions which nature and the heart point[ed] out" and chose mates according to "Private personal happiness," while the government had no more control over marriage than it did over other civil contracts. "In America," Pownall exclaimed, "Love and Liberty go hand in hand."[53]

Just as free individuals in America had full control over their own private lives, so, Old World commentators emphasized, did they collectively govern their public affairs through an equitable system of laws. To make and enforce those laws, to hold all "places of public trust," they chose people on the basis not of social status or property

50. Pownall, *Memorial to the Sovereigns of America*, 126–27.
51. Pownall, *Memorial to the Sovereigns of Europe*, 44–45.
52. Pownall, *Memorial to the Sovereigns of America*, 54–56, 122–23, 126–27.
53. Ibid., 56–59.

but of "merit."[54] Without "distinction[s] of rank" among them, with no "aristocratic class,"[55] and with simple and inexpensive governments that had no "lucrative places" that could generate "corrupt canvassings and ambitious intrigue,"[56] "no citizen," as Mazzei observed, could have "any power unless it" had "been given to him by his peers."[57] In polities in which only "Good Qualities," such as wisdom, judgment, and learning, and "a proper behaviour" were "necessary for procuring respect and esteem,"[58] there was nothing to prevent "men of merit but of modest means from seeking public office."[59]

The system of liberty Americans had established during the colonial period and then made the basis of their new republican governments during the Revolution thus seemed to contemporary British and European political writers to be "totally and intirely a New System of Things and Men." It was not, wrote Pownall, "that share of Dominion which a political Monarch throws into the hands of the People, in order to ally their power to his Force, by which to govern the Aristocracy." Nor was it "that share of Power, which an Aristocracy permits the People to amuse themselves with, and which they are taught to call Liberty." Rather, it was a liberty that extended widely throughout the free population of the colonies and was deeply and firmly rooted in the exceptional social circumstances in which Americans lived.[60] It was a liberty that, extending through every state, guaranteed to every citizen "the certainty of using" his "property in complete security, of having no superiors except the Magistrates one chooses annually, & practicing in public or in private the Religion of one's own choosing."[61]

Indeed, as they assessed the situation, the distinctive socioeconomic conditions and political arrangements that obtained in America seemed, to European commentators, to have made Americans "a different people from all others."[62] With each free man enjoying "the liberty of exerting his active powers of industry or ingenuity, as he can make them the most productive," and knowing that "his share

54. *View of North America*, 22.
55. Mazzei, *Researches*, 80, 140.
56. Price, *Observations on the Importance of the American Revolution*, 208–9.
57. Mazzei, *Researches*, 122.
58. *View of North America*, 22.
59. Mazzei, *Researches*, 146.
60. Pownall, *Memorial to the Sovereigns of America*, 54–56.
61. Burrows, " 'Notes on Settling America,' " 447.
62. Raynal, *Revolution of America*, 19.

of profit" would be "in proportion to his efficiency in creating it,"[63]
with all such autonomous men "trained to arms, instructed in their
rights," and "protected by laws . . . of their own will . . . and by

an equal government,"[64] the Americans seemed to have developed a
special "political Character" that, according to Pownall, was in every
way conformable to "such a System of Things" and deeply embedded
in their "Customs and manners." Shaped by the awareness among all
free individuals that each of them was an equal "Participant with his
fellow Citizens" in his own polity, that character, as Pownall defined
it, was most fully manifest in the view that "the full object and end
of man as a Citizen" was nothing more than the maintenance of his
"rights" to "perfect freedom" and the habit of extending no deference to any man except on the basis of his "place in those orders and
subordinations which the State gives."[65]

That people with "natural Principles" such as these should have first
"resist[ed] the unnatural violence" visited upon them by the British
ministry and then been able to achieve the "Unity, Wisdom, and perse-
vering firmness" that "gave strength to their own arms, and rendered
them impregnable to those of the Enemy" seemed entirely under-
standable.[66] In Raynal's words, people with such principles understood
"what was the dignity of man."[67] "Having his property secure, and
knowing himself his own governor," Price explained, every "member
of a free state" quickly acquired "a consciousness of dignity in himself
and" an impulse "to emulation and improvement to which the miserable slaves of arbitrary power must be utter strangers. In such a state,"
Price concluded, "all the springs of action" had "room to operate, and
the mind" was "stimulated to the noblest exertions."[68]

Notwithstanding their extraordinarily flattering portrait of an exceptional America with a distinctive body of free inhabitants, British
and continental observers of the Revolutionary years were not entirely uncritical in their efforts to describe—to identify—America.
Rather, they called attention to two principal flaws. The first was
America's cultural backwardness in relation to Europe. Some claimed

63. Pownall, *Memorial to the Sovereigns of Europe*, 105.
64. Price, *Observations on the Importance of the American Revolution*, 208–9.
65. Pownall, *Memorial to the Sovereigns of America*, 70–71.
66. Ibid., 23.
67. Raynal, *Revolution of America*, 19.
68. Price, *Observations on the Nature of Civil Liberty*, 74–75.

that Americans had "made little or no progress in the arts & sciences" and, as Gallatin remarked in the early 1780s, were "almost like their Fathers, that is to say a Century behind Europe." "Men of quality," he contended, were but "indifferently educated."[69] Although Price thought that Americans had moved well beyond that "first rude" stage of social and cultural development that characterized the early colonial settlements, he did not believe that they had yet advanced much beyond that "middle state of civilization" between "the savage and the refined or between the wild and the luxurious."[70]

Not all observers were so unimpressed by the cultural "progress of this new-world," however. The same social conditions—the breadth of opportunity, the encouragement of industry, and the absence of legal restraint—that had enabled so many free Americans to take charge of their lives, expand their social aspirations, and become militantly autonomous had also, Pownall claimed, produced "a turn of inquiry and investigation" that, no less than their ardor for political liberty, formed an essential ingredient in the American character. By sharpening "their wits" and providing "constant training to the[ir] mind[s]," he suggested, the "unabated application of the powers of [free] individuals" in America had nurtured a *"spirit of induction"* and an *"inquisitiveness"* that seemed to animate all Americans *"with the spirit of the new philosophy"* and to foster "a spirit of civilization" in which "all" was "enterprise and experiment."[71]

If it was not entirely *"peculiar to these people,"* Pownall declared, "this turn of character" was certainly "not to be met with" to such a degree anywhere else in the contemporary world. Nor, he thought, did it "ever . . . exist in any other [world] to the same degree, unless in some of the ancient republics, where the people were under the same predicament." To an exceptional extent, American culture seemed to be what Pownall referred to as *"an experimental culture."* Already, in his view, the "experimental application of the understanding, as well as labour to the several branches of the mechanics," had yielded "so many new and ingenious improvements" in "mechanick handicrafts," in "Arts and Sciences," and in "Legislation and Politics" as to suggest that America would become the leader of not just a revolution in poli-

69. Burrows, " 'Notes on Settling America,' " 451–52.

70. Price, *Observations on the Nature of Civil Liberty*, 102; Price, *Observations on the Importance of the American Revolution*, 208–9.

71. Pownall, *Memorial to the Sovereigns of Europe*, 42–47, 68–70.

America and Fame. The hope that America would become a nursery not only for liberty but also for the arts and sciences was widespread among Europeans and Americans after the Revolution. This engraving shows America as a young woman. With her shield resting by her side, her staff and liberty cap leaning against a tree, and, her foes vanquished, her bow and arrows lying upon the ground, she sits beside the shield of the United States in peace and plenty, represented by a cornucopia, with books and a globe. Pointing to a statue of Fame in a small temple behind them, an unnamed deity with a lyre, probably Apollo, calls upon her to exert herself to cultivate science and master the arts in a quest for fame. From the Columbian Magazine *(1789), frontispiece. Courtesy of the Library of Congress, neg. no.* LCUSZ62-45573.

tics but also *"a kind of instauration of science."* Who could doubt that a people whose whole "system of life" was "a course of experiments" would, once they had turned their thoughts "into the *active* channel of arts and manufactures" and cultural improvement, soon attain a degree of improvement that would be at least as impressive as that "to which the most enlightened parts of Europe have advanced."[72]

Condorcet agreed. With "no social distinctions" and "no beckoning ambitions" to "draw . . . men away from their natural desire to perfect their minds, to employ their intelligence in useful studies, and to seek that glory which is the reward of great ventures and discoveries," American society, he thought, contained nothing to confine any "part of humanity in an abject state of stupidity and poverty" and provided every stimulus to encourage "study and reflection." As a result, he predicted "that in a few generations" America would produce "almost as many men engaged in the task of adding to the mass of human knowledge as there will be in all of Europe" and that Americans would contribute to "both the useful arts and the speculative sciences."[73] There was, in short, every reason to suppose that America, whatever its remaining cultural deficiencies, would be, in Price's words, "a country where truth and reason" might "have fair play and the human powers find full scope for exerting themselves and for showing how far they" could "carry human improvement."[74]

In the view of many European writers, a far more serious problem

72. Ibid.
73. Condorcet, *Influence of the American Revolution*, 101.
74. Price, *Observations on the Importance of the American Revolution*, 189.

for the image of America was the continuing existence of racial slavery as a well-entrenched and vigorous institution in the American republic. The American Revolution was coeval with that vastly more radical revolution inherent in the growing antislavery movement. As David Brion Davis has shown, racial slavery, an institution that had long been accepted by Europeans and Americans with few objections and was still being practiced to a limited extent in many parts of Western Europe, suddenly, during the last decades of the eighteenth century, came to be widely condemned as a barbarous and barbarizing, un-European and uncivilized institution that, wherever it existed, both mocked and belied any celebrations of the freedom and equality of the unenslaved.[75]

With its condemnation of the African slave trade and its demand for the manumission of the vast slave populations of the New World, the antislavery movement dramatically directed attention to the incongruous attitudes of the free inhabitants of America, who on the one hand demanded liberty for themselves and on the other systematically denied it to the thousands of black slaves who constituted large and significant segments of the populations of most of the new American states, especially those states from Maryland south to Georgia. Notwithstanding the fact that "the principles embodied in the new state governments proclaim[ed] liberty and equality," wrote Mazzei, who in the 1770s had resided for several years in Virginia, a state with one of the largest slave populations, "slavery still" existed "in the United States."[76]

For abolitionists like the Quaker David Cooper, slavery seemed to be wholly incompatible with "the principles upon which the American revolution stands." "You, gentlemen," he lectured American leaders in 1783, "have, in behalf of America, *declared* to Europe, to the world, 'That all men are born *equal*, and, by the *immutable laws of nature*, are *equally* entitled to liberty.' We expect," he declared, "mankind expects, you to demonstrate your *faith* by your *works*; the sincerity of your *words* by your *actions*, in giving the *power*, with which you are invested, its utmost *energy* in promoting *equal* and *impartial* liberty to *all* whose lots are cast within the reach of influence," including slaves. "Every generous foreigner," he asserted, had to "feel a secret indignation rise in his breast, when he hears the language of Americans

75. David Brion Davis, *Slavery and Human Progress* (New York, 1984).
76. Mazzei, *Researches*, 344.

upon any of their own rights as freemen being in the least infringed, and reflects that these very people are holding thousands and tens of thousands of their innocent fellow men in the most debasing and abject slavery, deprived of every right of freemen, except light and air?" However congenial America had been to the aspirations and rights of free men, the "crying evil" of slavery, he predicted, would "[for]ever remain a stain" upon its "annals."[77]

Many others agreed. Until they had abolished slavery, Price wrote, Americans would never "deserve the liberty for which they have been contending." For "people who have been struggling so earnestly to save themselves from slavery" to prove so "very ready to enslave others," he warned, could only mortify "the friends of liberty and humanity in Europe" and make it clear that the American Revolution, the "event which had raised their hopes," was nothing more than the "introduction to a new scene of aristocratic tyranny and human debasement."[78] To keep "a great number of blacks" in slavery, added Turgot, was clearly "incompatible with a good political constitution."[79]

A few Europeans took a somewhat more sympathetic approach. Mazzei condemned the institution as it functioned in the five southern states as "the worst, the most humiliating, and the most difficult evil to correct," expressed his chagrin that "a great many" American whites yet "regard[ed] these unfortunates as a very inferior race" who could "never possess the attributes of free citizens," and joined most other Old World observers in calling upon Americans to "seize every opportunity . . . to promote the rights that all men without exception have to liberty." Yet, he acknowledged that the American states had many "excellent reasons for postponing the liberation of [such a] large number of slaves." Contending that only the dangers of suddenly altering the status of such a numerous and ill-prepared group had prevented Virginians from doing so in 1776, Mazzei believed that Americans wanted to give slaves "their liberty as soon as possible."[80]

Like Mazzei, Pownall displayed some appreciation for the problems

---

77. David Cooper, *A Serious Address to the Rulers of America, on the Inconsistency of Their Conduct Respecting Slavery* (London, 1783), 7, 19–20, 22.

78. Price, *Observations on the Importance of the American Revolution*, 213; Price to Thomas Jefferson, July 2, 1785, in Peach, *Price and the Ethical Foundations of the Revolution*, 330–31.

79. Turgot to Price, Mar. 22, 1778, 221.

80. Mazzei, *Researches*, 122–23, 344, 346.

involved in sudden abolition. Pointing out that it would behoove a country founded on the "Spirit of genuine Liberty" to "institute some mode, by which the *Slaves*, whom Providence hath suffered to come under their domination," could, "by proper means and in suitable time, [acquire] their Liberty," he suggested a gradual emancipation that would compensate owners for their property loss in slaves while putting the slaves under "certain limitations" that, while extending them liberty, would exclude them from holding landed property and prevent them from entering any occupations except those of "Labourers, Farmers upon rent, Mechanics, and Manufacturers," a scheme that would have consigned blacks to a permanent underclass and largely excluded them from sharing in the benefits of the exceptional social and political arrangements provided by America for free white people.[81]

Notwithstanding the qualifications offered by people like Mazzei and Pownall, most Old World commentators seemed to concur that black slavery constituted a gigantic and negative blot upon the positive identification of America. Whether or not it was abolished, they agreed, would determine whether the prosperous independent farmer of Connecticut or the proud and arrogant "negroe-drivers" of Virginia would become the most appropriate symbol for the New World of republican America.[82] Yet few of these writers saw the presence of slavery, exceptional though it may have been in comparison with Europe, as an institution that played a major role in defining and identifying republican America. With Price, many hoped that the black slaves would "either soon become extinct, or have their condition changed into that of freemen."[83] With Condorcet, they believed that "all enlightened" Americans felt "both the shame and the danger of this error" and suggested that it would "not for long stain the purity of American law."[84]

If British and continental writers stressed cultural backwardness and chattel slavery as the two principal elements that tarnished the bright image of the United States as a distinctive political society occupying an exceptional place in the annals of humanity, they noted other problems that might prevent the new republics from becoming "the seats of liberty, science, peace, and virtue" promised by their early history

81. Pownall, *Memorial to the Sovereigns of America*, 108–9.
82. *View of North America*, 23.
83. Price, *Observations on the Nature of Civil Liberty*, 102.
84. Condorcet, *Influence of the American Revolution*, 93.

Liberty Displaying the Arts and Sciences. Europeans especially called attention to the incongruity between white liberty and black slavery in the United States. This painting, sent from London to the Library Company of Philadelphia for its new building in 1792 by the expatriate painter Samuel Jennings, shows Liberty with her staff and cap in a temple of learning introducing some slaves to knowledge and the arts, while other slaves, one of whom is playing a banjo, congregate on a lawn. Courtesy of the Library Company of Philadelphia.

and by the American Revolution.[85] With Condorcet, they acknowledged that not all of the state constitutions had "been equally well written," that not "all the laws written since the Declaration of Independence" had "been equally just and wise," and even that the laws of some states still contained "vestiges of a fanaticism too embittered by long persecution to be erased by the first efforts of enlightenment." Nor did they deny that "these wise republicans" were to some extent "still hampered by some remnants of antiquated English notions" that

85. Price, *Observations on the Importance of the American Revolution*, 213.

prevented them from perceiving that "laws in restraint of trade, commercial regulations, and indirect taxes" were all "infringements on the [natural] right of property."[86]

With Price, they were also concerned lest "the pride of independence" and postwar dissipation destroy "those virtuous and simple manners" for which Americans had become famous and, they thought, "by which alone republics can long subsist." They were concerned that "clashing interests" and "excessive jealousy" might "distract their governments," "break the federal union,"[87] and, as Turgot put it, turn the states into "a mass of divided powers contending for territory and commerce." They worried that Americans might miss the opportunity to establish "a constitution under which man could enjoy his rights, freely exercise all his faculties, and be governed only by nature, reason, and justice,"[88] a constitution, wrote Pownall, that would stand as an "unequivocal demonstration to all mankind, that the spirit of freedom and a right sense of Government dwells in the Citizens of America."[89]

Whatever America's continuing defects, however, most European observers agreed that they were minor in comparison with those of the Old World. No "enlightened observer" who compared American laws with those "of even the wisest nations, and especially in the legislation of those ancient peoples whom we admire so greatly of whom we know so little," asserted Condorcet, could fail to appreciate the superiority of those of America. "Even though one may censure Americans for some things," he noted, "it is only for certain particular errors or for long-standing practices which they have not yet been able to correct." "Nowhere in the political or criminal legislation of the various states," he contended, could "one find gross errors or oppressive or destructive principles," and he had no doubt "that the love that Americans have for equality, their respect for liberty and for property, and the nature of their constitutions" would eventually enable them to "set right all their faults."[90]

The powerful consensus among Old World observers was that America would overcome all of its problems and fulfill the promise of

86. Condorcet, *Influence of the American Revolution*, 91–92, 107.

87. Price, *Observations on the Importance of the American Revolution*, 214.

88. Turgot to Price, Mar. 22, 1778, 222.

89. Pownall, *Memorial to the Sovereigns of America*, 19.

90. Condorcet, *Influence of the American Revolution*, 92, 107.

what Price referred to as "the fairest experiment ever tried in human affairs."[91] The social and political record of its various societies seemed to be in its favor. Pointing out that "NORTH AMERICA" had "ADVANCED" and was "EVERY DAY ADVANCING, TO GROWTH OF STATE, WITH A STEADY AND CONTINUALLY ACCELERATING MOTION, OF WHICH THERE HAS NEVER YET BEEN ANY EXAMPLE IN EUROPE," Pownall predicted that as long as America remained a place where people could find an outlet for their "active powers of industry or ingenuity," its "fostering happiness" would provide the basis for "the encreasing population, opulence, and strength" and the passion for liberty that had been its distinguishing features over the previous century.[92]

So assured did its success appear that many people in the Old World feared that "immediately, on the establishment of peace," the "spirit of emigration [from Europe], which so much prevailed at the commencement of the war," would "break out with renovated vigour."[93] They worried that "as peace and happiness prevail[ed], as liberty" flourished, and as "the arts and sciences . . . progress[ed],"[94] America would become so attractive as to generate "an almost *general Emigration to that New World*,"[95] an emigration that would not only entice more and more of the people who were then "wrestling with grim PENURY" in Europe to seek a "permanent inheritance, in that fertile and extensive country,"[96] but also carry off many of Europe's "most useful enterprizing Spirits, and much of the active property."[97]

"To what degree of happiness, splendour, and power," Raynal asked, could such an inviting and novel country "in time be raised?"[98] As "population and agriculture" continued to "flourish in America," he prophesied, the arts would "make a rapid progress" and "that country, rising out of nothing will be fired with the ambition of appearing with glory in its turn on the face of the globe and in the history of the world."[99] Operating "under a system so entirely new upon Earth," the

91. Price, *Observation on the Importance of the American Revolution*, 213–14.

92. Pownall, *Memorial to the Sovereigns of Europe*, 56, 105.

93. *View of North America*, viii–ix.

94. John King, *Thoughts on the Difficulties and Distresses in Which the Peace of 1783 Has Involved the People of England* (London, 1783), 32.

95. Pownall, *Memorial to the Sovereigns of Europe*, 87.

96. *View of North America*, viii–ix.

97. Pownall, *Memorial to the Sovereigns of Europe*, 87.

98. Raynal, *Revolution of America*, 172–73.

99. Guillaume Thomas François Raynal, *The Philosophical and Political History*

United States, as Pownall suggested, would continue to improve, in the process exerting "a Civilizing activity, beyond what Europe could ever know."[100] America, Price plausibly suggested, would "soon . . . become superior" even to its "parent state."[101]

Several Old World writers speculated about the role of Providence in the development of America over the period since its settlement by Europeans. To Pownall, "the peculiar blessings, . . . the special favours, . . . the singular happiness" that seemed to characterize free Americans all suggested that God had marked them out "as a chosen people" with special obligations to their posterity and to the rest of humanity. By placing them "in a New World, separate and removed far from the regions and wretched Polities of the Old one," a world in "a land of plenty and liberty" with "so many sources of enjoyments," and by permitting them to enjoy "a System of police that" gave "activity to their powers" and provided them with so much liberty, God, Pownall suggested, had entailed upon Americans the duty to "consider themselves as the means in the hands of Providence" to extend "the Civilization of human Society" and "by their example" to become "the Teachers . . . of those Political Truths, which are meant, not to enslave, but to render men more free and happy under Government."[102] "Perhaps," added Price, "there never existed a people . . . to whom a station of more importance in the plan of Providence" had "been assigned."[103]

Having long been valued for the gold, silver, sugar, tobacco, rice, wheat, fish, naval stores, and other products that they sent back to enrich the Old World, the colonies of British North America as they were reorganized into the new United States had thus come to be celebrated by Britons and continental Europeans because they seemed to represent an "immediate [and working] application of most of the controversial social and political ideas [then] under discussion in Europe."[104] As such, the former colonies suddenly became "living, heartening proof that men had a capacity for growth, that reason and

---

of the Settlements and Trade of the Europeans in the East and West Indies, 4 vols. (London, 1776), 4:390–91.

100. Pownall, *Memorial to the Sovereigns of America,* 72–73.

101. Price, *Observations on the Nature of Civil Liberty,* 82.

102. Pownall, *Memorial to the Sovereigns of America,* 69, 137–38.

103. Price, *Observations on the Importance of the American Revolution,* 184.

104. Echeverria, *Mirage in the West,* 3.

humanity could become governing rather than merely critical principles,"[105] and that, in the manner of Plato's republic, philosophers of the kind who produced the American Declaration of Independence, the new republican state constitutions, and the federal Constitution of 1787 could become governors. Such a flattering evaluation powerfully beckoned Americans themselves to exhibit a greater appreciation of the many positive, and exceptional, features of the societies in which they lived and of the polities they were creating.

105. Peter Gay, "The Enlightenment," in *The Comparative Approach to American History*, ed. C. Vann Woodward (New York, 1968), 41.

CHAPTER SIX

Explanations

REVOLUTION AND REDEFINITION,

1774–1800

Not just in Europe but in America itself, the momentous events of the last four decades of the eighteenth century gave rise to a major reassessment of the character and promise of America as represented by the rising American republic. For a century and a half, the status of the Anglophone colonies as cultural provinces of England and their failure to measure up to the social and cultural standards of metropolitan Europe had prevented Anglo-Americans from achieving a fully positive sense of corporate self. However, as these British-American societies during the 1760s and 1770s first defiantly stood up for their rights and then revolted and moved to secure independent nationhood and establish republican forms of government, their inhabitants also defined more fully than ever before what made their societies both different from those of the Old World and similar to each other. In the process of thus elaborating their Americanness, they quickly began to develop an infinitely more favorable sense of collective self.

Well before the revolutionary era, the "amazingly rapid . . . growth and progress" of the colonies had given Americans and their inter-
162   preters a profound appreciation of the extraordinary extent to which

their country seemed to have been "[well]-adapted to health, vigour, industry, liberty, genius, and happiness." It gave them as well an equally strong and positive understanding of the degree to which, in the words of Samuel Williams, then Congregational pastor in Bradford, Massachusetts, in December 1774, it offered the diligent "labourer what neither Europe nor Asia" would "afford him, a comfortable support for the wages of his work." By enhancing their awareness of the extent to which their prosperity and happiness also had been a function of "the spirit and tendency of" their own internal "civil government[s]," the controversies with Britain in the decade beginning with the Stamp Act crisis of 1764–65 intensified both their respect for and their attachment to those governments.[1]

Moreover, as, in the process of defending themselves in these controversies, American leaders fixed their attention upon more general "matters of history, jurisprudence, and policy," they also acquired a strong appreciation of the uniqueness of their political situation. As they surveyed conditions over the rest of the globe, they came to understand that they were almost the only people who did not live in "total subjection to their rulers." "To such a degree of abasement and degradation" had Asia's "wretched inhabitants [been] reduced," declared Williams, in passages that anticipated by a year Thomas Paine's similar observations in *Common Sense*, "that the very idea of Liberty" was "unknown among" its inhabitants. "In *Africa*," he continued, "scarce any human beings are to be found but barbarians, tyrants, and slaves: All equally remote from the true dignity of human nature, and from a well-regulated state of society." Nor, in his view, was the situation much better in Europe, where "the vital flame" of liberty seemed about to die, as one country after another either forfeited or lost its freedom. Even in Britain, whose constitution had political liberty for its "main aim and end," freedom seemed to be in danger of being swept away in a tide of corruption. "*Switzerland* alone," it seemed to Williams, was "in the full and safe possession of her freedom."[2] From the perspective of their altercation with Britain, Americans came more and more to the realization that "the North-American provinces" were virtually the only polities that "yet remain[ed] *the country[s] of free men*." Increasingly, they began to develop the intoxicating sense that

1. Samuel Williams, *A Discourse on the Love of Our Country* (Salem, Mass., 1775), 20, 22–23.
2. Ibid., 21, 24.

Maryland State Seal. Like the new seals of several other states, that of Maryland sought to encapsulate the meaning of the American experience. The front of the seal shows a female figure upholding justice and peace, with the scales of justice in one hand and an olive branch in the other. In the foreground, another olive branch and a fasces holding the staff of liberty are crossed. On the reverse side two bundles of wheat, a hogshead of tobacco, a ship, and a cornucopia illustrate the connection between industry and plenty emphasized by the motto: "Industry the Means and Plenty the Result." From Eugene Zieber, Heraldry in America *(Philadelphia, 1909), 138. Courtesy of The Johns Hopkins University Library.*

America not only might, as Williams announced, be moving toward the achievement "of greater perfection and happiness than mankind has yet seen" but also was well positioned to inaugurate "a new aera, and give a new turn to human affairs" all over the globe.[3]

As the "inspiring voice of LIBERTY" echoed "from province to province" and flashed "like lightning through the distant regions of" their "vast continent" and as their resistance brought them "increased fame" in the Old World, American observers more and more began to entertain the possibility that their country might have a distinctive role to play in the course of human affairs. Noting that the colonies had long served as an asylum for the impoverished and the oppressed, they now began to speculate that they might some day become the sites at which "the streams of wealth, the beams of science, the stars of wisdom, the light of virtue, and the sun of liberty" would "all unite their rays, and form the sublime circle of human splendor and felicity." By the mid-1770s, they found it plausible to envision the day "when the knee of empires and splendid kingdoms" would "bow to" their "greatness"; when "the spirit of freedom" exemplified by the colonies would spread "from pole to pole, and rouse up a world of slaves"; when America would "be the glory and the astonishment of the whole earth"; and when the very "name of AMERICAN," would "carry honour and majesty in the sound—and men" would "esteem it a blessing to wear" that "venerable and commanding stile."[4]

Yet, at the time of independence, such visions of present and future greatness existed in uneasy tension with probably even deeper and much more widely manifest convictions about the deficiencies of the New World in comparison with the Old. In the mid-1770s, Paine

3. Ibid., 22, 16.
4. *Royal American Magazine* 1 (1774): 10.

still felt that he had to address those convictions explicitly. In *Common Sense* and other early writings, he systematically endeavored both to undermine all those cherished misconceptions about Britain that caused so many Americans, in his words, to "think better of the European world than it deserves" and to teach Americans what he subsequently referred to as "the manly doctrine of reverencing themselves."[5]

To that end, Paine sought to persuade Americans that many of the features of American society for which they had traditionally apologized—its simplicity, its newness, its rusticity, its innocence—were not deficiencies but advantages. The highly differentiated society of England, he informed his American readers, only meant that it had a few overwhelmingly rich people and a very large "class of poor and wretched people," while its "exceedingly complex" government caused "the nation [to] . . . suffer for years together without being able to discover in which part the fault lies." Nor when it came to size did the disadvantages outweigh the benefits. The vastness of their country, Paine contended, merely made it easier for Americans to "forget the narrow limits of three hundred and sixty miles (the extent of England)" and, "triumph[ing] in the generosity of . . . sentiment" that was the natural result of living in such an "extensive quarter of the globe," to "surmount the force of local prejudices."[6]

Through his writings, Paine helped to give Americans an appreciation of their own social virtues, inner worth, and what he thought was their superiority over the Old World. In the process, he held out to them a powerful, self-legitimating, and exhilarating vision that catered to their own rising feelings of worth and their growing sense that they might yet hold a place of first importance in the unfolding course of human history. "As the independence of America became contemplated and understood," Paine subsequently wrote in his *Letter to the Abbé Raynal*, "the numerous benefits it promised mankind, appeared to be every day increasing; and we saw not a temporary good for the present race only, but a continued good to all posterity."[7]

If after 1776 Paine played a critical part in revising the intellectual

5. Thomas Paine, *Common Sense*, in *The Complete Writings of Thomas Paine*, ed. Philip S. Foner, 2 vols. (New York, 1945), 1:21; Paine to Mr. Secretary Dundas, June 6, 1792, in ibid., 2:452.

6. Paine, *Common Sense*; Paine to Dundas, June 6, 1792, in ibid., 1:6–7, 19, 36, 2:451.

7. Paine, *Letter to the Abbé Raynal*, 1782, in ibid., 2:238.

construction of America on the western side of the Atlantic as well as on the eastern, Americans themselves took an active role in the process. As the new United States came to be celebrated as a "laboratory for Enlightenment ideas" and the "workshop for liberty"[8] by European thinkers, it acquired the respect not only of the outside world but also of its own people. For virtually the entire existence of the British-American colonies, their inhabitants had measured their societies against metropolitan Britain and had found themselves wanting. Now, in view of their heroic achievements during the last quarter of the eighteenth century, they learned to think infinitely better of themselves. No longer did Europe seem to be the center of the world. Now, instead of Americans going to school to Europe, Europe was going to school to America, which, as a result of its achievements during the American Revolution, seemed to have acquired a special place in the creation of a new, enlightened world order.

When they themselves explored the general meaning of their social and political achievements, American writers affirmed and elaborated the expanding, intensifying, and highly positive identification, championed by their contemporary Old World interpreters, of America as an exceptional place and of Americans as an exceptional people. Ecstatic that this "great American Revolution, this recent political phenomenon of a new sovereignty arising among the sovereign powers of the earth," had been, as Ezra Stiles, president of Yale College, wrote in 1783, "attended to and contemplated by all nations,"[9] they were especially pleased that, in the words of a later observer, "a great part of the civilized world" had "embarked [so] deeply in the American cause."[10] Nor did the admiration of American interpreters for the Revolution diminish over time. Among those few events, "which, scattered at distant intervals in the long trash of human record," "adorn[ed] the history and honour[ed] the nature of man," a Rhode Island orator proudly declared in 1802, "the American revolution holds a high and distinguished place."[11]

8. Peter Gay, "The Enlightenment," in *The Comparative Approach to American History*, ed. C. Vann Woodward (New York, 1968), 42.

9. Ezra Stiles, *The United States Elevated to Glory and Honor* (New Haven, Conn., 1783), in *The Pulpit of the American Revolution*, ed. John Wingate Thornton (Boston, 1876), 463.

10. Timothy Dwight, *A Discourse on Some Events of the Last Century* (New Haven, Conn., 1801), 23.

11. Nathaniel Bowen, *An Oration* (Providence, R.I., 1802), 4.

In the emerging American understanding of that event, the entire course of the Revolution seemed to redound to the credit of themselves and their country. The "active instruments of carrying on the revolution," wrote the South Carolina physician and historian David Ramsay approvingly, had been drawn from among those many "self-made, industrious men" who, "by their own exertions" in their private capacities, had previously "established or laid a foundation for establishing personal independence"[12] and during the Revolution had deeply engaged themselves in "the cause of justice and rational liberty against the unjust encroachments of arbitrary power."[13] Under the leadership of such men, Americans, their interpreters emphasized, had stood up for their liberties, "raised armies without compulsion, and supported them almost without means."[14] Wading through "a sea of trouble" with "unexampled patience" during the war, Americans had, despite much loss of life and personal sacrifice, fought on until they had secured their "independent station among the nations of the earth."[15]

Even more impressive, Americans, employing the many "talents for great stations" that emerged during the Revolution as a result of what Ramsay referred to as a "vast expansion" of human capacities,[16] had also successfully managed to "set up governments for themselves"[17] that had "effectually secured" individual liberty in "all the polities of the United States"[18] and everywhere exhibited the "certain marks of a good government," including "peace, happiness, and prosperity, the increase, and the affections of the people."[19] To their "Infinite credit," the "conductors of our American Revolution," the cultural nationalist Joel Barlow observed during the first years of the nineteenth century,

12. David Ramsay, *The History of the American Revolution*, ed. Lester H. Cohen, 2 vols. (Indianapolis, 1990), 2:630.

13. Zephaniah Swift Moore, *An Oration on the Anniversary of the Independence of the United States of America* (Worcester, Mass., 1802), in *American Political Writing during the Founding Era, 1760–1805*, ed. Charles S. Hyneman and Donald S. Lutz, 2 vols. (Indianapolis, 1983), 2:1207.

14. Ibid.

15. Zabdiel Adams, *An Election Sermon* (Boston, 1782), in Hyneman and Lutz, eds., *American Political Writing*, 1:546.

16. Ramsay, *History of American Revolution*, 2:630.

17. Samuel Williams, *Natural and Civil History of Vermont*, 2 vols. (Walpole, N.H., 1794), 2:415.

18. Stiles, *United States*, 421.

19. Williams, *History of Vermont*, 2:415.

had "seized the occasion" to establish "our interior and federal governments" on the "two most consoling principles that political experience has yet brought to light," the principles of *representative democracy, and the federalizing of States."* [20]

By these efforts, American writers pointed out, American leaders had insured that American governments would have no power except that "derived from the public opinion." [21] "Our free and happy constitutions," one speaker explained in 1790 in one of the many Independence Day orations that contributed so powerfully to the construction of the postrevolutionary American definition of America, ordained that government should "be for the people, and not the people for government; or agreeable to the apostolick institutions." "However exalted in power, or respectable from official character," he noted, "those intrusted with authority for the common good" were

> nevertheless considered as the servants and ministers of the rest. Instead of domineering over us, like the lords of our enslaved earth, they are amenable to us for their conduct, and accountable to us as their masters. We are, in short, a nation of princes—and more than princes—for we have more liberty. We are privileged to do all things whatsoever that are in themselves right; and are prohibited from nothing but what is in itself morally evil. We are amenable only to the laws of our own making, and are not humbled by the appellation of subjects, servants or slaves to any man, king, or potentate whatsoever: but we call ourselves free citizens.

Glorying in "the honor, the dignity, and happiness necessarily connected with the character of a free citizen" and "the distinguished majesty, grandeur, and felicity of a nation thus privileged," [22] American interpreters were "most deeply persuaded" that their free countrymen, in the words of the New York legal theorist James Kent, were "favoured with the best Political Institutions, *take them for all in all,* of any People that ever were united in the Bonds of Civil Society." [23]

This revolutionary achievement, such analysts never tired of stress-

20. Joel Barlow, *To His Fellow Citizens of the United States. Letter II* (Philadelphia, 1801), in Hyneman and Lutz, eds., *American Political Writing,* 2:1106.

21. Williams, *History of Vermont,* 2:394.

22. James Tilton, "Oration," July 5, 1790, *Columbian Magazine* (Dec. 1790): 369–70.

23. James Kent, *An Introductory Lecture to a Course of Law Lectures* (New York, 1794), in Hyneman and Lutz, eds., *American Political Writing,* 2:949.

ing, distinguished Americans from all other peoples in the history of the world. "Such an amazing effort of deliberation as the peaceable adoption of" these governments, Kent observed, was "literally without example."[24] "In no age before, and in no other country," said Ramsay, "did man ever possess an election of the kind of government under which he would choose to live. The constituent parts of the antient free governments were thrown together by accident. The freedom of modern European governments was, for the most part, obtained by the concessions, or liberality of monarchs, or military leaders. In America alone, reason and liberty concurred in the formation of constitutions."[25] For "every American" who reflected "seriously on the immensity of the undertaking, the manner in which it was conducted, the felicity of its issue, and the fate of similar experiments," such momentous accomplishments, said Kent, "must indeed be a source of high satisfaction."[26]

Postrevolutionary American interpreters often expressed wonder at these developments. With Noah Webster, they marveled that, "after the experience of four or five thousand years, and numberless forms of government," it "should . . . happen to be reserved for America to discover the great secret," a system of government that had "eluded all form of inquiry"[27] and had "no where been suffered to prevail but in America."[28] Mankind had tried "all the forms of civil polity . . . except one," Stiles boasted, "and that seems to have been reserved in Providence to be realized in America." Who, even a generation earlier, he asked, would have thought "that the world should ever look to America for models of government and polity?"[29]

As they surveyed their new country, American interpreters witnessed the benefits of its political institutions in every aspect of life. Everywhere, Americans seemed to be "flourishing, and rapidly increasing in their wealth, and numbers."[30] "Religious freedom," "ban-

24. James Kent, *Dissertations: Being the Preliminary Part of a Course of Law Lectures* (New York, 1795), 47–48.

25. Ramsay, *History of American Revolution*, 1:331.

26. Kent, *Dissertations*, 47–48.

27. Noah Webster, *An Oration on the Anniversay of the Declaration of Independence* (New Haven, Conn., 1802), in Hyneman and Lutz, eds., *American Political Writing*, 2:1222–23.

28. Williams, *History of Vermont*, 2:393.

29. Stiles, *United States*, 412, 468–69.

30. Williams, *History of Vermont*, 2:415.

ished from every other corner of the earth," had "erected her standard in these states," where there was "no fire and faggots, no pains and emoluments of any kind" to force any religious sentiments upon anyone.[31] Enjoying "the tranquility of an efficient government"[32] and "having but few objects of ambition or contention among themselves" in either religion or politics, all Americans could absorb themselves "in the ordinary cares of domestic life"[33] and every individual, American analysts proclaimed in invoking an ancient American cultural ideal, could rest quietly "under his own vine and under his own fig-tree," with "none to make him afraid."[34] In the "calm retreat" in which they lived, "Peace, independence, and a joyous heart" seemed to invite every one "to freedom, joy, and blest repose."[35] Of the four seasons, "the radiant summer" seemed to a commencement speaker at the University of Pennsylvania in May 1784 to be the only appropriate "emblem . . . of what as a people, we have been; are now; and expect eventually to be made perfect in."[36]

Soberly, but with obvious pride, American interpreters contrasted their own fortunate situation of freedom, peace, happiness, and prosperity with the dark situation that characterized "the great bulk of mankind," few of whom enjoyed "even the shadow of liberty."[37] In the Old World, wrote Ramsay, the vast majority of people lived "under the galling yoke of oppression" in "a state of dependency" that debased "human nature," while "a few among them" were "exalted to be more than men."[38] From the emerging perspective of American developments at the end of the eighteenth century, the Old World seemed mostly to be the "residence of despotism" in which ignorance unavoidably pervaded a "populace, who, never having enjoyed the genial rays of liberty," had early learned to "endure its extinction

31. William Linn, *The Blessings of America* (New York, 1790), 20.

32. Tilton, "Oration," 369.

33. Ramsay, *History of American Revolution*, 1:33.

34. Tilton, "Oration," 369.

35. W. K., "The Happiness of America," *Columbian Magazine* (Jan. 1791): 52.

36. "The Former, Present, and Future Prospects of America," *Columbian Magazine* (Oct. 1786): 83.

37. Linn, *Blessings of America*, 18.

38. David Ramsay, *An Oration in Commemoration of American Independence* (Charleston, S.C., 1794), in Robert L. Brunhouse, ed., "David Ramsay, 1749–1815: Selections from His Writings," *American Philosophical Society Transactions*, n.s., 55 (1965): 193.

An American New Cleared Farm. This engraving represents the first stage of settlement on an American frontier when the fields had only just been cleared of the original forest growth and were still full of stumps. It shows four different styles of fencing and two different kinds of houses, a log house on the right and a more pretentious house with wings as well as several different kinds of barns and shelters on the left. The presence of Amerindians in birchbark canoes, one with a farmer being poled by an Amerindian and the other with four Amerindians, including a "Baboose, or Indian Child," being paddled by two "squaws," emphasizes the proximity of the farm not just to the wilderness but to its native inhabitants. From Patrick Campbell, Travels in the Interior Inhabited Parts of North America *(Edinburgh, 1793). Courtesy of the Library Company of Philadelphia.*

with slavish insensibility."[39] For all but a few privileged members of society, asserted one writer, Europe was only a *"furnace of affliction and [a] gaol of oppression."*[40]

Nor, they mostly agreed, had much of the Old World ever been any

39. "The Worcester Speculator, No. VI," *Worcester Magazine* (Oct. 1787), in Hyneman and Lutz, eds., *American Political Writing*, 1:701.

40. Morgan J. Rhees, *The Good Samaritan: An Oration* (Philadelphia, 1796), 12–13.

different. "In most of the ancient and populous nations of Europe," wrote Samuel Williams in the early 1790s in the most systematic and extended attempt by an American to define the special character of American society, "their forms of government, their ecclesiastical establishments, the extreme luxury of one part of the people, and the extreme poverty of the other, their long and bloody wars, their numerous fleets and armies," and "the impious institution of celebacy" had reduced most men "to servitude," rendered them "incapable of supporting families," and "nearly destroyed the natural increase of mankind."[41]

As they continued to ruminate upon the dramatic "contrast[s] between the Old and the New World," American interpreters developed an ever deeper appreciation of the fortunate situation of their "rising republic,"[42] and they eagerly endorsed the opinion of contemporary British and European writers that the Revolution had introduced "a new era . . . in human things"[43] during which "the rest of the world" would "follow the laudable example of America and . . . construct governments, that" would "embrace the happiness of the many, and not [just] of the few,"[44] wherein " 'the iron rod of the oppresser' " would be "broken, and" the "oppressed . . . be universally set free."[45] By thus kindling such a powerful flame of liberty that could eventually be expected to spread even into "the darkest and remotest corners of the earth,"[46] Americans, their local interpreters stressed, had contributed "most eventful[ly] to" their own "fortune and glory."[47]

Whether or not America ever became a model for the polities of the Old World, American interpreters following the Revolution had no doubt that it would continue to offer a welcoming sanctuary for refugees from that world, and the depiction of the United States as an asylum for the oppressed became one of the most conspicuous features in the emerging image of America. For the millions of Europeans whose lives were "imbittered by the cruel impositions of men" and who, despite perpetual labor, could manage to "obtain only a scanty

41. Williams, *History of Vermont*, 2:424–25.

42. Rhees, *Good Samaritan*, 13, 17.

43. Timothy Dwight, *Discourse*, 23.

44. Robert Porter, "An Oration to Commemorate the Independence of the United States of America," *Columbian Magazine* (Sept. 1791): 190.

45. Timothy Dwight, *Discourse*, 23.

46. Linn, *Blessings of America*, 33.

47. Kent, *Dissertations*, 47–48.

subsistence" for themselves and their families, the happy governments and "fertile plains of America," American writers reiterated again and again, continued to offer what America had always offered, the chance for a new beginning.[48] While some interpreters worried that such an inviting country would "excite the discontented of other countries to swarm in upon us" in such numbers as to make the existing inhabitants a "minority in their own country,"[49] most commentators looked forward, with Ramsay, to the time when the whole country would be "filled with freemen—with citizens of the United States," living under governments "founded on reason and equality" and devoted to perpetuating "the happiness of the people" who composed them. The favorable prospects for such a "great extension of human happiness"[50] made it almost impossible, as one orator announced, for even the "most brilliant imagination" to predict the extent "of human greatness which the united states" might eventually attain.[51]

But many interpreters took special pains to emphasize that America's fortunate situation was by no means a new phenomenon. Virtually from the beginning of English settlement, they stressed, both liberty and abundance had characterized the colonies. Their very distance from Britain, Ramsay noted, "generated ideas . . . favourable to liberty." In an "extensive or detached empire," he explained, "the circulation of power" had inevitably been "enfeebled at the extremities,"[52] with the result that the settlers quickly "acquire[d] ideas of liberty and independence, and their own importance" which the metropolitan government "in vain endeavour[ed] to restrain."[53] In this situation, the colonists soon developed "just ideas of law, liberty and government" and learned to maintain "a watchful jealousy . . . over the encroachments of arbitrary power."[54] By the time of the Revolution,

48. Linn, Blessings of America, 20.

49. Rudiments of Law and Government Deduced from the Law of Nature (Charleston, S.C., 1783), in Hyneman and Lutz, eds., American Political Writing, 1:597.

50. David Ramsay, An Oration, on the Cession of Louisiana (Charleston, S.C., 1804), 21.

51. Porter, "Oration," 190.

52. Ramsay, History of American Revolution, 1:28.

53. "Observations in Response to an 'Enquiry Whether the Discovery of America Has Been Useful or Hurtful to Mankind,'" Boston Magazine (May 1784), republished in Columbian Magazine (June 1788): 308.

54. Ibid., 305.

then, "Freedom," as Williams put it, "had been the constant product and effect of the state of society in the British colonies" for almost "a century and a half."[55]

To an even greater extent than contemporary British and European commentators, American writers traced the special fortunes of the United States to what Williams called "the state of society in America" as it had developed during the colonial era. Well before "the American war came on," Williams explained, Americans lived in "that natural, easy, and independent situation, and spirit" that had, with the American Revolution, become the envy of people in the Old World. "Long before the nations of Europe had any suspicion of what was taking place in the minds of men" in the colonies, he noted, "the foundations of . . . freedom" had been thoroughly established "in the state of society which had taken place in America."[56]

The primary determinants of that society were those to which observers had long attributed the distinctiveness of colonial British America: "immense tracts of uncultivated lands,"[57] high wages for labor, and a beneficent climate that provided inhabitants with not only "necessaries, but even indulgencies, in abundance."[58] Such inviting conditions, they explained, offered "every temptation . . . to emigration," generously rewarded "industry . . . with competency,"[59] and "cooperate[d] to the sure acquest of gain."[60] As a consequence of these conditions, all but a few of the free settlers of the British colonies, they explained, had managed, "from no other source but the earth and" their "own industry," to acquire an "independent subsistence" that in just a few years supplied them with a "very comfortable living" and "sufficient property to maintain a family."[61]

Also more than contemporary European commentators, Americans appreciated the enormous amount of labor that lay behind these developments. America, they stressed, did not offer its inhabitants "the

55. Williams, *History of Vermont*, 2:431.

56. Ibid., 426, 430.

57. Charles Pinckney, Speech, June 25, 1787, in *Colonies to Nation, 1763–1789: A Documentary History of the American Revolution*, ed. Jack P. Greene (New York, 1967), 530.

58. "An Enquiry into the Most Advantageous Occupations to Be Followed by Persons Emigrating to America," *Columbian Magazine* (Oct. 1787): 699–700.

59. Pinckney, Speech, June 25, 1787, 530.

60. *Rudiments of Law and Government*, 593.

61. Williams, *History of Vermont*, 2:354, 367.

View from Bushongo Tavern. At a later stage of settlement after stumps had rotted and fields had been cultivated for some time, rural landscapes took on a somewhat more settled appearance. Still adjacent to large forested areas, such landscapes had log and plank houses arranged along dirt roads with narrow bridges to enable travelers to cross streams. This view from the Bushongo Tavern along the road from York to Baltimore in northern Maryland or southern Pennsylvania depicts such a scene. Columbian Magazine *(July 1788), frontispiece. Courtesy of the Library of Congress, neg. no.* LCUSZ62-31149.

pleasures of Arcadia." "The moderate price of land, the credit which arises from prudence, and the safety from our courts of law, of every species of property," explained an anonymous author in the *Columbian Magazine* in 1786, put "affluence, independence, and happiness . . . within the reach of every man." But great "patience, industry, and labour" were necessary to secure them.[62] "The cup is within the reach of every man, full to the brim," said another writer in the same periodical, "but the exertion to take it must arise from himself." "The necessaries, the comforts, and the indulgences of life, may be procured by labour; but even the necessaries," he insisted, were "not to be procured without it." "Activity and industry" were "indispensably requisite to success." Neither America nor the industrious Americans who were creating it smiled on indolence. Every individual, most

62. "An Account of the Progress of Population, Agriculture, Manners, and Government in Pennsylvania," *Columbian Magazine* (Nov. 1786): 120.

American commentators agreed, had to "work in some shape or other, either by his head or his hands."[63]

If only the "industrious and [the] enterprising"[64] could be "sure of acquiring, in a short time, large and profitable farms"[65] and "enriching themselves"[66] in America, the conditions that Europeans and their descendants found and created there, American writers emphasized in reinforcing a long-standing conception, had encouraged so many of them to develop those qualities that they produced a society that was wholly exceptional. "The people of the U[nited] States," the South Carolina lawyer Charles Pinckney told his fellow delegates to the Philadelphia convention in 1787, "are perhaps the most singular of any we are acquainted with." With "very few rich men among them" and with "few poor and few dependent" among the free population, Americans, Pinckney said, had "fewer distinctions of fortune & less of rank, than among the inhabitants of any other nation."[67] With the "best part of the American terra firma . . . [as] yet not only uncultivated, but unappropriated,"[68] the United States had such a "vast extent of unpeopled territory" to provide "the frugal & industrious [with] a sure road to competency" that, Pinckney predicted, American society "must . . . for centuries" continue to be, as it had always been, "unfavorable to the rapid distinction of ranks" and favorable to the preservation of "that equality of condition which so eminently distinguishes us."[69]

The social effects of these conditions, American observers mostly agreed, were profound. Unlike Europe, Pinckney noted in reiterating a by then ancient point, the United States had "no distinct . . . Class of Citizens" with special "rights, privileges & properties."[70] "Patrician and plebian orders," echoed Charles Jared Ingersoll two decades later in spelling out the many features of American society that he thought made it superior to those of Europe, were "unknown." "The proportion of persons of large fortunes" was "small; that of paupers next to nothing." Because "Luxury" had "not yet corrupted the rich" and

63. "Enquiry into the Most Advantageous Occupations," 699.
64. "Former, Present, and Future Prospects of America," 84.
65. "Enquiry into the Most Advantageous Occupations," 698.
66. "Former, Present, and Future Prospects of America," 84.
67. Pinckney, Speech, June 25, 1787, 530–32.
68. "Observations in Response to an 'Enquiry,'" 305.
69. Pinckney, Speech, June 25, 1787, 530–32.
70. Ibid.

there was none "of that want, which classifies the poor," the United States, he contended, had "no populace. . . . All are people. What in other countries is called a populace, a compost heap, whence germinates mobs, beggars, and tyrants," he explained, "is not to be found in the towns; and there is no peasantry in the country. Were it not for the slaves of the south, there would be but one rank."[71]

In turn, the absence of ranks among the free population meant, American analysts explained, that social dynamics in America operated in an entirely different way than they did in the Old World. With no "great inequalities in privileges" and no distinctions deriving "from birth, blood, [or] hereditary titles and honors," as Williams contended, there were "no family interests, connexions, or estates large enough to oppress" the broad body of the people, and "pride of families, the ambition of ostentation, or the idle notions of useless and dangerous distinctions, under the name and honor of titles," were largely unknown.[72] "Led by [neither] powerful families, nor by great officers, of church and state," Americans, said Ramsay, "were . . . separate independent individuals," who lived "under no general influence, but that of their personal feelings and opinions."[73]

Under such conditions, American interpreters explained, government was "highly democratic."[74] No free white adult male was "excluded by birth, & few by fortune, from voting for proper persons to fill the offices of Government," and, in Pinckney's words, the "whole community . . . enjoy[ed] in the fullest sense that kind of political liberty which consists in the power the members of the State reserve to themselves, of arriving at the public offices, or at least, of having votes in the nomination of those who fill them."[75] "In such circumstances," noted Williams, "the common farmer in America had a more comprehensive view of his rights and privileges, than the speculative philosopher of Europe . . . ever could have of the subject."[76] No wonder that, according to America's observers, this extensively empowered population insisted that "Every freeman" have "a right to

71. Charles Jared Ingersoll, *Inchiquin, the Jesuit's Letters* (New York, 1810), 120, 122–23.

72. Williams, *History of Vermont*, 2:371, 374–75, 376, 393.

73. Ramsay, *History of American Revolution*, 1:31–32.

74. Williams, *History of Vermont*, 2:423.

75. Pinckney, Speech, June 25, 1787, 530.

76. Williams, *History of Vermont*, 2:394, 430.

the same protection & security,"[77] that laws be "uniform and equal in their operation,"[78] that taxes be "no more than what" were "unavoidably necessary," and that "Every family" be permitted to enjoy "nearly the whole produce of their labor."[79]

A political society with such "a great degree of equality"[80] obviously had no place for "a proud and factious Aristocracy." "That unnecessary distinction between the rich and the poor, the great and the small, which aggrandizes a few, and enslaves the rest of mankind, as far as the wide limits of monarchy extend," declared a Connecticut writer in 1796, had "ever been the abhorrence of Americans."[81] For that reason, during the Revolution, Kent noted, Americans had taken pains to insure that "every part" of their political system had been based on "the principle[s] of representation and responsibility" and that "hereditary orders with all the dangers of their destructive influence and unequal appendages" had thereby been "entirely" excluded.[82] By prohibiting primogeniture and other inheritance practices that European aristocracies had used to sustain themselves, Americans had deliberately sought, Kent said, to give "Property . . . a free circulation, and free employment, with out any of the fetters of entailments and perpetuities" that in Europe had "foster[ed] excessive inequalities of power and property, invite[d people] to indolence, damp[ened] enterprize, facilitate[d] corruption, unduly widen[ed] distinctions, and humble[d] the poor under the proud superiority of the rich."[83]

No American commentators claimed that the United States did not have considerable variations in wealth. Rather, they recognized that, no matter how equal American society appeared in comparison with societies in the Old World, differences in the "original powers, capacities, and talents" of individuals inevitably resulted in social inequalities.[84] But Americans regarded such inequalities as the just

77. Pinckney, Speech, June 25, 1787, 530–32.

78. Kent, *Dissertations*, 20.

79. Williams, *History of Vermont*, 2:423.

80. Frederick William Hotchkiss, *Our National Greatness* (New Haven, Conn., 1793), 9–14.

81. Israel Beard Woodward, *American Liberty and Independence* (Litchfield, Conn., 1796), 6.

82. Kent, *Dissertations*, 17–18.

83. Ibid., 20.

84. Williams, *History of Vermont*, 2:376.

consequences of different rates in the acquisition of property "by different talents and industry."[85] American "men of wealth," Timothy Dwight told a Connecticut audience in 1801, were nothing more than "industrious farmers, mechanics, merchants, and professional men" who had lived "lives of labour, and frugality" and could never credibly "be branded as an aristocratic nobility."[86] So long as "no one" was empowered to "exercise any authority by virtue of birth," so long as everyone, in Ramsay's words, started "equal in the race of life,"[87] so long as talents had "fair play" and merit was "unrestrained,"[88] so long as private economic endeavors and public offices were "open to [all] men of merit, of whatever rank or condition,"[89] Americans had no objections to, indeed, mostly only admiration for, some individuals rising to higher social positions. They agreed with Samuel Williams that "nothing ever did or ever can produce an equality of power, capacity and advantages, in the social, or in any other state of man."[90] Believing that people ought "to be distinguished by their talents and their virtues,"[91] they found "superiority . . . galling and insuferable" only when it arose solely "from incidental circumstances" such as birth and was "not annexed to merit."[92]

Like Pownall and many earlier writers, American observers during and after the Revolution also emphasized that the expansive and empowering conditions of American society had functioned to enlarge the aspirations and give a distinctive shape to the character of free Americans. Whereas social arrangements in the Old World, in Joel Barlow's words, habituated "people to believe in an inequality in the rights of men" and thereby taught them to acknowledge "the birth-right of domineering" and prepared "them for servility and oppression,"[93] the "facility of subsistence and high price of labour" in

85. *Rudiments of Law and Government,* 577.

86. Timothy Dwight, *An Oration* (Hartford, Conn., 1801), 25.

87. Ramsay, *Oration* (1794), 192, and *An Oration on the Advantages of American Independence* (Charleston, S.C., 1778), in Brunhouse, ed., "David Ramsay," 183.

88. Tilton, "Oration," 370.

89. Ramsay, *Oration* (1794), 192, and *Oration* (1778), 183.

90. Williams, *History of Vermont,* 2:374–75.

91. Tilton, "Oration," 370.

92. *Rudiments of Law and Government,* 578.

93. Joel Barlow, *Advice to the Privileged Orders in the Several States of Europe* (London, 1792), in *The Works of Joel Barlow,* ed. William Bottoroff and Arthur L. Ford, 2 vols. (Gainesville, Fla., 1970), 1:111–12.

Seat of Moses Gill. The prosperity achieved by some farmers can be seen in this engraving of the property of Moses Gill in Worcester County, Massachusetts. It shows a large, by colonial standards, two-story rural mansion with a coach house and other outbuildings and a lawn and adjacent garden surrounded by an intricate wooden fence. A group of farm workers with a cart drawn by two oxen are haying in a field in front of the house, while a stately coach drawn by two horses passes by on the road to one of the many other houses in the neighborhood. In the parlance of the day, such a property was called a seat. From the Massachusetts Magazine *(1791). Courtesy of the Library Company of Philadelphia.*

America rendered "almost every man an independent property holder and a citizen,"[94] who was "perfectly free of the will of every other citizen."[95] Along with light taxes and the absence of either an extensive military force or a legally privileged social order, this widespread empowering process in turn "remove[d] every sensation of restraint" and made each man "sensible of his individual importance,"[96] strength-

94. Ingersoll, *Inchiquin*, 120.
95. Ramsay, *Oration* (1794), 192.
96. Ingersoll, *Inchiquin*, 120, 122–23.

ened his "natural desire of freedom," "impressed [him] with an opinion, that all men" were "by nature equal," and made him deeply
resistant to any "idea of subjection."[97] "Secure in life, liberty, and
property, [and] uninterrupted in civil or religious privileges, every"
American freeholder, said one writer, felt that "dignity of nature and
of character" that was "peculiar to free citizens,"[98] and all were encouraged to lives of "activity" and "lively, vigorous exertion[s] of
energy."[99]

Indeed, the adjective American writers most often used to describe
the emerging character of Americans throughout the continent was
active. The American people, said Pinckney, were "as active . . . as
any people in the world."[100] In contrast to Europeans whose small
hopes of ever "acquiring ease or property" or improving their material lives through their labor had rendered them passive,[101] all free
men in America knew, as Stiles put it, that they would reap "the fruits
of" their "labor and . . . share in the aggregate system of power."[102]
That knowledge, the prospects that their own labor could bring them
"subsistence, and estate"[103] and that property would guarantee them
"Liberty, [both] civil and religious," Stiles wrote, had from the beginning "filled the English settlers in America with a most amazing
spirit." Operating "with great energy,"[104] this "spirit of universal activity, and enterprize," wrote Williams, focused men's attention on
the active pursuit of "their own employments and business," taught
them to suffer "No other pursuits . . . to divert their attention,"[105] and
so engaged their energies that, another writer declared, people from
"every nation, kindred, and tongue under heaven" soon forgot "their
ancient animosities, and form[ed] one race of *republicans*."[106]

To American writers engaged in the process of constructing and
identifying America, the United States thus seemed to be a society in
which opportunity, freedom, equality, and individual autonomy and

97. Ramsay, *History of American Revolution*, 1:30–31.
98. Tilton, "Oration," 370.
99. Stiles, *United States*, 431.
100. Pinckney, Speech, June 25, 1787, 533.
101. Williams, *History of Vermont*, 2:368.
102. Stiles, *United States*, 439.
103. Williams, *History of Vermont*, 2:372.
104. Stiles, *United States*, 439.
105. Williams, *History of Vermont*, 2:372.
106. Rhees, *Good Samaritan*, 14.

activity were "the leading feature[s]."[107] "Universality of successful employment" had diffused "alacrity and happiness throughout the community," and, wrote Ingersoll, as each individual felt "himself rising in his [personal] fortunes," the "nation, rising with the concentration of all this elasticity," rejoiced "in its growing greatness."[108] With nearly universal suffrage, "a general diffusion of knowledge, a tolerably equal distribution of wealth, and a moral character formed in mildness and with a love of order," the United States, Kent was persuaded, had "peculiar advantages . . . as a nation."[109] America, Stiles said triumphantly, appeared to have realized all "the capital ideas of Harrington's Oceana," the late seventeenth-century tract that had inspired the founders of Carolina, Jersey, and Pennsylvania.[110] Indeed, as they contemplated the favorable conditions America offered to all free people, American observers found it extremely difficult to understand why anybody, in Ramsay's words, "would remain in Europe, a dependant on the will of an imperious landlord, when a few years industry can make him an independent American freeholder" and earn him the full "enjoyment of the sweets of American Liberty."[111]

In their efforts to define and identify America, American writers laid little emphasis on its deficiencies. Although few claimed that American society was as yet equivalent to Europe in terms of its cultural achievements, and most admitted that Americans still had to content themselves "with admiring the works of nature" rather than their own "works of art,"[112] they tended to attribute America's alleged "inferiority" in the "arts and sciences" largely to the effects of its long subjection to Britain and to a "state of society" in which the attention of most people was still "engrossed by agriculture, or directed by the low pursuit of wealth,"[113] conditions that they did not regard as permanent. Because Americans were people of "clear and sound understanding, and of acute and solid judgment" and because more and more of them possessed "extensive learning" and "comprehen-

107. Pinckney, Speech, June 25, 1787, 530–32.

108. Ingersoll, Inchiquin, 122–23.

109. Kent, Dissertations, 17–18.

110. Stiles, United States, 404.

111. Ramsay, Oration (1778), 188.

112. "Enquiry into the Most Advantageous Occupations," 700.

113. Ramsay to Thomas Jefferson, May 3, 1786, in Brunhouse, ed., "David Ramsay," 183–85, and Ramsay, Oration (1778), 101.

sive minds,"[114] these writers predicted that in an independent America "philosophy and literature" would soon find "a peaceful residence"[115] and be "cultivated, extended, and improved" until they had "spread far and wide" and "reached the remotest parts of this untutored continent."[116]

America's interpreters were far more critical of their country's continuing cultural dependence on the Old World. For several decades after the Revolution, they complained about the "common practice" of reverting "to Grecian, Roman and British customs, for precedents and models, whereby to build our political edifice"[117] and lamented the tendency of Americans "to imitate European manners; to copy the extravagant fashions, and absurd customs, to which refined luxury and perverted taste had given birth, in foreign monarchies."[118] "We behold our houses accomodated to the climate of Great Britain," complained a contributor to the Columbian Magazine in 1790. "We behold our ladies panting in a heat of ninety degrees, under a hat and cushion, which were calculated for the temperature of a British summer. We behold our citizens condemned and punished by a criminal law, which was copied from a country where maturity in corruption renders public executions a part of the amusements of the country."[119] "Why should the habits of Europe, base in their origin, and debasing in their continuance, become laws to the sons of freedom?" asked another writer.[120] "Is there a necessity for our being always a dependent people?" asked still another. "And when our bodies and property are rescued from the controul of others, must our minds shew submission still?"[121]

To remedy this situation, American writers called upon "the people

114. "Enquiry into the Most Advantageous Occupations," 699.

115. "Former, Present, and Future Prospects of America," 85.

116. Ramsay to Jefferson, May 3, 1786, 183–85, and Ramsay, Oration (1778), 101.

117. Rudiments of Law and Government, 566.

118. "Impartial Review of Late American Publications," Columbian Magazine (June 1790): 372.

119. "Thoughts upon Female Education," Columbian Magazine (May 1790): 289–90.

120. "Letter from a Gentleman in Wilmington, Delaware," Oct. 21, 1790, Columbian Magazine (Nov. 1790): 317.

121. Rudiments of Law and Government, 566.

of the United States" to undertake "a reformation in manners and customs" as "great . . . as they have made in government."[122] In the language of Thomas Paine, they admonished Americans "to *reverence yourselves*"[123] and to stop being "the servile copyists of foreign manners, fashions, and vices."[124] They exhorted them to "consider yourselves as what you are, of judgment equal to the rest of mankind, with the advantage of their experience."[125] "It is high time," declared an anonymous writer in 1790, for us "to awake from this servility— to study our own character—to examine the age of our country—and to adopt manners in every thing, that shall be accommodated to our state of society, and to the forms of our government."[126]

Nor was their country's continuing cultural dependence on the Old World the only source of worry for those Americans who took upon themselves the task of identifying America. In times of unusual political volatility, they fretted that their countrymen were not "act[ing] like men" who "deserve[d] to be free" and were taking too long to "learn the art of governing well."[127] Fearing that their "revolutionary schemes" had been "too visionary" and their "hopes too sanguine," some commentators despaired that "the mass of citizens" would ever acquire the "knowledge and independence of mind, which" seemed to be "absolutely essential to render an elective government a public blessing."[128]

Still others worried that the growing concentration of land in some areas was beginning to produce a more European-style social structure. They feared that, notwithstanding "the best and most intelligent Constitution with principles of freedom and equality," America would through law, habit, and public opinion slowly reproduce what one Polish visitor called that great European "public ill," the "dominating and the dominated, in a word," the "influence of the landlord and the dependence of the renters." In America, as everywhere, he predicted,

122. "Letter from a Gentleman," 317.
123. Tilton, "Oration," 373.
124. "Impartial Review," 372.
125. *Rudiments of Law and Government*, 566.
126. "Thoughts upon Female Education," 289–90.
127. Pro Republica, "Thoughts on the Present Situation of the Federal Government of the United States of America," *Columbian Magazine* (Dec. 1786): 172–74.
128. Webster, *Oration on the Declaration of Independence*, 1235–36.

*View of Mulberry Plantation. Expressive of the same social values, an afflu-
ent estate in the Lower South, where most agricultural work was performed by
slaves, looked far different from one in rural New England. At Mulberry Plantation in South Carolina, depicted here in an oil painting, an imposing planter's
house is flanked by two rows of slave houses with thatched roofs, and slaves
are shown walking along the path and doing chores in the yard. Courtesy of the
Gibbes Museum of Art, CAA Collection, Charleston, South Carolina.*

"wealth, power, and higher education" would eventually "have the
ascendancy."[129]

Far more damaging to the positive image of America limned by
its own interpreters during the decades after the Revolution was the
tragic situation of enslaved blacks and Amerindians, albeit neither of
these "others" figured centrally in their intellectual constructions.

But the growing antislavery movement in Europe and America
made it difficult for American observers to ignore the powerful presence of slavery in the new republic or to give that institution a positive
evaluation. They acknowledged that the *"Negroes of Africa"* had "ex-

129. Julien Niemcewicz, *Under Their Vine and Figtree: Travels through America
in 1797–1799*, trans. Metchie J. E. Budka, *Collections of the New Jersey Historical
Society* 14 (1965): 105–6.

perienced the most fatal *disadvantages* by the discovery of America."[130]
That discovery, said Ramsay, had "furnished the temptation" for a
major expansion in "the slavery of the Africans," occasioned "many
long and bloody wars," and visited "such a crowd of woes" upon the
African continent as to raise the "apprehension, that the evil" arising
out of Europe's encounter with America far "outweighed the good."[131]

Nor did many observers deny that their transportation to America
had thrown slaves into "a wretched life in servitude."[132] In America,
wrote Ramsay, slaves had been consigned to the most "humiliating"
and degrading "degree of dependence" upon their masters.[133] "Forced
from their country, their friends, and their families," the "negroes
whom our fathers, and ourselves have enslaved," declared the Connecticut abolitionist Theodore Dwight in 1794, had been "dragged to
the sufferance of slavery, of torture, and of death, with no eye, and
no arm, but the eye and arm of God, to pity, and to punish their
wrongs." Providing them with "no tribunal to listen to their complaints, or to redress their injuries," the slave societies of the United
States, Dwight lamented, recognized "their existence, only for the
purposes of injustice, oppression, and punishment."[134]

American interpreters readily acknowledged that the experiences
of Europeans and Africans in America had been totally opposite.
Whereas Europeans had found "an asylum from persecution" and
want in America, declared the Maryland political leader William
Pinkney in 1790, Africans had discovered only "an eternal grave for
the liberties of themselves and their posterity."[135] "Whilst America
hath been the land of promise to Europeans, and their descendants,"
echoed the Virginia jurist St. George Tucker six years later, "it hath
been the vale of death to millions of the wretched sons of Africa. The
genial light of liberty, which hath here shone with unrivalled lustre
on the former" while conducting them "to the most enviable state of

130. "Observations in Response to an 'Enquiry,'" 306.
131. Ramsay, *History of American Revolution*, 1:14.
132. "Observations in Response to an 'Enquiry,'" 306.
133. Ramsay, *History of American Revolution*, 1:29–30.
134. Theodore Dwight, *An Oration, Spoken before the Connecticut Society, for
the Promotion of Freedom and the Relief of Persons Unlawfully Holden in Bondage*
(Hartford, Conn., 1794), in Hyneman and Lutz, eds., *American Political Writing*,
2:887.
135. William Pinkney, *Speech* (Philadelphia, 1790), 8.

human existence," Tucker asserted, "hath yielded no comfort to the latter, but to them hath proved a pillar of darkness."[136]

Convinced that liberty, security, and peace could "never flourish" in "the bleak and barren soil of Slavery,"[137] some observers decried the fact that the Revolution had not put an end to the institution. They condemned it as "a standing monument of the tyranny and inconsistency of human governments"[138] and pointed out the "horrid inconsistency" of "the American continent . . . fighting for its own liberty with one hand, and holding fast its slaves with the other."[139] "Whilst we were offering up vows at the shrine of Liberty," Tucker observed, "we were imposing upon our fellow men, who differ in complexion from us, a *slavery*, ten thousand times more cruel than the utmost extremity of those grievances and oppressions of which we complained."[140] To declare through "the united voice of America" that all people were "by nature free, and entitled to the privilege of acquiring and enjoying property" while simultaneously passing and enforcing laws by which large numbers of people were "retained in slavery, and dispossessed of all property and all capacity of acquiring any" seemed to the Kentucky abolitionist David Rice to furnish "a striking instance of a people carrying on a war in defence of principles, which they are actually and avowedly destroying by legal force; using one measure for themselves and another for their neighbours."[141]

By such inconsistency, several commentators charged, the American republic had, in William Pinkney's words, fatally "poison[ed] the fair Eden of Liberty with the rank weed of individual bondage" and insured that it would at once be both "the fair temple of freedom, and the abominable nursery of slaves; the school for patriots, and the foster-mother of petty despots; the asserter of human rights, and the patron of wanton oppression."[142] So long as "Domestic despotism" rode "triumphantly over the liberties, and happiness of thousands of our fellow-creatures," the states that still retained slavery, asserted Theodore Dwight, could never be any more than "pretended repub-

136. St. George Tucker, *A Dissertation on Slavery* (Philadelphia, 1796), 9–10.

137. Theodore Dwight, *Oration*, 898.

138. David Rice, *Slavery Inconsistent with Justice and Good Policy* (Augusta, Ky., 1792), in Hyneman and Lutz, eds., *American Political Writing*, 2:866.

139. "Observations in Response to an 'Enquiry,' " 306.

140. Tucker, *Dissertation on Slavery*, 9–10.

141. Rice, *Slavery Inconsistent with Justice*, 866.

142. Pinkney, *Speech*, 6, 8.

lics."[143] Not until slavery had been entirely abolished, agreed Tucker, could "the golden age of our country . . . begin."[144]

As Tucker's remark implies, the widespread depiction of slavery as an anomaly "in this land of liberty" carried with it the hope, if not the conviction, that the days of slavery in the American republic were numbered. Ramsay was not the only one to predict, as he did in 1779, that there would "not be a slave in these states fifty years hence."[145] Many of America's interpreters seemed to have nourished a vague hope that the institution would somehow disappear. In the early 1780s, Stiles took encouragement from the mistaken supposition that, like the Amerindians, the "Africans in America" were "decreasing as rapidly" as the whites were increasing and speculated that this development might eventually lead to the disappearance of both groups and to the abolition of "an unrighteous slavery."[146]

Notwithstanding the frequent use of Amerindians in the emerging iconography of the new nation, they occupied an even smaller place than blacks in the literature of American definition. David Ramsay was one of the few even to acknowledge, much less to lament, that "the neighbourhood of Europeans" had been responsible for all of "the principal causes" that had brought about the "destruction" and "extirpation" of so many of the native inhabitants of America. By abridging the territory of "a people whose mode of life needed an extensive range," white settlers, Ramsay noted, had "By degrees . . . circumscribed" the "old inhabitants . . . within narrower limits" at the same time that "Spiritous liquors, the small pox," and "some [other] strange fatality" were "consistently lessening" their numbers. As a consequence, Ramsay observed, the "names of several nations who in the last century boasted of several thousands, are now known only to those who are fond of curious researches. Many are totally extinct, and others can shew no more than a few straggling individuals, the remnants of their fallen greatness. That so many tribes should, in so short a time, lose both their country, and their national existence," he wrote, was "an event scarcely to be paralleled in the history of the world."[147]

143. Theodore Dwight, *Oration*, 892.

144. Tucker, *Dissertation on Slavery*, 106.

145. Ramsay to Benjamin Rush, June 20, 1779, in Brunhouse, ed., "David Ramsay," 60.

146. Stiles, *United States*, 405, 412.

147. Ramsay, *History of American Revolution*, 1:14, 2:463–64.

The Beckoning West. During the early years of the new American republic, iconographers continued to use Amerindian figures to represent America. In this figure, taken from a map illustration, an Amerindian man and woman with a child on her back are posed with typical American wildlife, including a bison and an opossum, as two Amerindian men pour water, representing the western waters of the Mississippi River, from a cornucopia, emblematic of the rich abundance associated with the interior lands west of the Appalachian Mountains. From Erben Homann, Atlas Geographicus Maior *(Norimbergae, 1759–81). Courtesy of the Library of Congress, neg. no.* LCUSZ62-460872.

But Ramsay's sympathetic appreciation of the situation of the Amerindians was atypical. More commonly, American observers depicted
them as savages whose "distinguishing characteristics" were "Cruelty,
and a base barbarity"[148] and looked forward, with little regret, to
the time when the aboriginal inhabitants would "gradually vanish"
from the continent.[149] Still others, dismissive of the possibility that
an Amerindian culture could have integrity or worth, deplored the
continuing failure of white culture to incorporate Amerindians. Such
people acknowledged that Amerindians found "Civilization . . . such a
perpetual restraint on the[ir] native genius" that most of them seized
"the first opportunity to throw it off and return to a savage life."
But they nevertheless insisted that measures be taken "to civilize and
improve the morals of the *Savage Americans.*"[150]

However regretful some observers may have been because of the
miseries that had been inflicted upon blacks and Amerindians during the three centuries following the initial European encounter with
America, American interpreters of the revolutionary era neither defined America in reference to those groups nor displayed much ac-
knowledgement of their points of view in the intellectual construction
of America. Insofar as they could assess white treatment of these
"others" negatively, most American writers regarded that treatment
and the plight of the others as far less central to the definition of
America than the many achievements of the white settlers and the
exceptional characteristics of their society and its inhabitants.

What they, like their predecessors before the Revolution, found
most impressive about America was its impressive growth and development. Landing in "a dismal wilderness; the habitation of wild
beasts, and of savage men,"[151] European settlers and their descendants, American analysts approvingly recounted, had proceeded to
turn "the wilds of America . . . into beautiful pastures . . . filled with
inhabitants."[152] "Where now the populous city lifts its spires," said
one writer, "the solitary wigwam stood; where commerce spreads its
sails, was seen the bark canoe; and where the sound of industry is
heard, and all the arts of civilized life flourish, indolence, rudeness,

148. "The Former, Present, and Future Prospects of America," 83–84.
149. Stiles, *United States,* 412.
150. "Observations in Response to an 'Enquiry,' " 306–7.
151. Linn, *Blessings of America,* 10.
152. "Enquiry into the Most Advantageous Occupations," 701.

A Settled Rural Landscape. This "Perspective View of the Country between Wilmington and the Delaware" presents a panoramic winter view of a countryside at a still later stage of occupation. Few woods are left, and most of the land has been converted into fields or pasture. With the river in the background, houses, roads, and fences form a settled rural landscape. From Columbian Magazine (October 1789). Courtesy of the Library of Congress, neg. no. LCUSZ62-45578.

and ignorance, held a gloomy sway."[153] "Neither antient nor modern history can produce an example of colonies . . . flourishing with equal rapidity," Ramsay proudly proclaimed. "In the short space of 150 years their numbers increased to three millions, and their commerce to such a degree, as to be more than a third of that of Great Britain. They also extended their settlements 1500 miles on the sea coast, and 300 miles to the westward."[154]

At least "in some degree," even to a person as sensitive to Amerindian misfortune as Ramsay, these achievements seemed to justify "the havoc made among the native proprietors of this new world." "While one set of inhabitants was insensibly dwindling away," he wrote, another was "growing in numbers, and gradually filling up their places." Even more important from the point of view of American writers, Euroamericans, through their steady expansion, were

153. Linn, *Blessings of America*, 10.
154. Ramsay, *History of American Revolution*, 1:19–20.

making great improvements "in the arts of civil and social life" in the spaces vacated by the Amerindians.[155] Even while Amerindians were rejecting this new civilization, Stiles suggested, they could take some consolation for the loss of so much of their lands to the whites from the fact that white occupation and development had significantly raised the price of the lands that remained in Indian hands.[156]

Such Eurocentric judgments rested on the theory of cultural development associated with Scottish conjectural history and discussed in chapter 4. As one writer adumbrated that theory in 1786 in an article in the *Columbian Magazine*, each society "progress[ed] from the savage to the civilized life" through an evolutionary process that could be divided into a series of "regular stages" defined according to the cultural level of the predominant inhabitants. From the aboriginal people to a group of settlers who were "nearly related" to the Amerindians "in their manners" through more and more refined types of settlers, each society, according to this theory, evolved ineluctably in the direction of a "completed" civilization with stable civil government, roads, schools, churches, "spacious stone houses, and highly cultivated farms."[157]

Few Americans involved in the effort to identify America had any doubt that this evolutionary sequence was rapidly changing America for the better. Indeed, they eagerly looked forward to the time when the whole of America's "vast wilderness" would have been similarly converted into "*Eden, and the deserts of the West*"[158] would have been entirely conquered by "the implements of husbandry . . . and the [civilized] virtues which direct them."[159] When they also reflected upon their "successful efforts in the cause of liberty" in winning their independence and forging a continental constitution, considered that Americans enjoyed "advantages, rights and privileges superior to most, if not to all of the human race,"[160] and reviewed the fact that their "progress, since the revolution, in population, in wealth, and in the useful arts" had "never been equalled by any nation, of which we have an account in the records of time,"[161] they found it easy, what-

155. Ibid., 2:464.
156. Stiles, *United States*, 405.
157. "Account of the Progress of Population," 120–21.
158. Rhees, *Good Samaritan*, 12.
159. "Account of the Progress of Population," 120–21.
160. Ramsay, *Oration* (1778), 188, and *Oration* (1794), 191.
161. Moore, *Oration*, 1209.

Seat of Colonel George Boyd. Situated on the sea, the seat of Colonel George Boyd in Portsmouth, New Hampshire, was surrounded not by fields but by beaches, water, and a variety of buildings having to do with fishing and shipping. The three-story house, still a rare phenomenon, and the enclosed formal garden manifest the same pride in the successful pursuit of wealth and the same striving for order and elegance that are represented by the large landed estates elsewhere in the colonies. Dating from 1774, the painting is the work of a unknown artist. Courtesy of the Lamont Gallery, Phillips Exeter Academy, Exeter, New Hampshire.

ever America's remaining deficiencies, to champion a highly positive identity for Americans and their society.

Indeed, as they began from the perspective of the Revolution to articulate their role in enlarging "the happiness of mankind, by regenerating the principles of government in every quarter of the world" and, in the late 1780s, witnessed France "imitating" their "example," these American observers proudly arrogated to themselves "the merit of having enlightened mankind in the art of government." As "the benefits acquired by this country from its independence" and its "excellent constitution" became increasingly obvious to the world, Ramsay predicted, other nations would almost certainly be inspired "to new model their own, on similar principles," with the consequences "that revolutions" would "follow revolutions, till despotism" was "banished from the globe." "The cause of America," Ramsay speculated, would quickly become "the cause of Human Nature" and "extend its influence to thousands who will never see it, and procure them a mitigation of the cruelties and impressions imposed by their arbitrary task-masters."[162]

As the French Revolution began to display an ugly side and many thinkers on both sides of the Atlantic became more skeptical about revolution as a device for salutary change, America's interpreters increasingly recommended to the attention of the rest of the world not just America's "successful exertions in the cause of liberty" but also its peaceful social accomplishments. "The happiness [Americans] enjoyed under our new system, in this new world," where "the poor of all nations" could find refuge, "become independent citizens, on their own lands, and [live] in peaceable enjoyment of every earthly comfort," said Ramsay, rendered America "the noblest experiment ever made for meliorating the condition of man." "If this happiness increases, and extends with the increase," he concluded, it could scarcely fail to bring "incalculable" benefits to the distressed of the Old World. By exhibiting a superior form of social arrangements and serving as a vent for the distressed, America would teach even tyrants that it was in their own best interest to "relax in their oppression—curb their ambition, and study the things that make for the peace and happiness of their subjects." In that way, he thought, the American experience carried within it "a direct tendency to regenerate the old [world], without the horrors and bloodshed of revolutions."[163]

As they contemplated their past glories and future promise, as they developed this conception of America as an exemplary nation and society, American interpreters of the revolutionary generation could scarcely avoid the conclusion that Providence had been active in their behalf. Reflecting upon "how wonderful, how gracious, how glorious" had "been the good hand of God upon us, in carrying us through so tremendous a warfare," and considering that, of "all the forms of civil polity" that had "been tried by mankind," Providence had "reserved" one, and that the best one, "to be realized in America,"[164] they did not find it implausible to speculate that "the American revolution"

162. Ramsay, *Oration* (1794), 196, and *Oration* (1778), 188, 191.
163. Ramsay, *Oration, on the Cession of Louisiana*, 24–25.
164. Stiles, *United States*, 412, 441.

had been "effected by the special agency of God"[165] and that they had benefited from the "special interposition of Providence."[166]

Some evangelical clergy even evoked the millennial expectations of the early puritan settlers and once again touted their country as "God's American Israel" for whom "the honor" of giving "the true religion" to the world had been "reserved."[167] Its "rapid increase of population; and advancement in civilization; its remote situation from the great powers of the old world, with all the advantages it possesses, of climate, soil, and extent of territory; and above all, the excellent constitution of its government, with the prevailing principles of religion among its inhabitants," said the Baptist minister Richard Furman in 1802, were all "favourable to the sentiment" that, "in the scheme of Divine Providence," America had been "originally designed as an asylum for religion and liberty; and a theatre, on which the power and excellence of both were to be exhibited to the greatest advantage." Such thoughts encouraged Americans of Furman's persuasion "to look forward, with pleasing hope, to a day when America will be the praise of the whole earth; and shall participate, largely, in the fulfillment of those sacred prophecies which have foretold the glory of Messiah's kingdom."[168]

Much more pervasive was the secular vision of the United States as a place whose inhabitants would continue to be "the happiest and freest people in the world for ages to come."[169] As they pondered their country's extraordinary achievements during the Revolution and considered its happy social and political state, in which the inhabitants were "more upon an equality in stature and powers of body and mind than the subjects of any government in Europe"[170] and "*liberty and equality* . . . reigned,"[171] they were increasingly drawn to the heady

165. Richard Furman, *America's Deliverance and Duty* (Charleston, S.C., 1802), 7.

166. Ramsay, *Oration* (1778), 189.

167. Stiles, *United States*, 403, 486. On the revival of millennialist thought after 1750 in New England and its spread among evangelicals, see Ruth H. Bloch, *Visionary Republic: Millennial Themes in American Thought, 1756–1800* (Cambridge, 1985).

168. Furman, *America's Deliverance and Duty*, 13–14.

169. Ramsay, *Oration* (1778), 190.

170. Robert Coram, *Political Inquiries* (Wilmington, Del., 1791), in Hyneman and Lutz, eds., *American Political Writing*, 2:801.

171. Rhees, *Good Samaritan*, 17.

notion that, in addition to being the exemplar of liberty, America was destined for an even grander role on the world stage as "the garden of philanthropy, the theatre of virtue, the temple of science," perhaps even "the seat of elysium."[172]

At least temporarily, the new appreciation growing out of the Revolution and its celebration by Old and New World analysts alike had thus contributed powerfully to liberate Americans from the sense of dependence and cultural inferiority that had for so long prevented them from achieving a positive sense of corporate self. As they thus anticipated the "future glory" of their country "and the illustrious figure it will soon make on the theatre of the world," they could scarcely avoid taking a "generous pride" in being . . . Americans."[173] They found it entirely credible to entertain the flattering prediction by the Philadelphia artist Charles Willson Peale that the Pennsylvania statehouse, now Independence Hall, would be "a building more interesting in the history of the world, than any of the celebrated fabrics of Greece and Rome!"[174] "When we compare the growing light and liberty of our country with that of any other, that does or ever did exist: when we reflect upon the probable growth of our empire, in extent, happiness, and fame," one writer announced in the *Columbian Magazine*, "how natural it is for us . . . to regard *America*, as more favoured of heaven, more glorious among men, than a former *Greece*!"[175]

"No new idea," the concept of America as an exceptional place thus grew "increasingly stronger" during and after the Revolution.[176] As writers on both sides of the Atlantic came to identify America in the decades after the Revolution, it appeared even more distinctive than it had to observers in earlier generations. "A country prolific in all the articles either of necessity or luxury; . . . every where furnished with ports and inviting the inhabitants to industry and commerce: together with the extent of fertile soil, which seemed to allow the human species liberty to expand for ages yet to come," wrote the Englishman Thomas Day in 1782, "were such advantages as no period

172. "Observations in Response to an 'Enquiry,' " 308.

173. Ramsay, *Oration* (1778), 190.

174. Edgar P. Richardson, Brooke Hindle, and Lillian B. Miller, *Charles Willson Peale and His World* (New York, 1982), 60, 92, 183.

175. Tilton, "Oration," 373.

176. Edwin G. Burrows, ed., " 'Notes on Settling America': Albert Gallatin, New England, and the American Revolution," *New England Quarterly* 58 (1985): 448–49.

Philadelphia Public Buildings. The small area of Philadelphia represented in this engraving by James Trenchard from a work by Charles Willson Peale included the largest concentration of public buildings anywhere in the United States and was the site of many of the great public transactions of the American Revolution. At the center is the Pennsylvania Statehouse, now Independence Hall, the place in which the federal Constitution of 1787 was composed. To the left are the American Philosophical Society, the Library Company of Philadelphia, and Carpenters' Hall. To the right are the Protestant Episcopal Academy and the courthouse. From Columbian Magazine *(January 1790). Courtesy of the Library Company of Philadelphia.*

of recorded time has ever seen attached to any other people in the universe."[177] "The people of this country," Pinckney concurred, "are not only very different from the inhabitants of any State we are acquainted with in the modern world . . . but . . . distinct from either the people of Greece or Rome, or of any State we are acquainted with among the antients. . . . They are," he emphasized, "perfectly different, in their distinctions of rank, their Constitutions, their manners & their policy."[178]

Stretching back to the first encounters between Europe and America at the end of the fifteenth century, the conceptions of America as a special place and of Americans as different from all other peoples in

177. Thomas Day, *Reflexions upon the Present State of England, and the Independence of America* (London, 1782), 2.

178. Pinckney, Speech, June 25, 1787, 532.

the history of the world were by the end of the revolutionary era more pervasive and more fully elaborated than they had ever been. Throughout the first three centuries of European interactions with America, a sense of exceptionalism had remained the principal component in the identification of America, particularly as it was represented first, after 1606, by the English colonies in North America and then, after 1776, by the republican United States. By 1800, those conceptions, no longer just "speculative Theorem[s],"[179] were deeply etched into the understandings of both Europeans and Americans.

179. Thomas Pownall, *Memorial Addressed to the Sovereigns of America* (London, 1783), 55.

Epilogue

An examination of changing contemporary definitions of America from Columbus's first encounter with the New World in 1492 through the American Revolution and establishment of the American republic during the closing decades of the eighteenth century reveals that the concept of American exceptionalism was by no means, as one historian has recently suggested,[1] entirely a product of the nineteenth century. In one form or another, a notion of distinctiveness was a significant component in intellectual constructs of America from the beginning.

Throughout much of the early modern era, the vast unexplored and, from a European perspective, unorganized spaces of America helped to excite and to sustain the dreams of Europeans for making a new beginning for humanity. As it developed from 1607 to 1775, British North America seemed to contemporary social analysts to provide the exceptional social conditions that made it possible for thousands of free Europeans and Euroamericans to achieve lives of a quality that few of them could have found in the Old World and, in the process, to construct the increasingly elaborate but still distinctive social entities that had come to exist by the late colonial period.

In their efforts to conceptualize and identify these entities, analysts devoted especial attention to explaining the many ways in which they seemed to be exceptional in relation to the societies of the Old World—in particular, the ways in which they appeared both superior and inferior to the metropolitan society to which they were attached. With the American Revolution and its attendant developments beginning in the mid-1770s, the societies and free inhabitants of the United

1. Ian Tyrrell, "American Exceptionalism in an Age of International History," *American Historical Review* 96 (1991): 1035.

States became objects of great curiosity and elicited considerable admiration among British and continental social thinkers. Combined with the success of the Revolution, that admiration helped Americans both to put what they had long regarded as their many continuing deficiencies in a new perspective and to fabricate a more positive sense of collective self. This development in turn functioned to sharpen and intensify the by then old and well-established concept of America as an exceptional country.

The modern concept of American exceptionalism rests on two important propositions. First is the "insistence on American divergence from 'fixed patterns of historical development,'"[2] the idea that, in Daniel Bell's words, America was "an *exempt* nation" that had been freed "from the laws of decadence or the laws of history."[3] Behind this proposition is the assumption that America was born modern without a deeply entrenched traditional socioeconomic and political structure and did not, therefore, ever have to undergo a wrenching transition to modernity. Because America had a largely middle-class society, relatively little residual poverty, high levels of economic opportunity for individuals, and a highly permeable class system, according to this line of analysis, social conflict, contrary to the case in much of Europe throughout the late early modern and modern eras, neither revolved around class struggle nor produced deeply antagonistic and class-based social ideologies. A second proposition underlying contemporary notions of American exceptionalism is the assumption of "American 'national superiority'"[4] contained in the idea of the United States as an *"exemplary* nation."[5]

From the sixteenth century on, the first of these propositions, expressed in the conception of America as a place of vast unoccupied or underutilized spaces where the inhabitants of the Old World could escape its trammels and form a distinctive new social order in which the inhibiting conditions and rules governing the Old World would not apply, was fundamental to the images of America limned by early advocates of colonization and promotional writers. During the eigh-

2. Michael McGerr, "The Price of the 'New Transnational History,'" ibid., 1057.

3. Daniel Bell, "'The Hegelian Secret': Civil Society and American Exceptionalism," in *Is America Different? A New Look at American Exceptionalism*, ed. Byron E. Shafer (Oxford, 1991), 51.

4. McGerr, "Price of the 'New Transnational History,'" 1057.

5. Bell, "'Hegelian Secret,'" 51.

Invitation from America. The conception of America as an asylum for the op-
pressed, impoverished, and frustrated of the Old World assumed that North
America was a welcoming continent of vast proportions that would over time
be slowly and easily yielded up by its Amerindian inhabitants. This notion
was depicted in this engraving, which shows an Amerindian presenting a figure
standing for Euroamerica with a map of tribal lands. In return, she, though hel-
meted, offers liberty and a calumet. At her feet, a cherub measures distances in
the Gulf of Mexico on a map of West Florida, while a map of East Florida stands
by its side. Neptune sits between two jugs, one marked Mississippi and the other
Tombigbee, the two major rivers pouring water into the gulf. A settlement of
Euroamericans can be seen in the distance. From Bernard Romans, A Concise
Natural History of East and West Florida *(New York, 1775). Courtesy of the*
Library of Congress, neg. no. LCUSZ62-45536.

teenth century, several developments, specifically the growth in all
areas of British American colonial life and the behaviors that growth
represented, seemed to provide a strong empirical base for the conceptual ordering of America around an idea of exceptionalism.

As a result, virtually all contemporary analysts who systematically
addressed themselves to the task of defining America during the late
colonial and revolutionary eras contrasted it with the Old World in
terms of its unusual social elasticity and its abundant life chances for
individuals. They depicted America as a place in which a much higher
proportion of the male population than in Europe had independent
freeholds, married, created families, lived without want and in some
abundance, participated in public affairs when they wished, and had all
of the satisfactions—and the anxieties—of being authors and masters
of their own lives and families, independent of the control and the
patronage of others.

At the same time, they characterized American societies in terms
not only of this broad diffusion of property among the free population
but also of several other features that seemed radically to differentiate
them from most societies in the Old World. These included much less
poverty, much less social differentiation, a much less uneven distribution of property, much less rigid social structures, much less patronage
and deference, much less government, much less monolithic and costly
religious establishments, and somewhat less patriarchal authority.

Contemporary observers attributed these striking differences to the
extensive space and the broad opportunities for achieving personal
economic self-sufficiency and independence, political empowerment,

and mastery that America provided for its free inhabitants. These conditions, they emphasized, incited individuals to industry, activity, and schemes of improvement; provided no social foundations for either an aristocracy or the organization of society into legally established ranks; gave government a broad popular base; produced a citizenry with an unusual degree of political enlightenment and an intense preoccupation with the pursuit of domestic happiness; and resulted in a public realm that was laudably inexpensive, small in scope, and relatively unobtrusive.

Some early American historians have recently suggested that these contemporary observers were wrong. Although no one yet seems to have worked out the case against them systematically or in detail, the emerging antiexceptionalist position seems to rest upon two related implications of the findings of early American social historians. The first is that in terms of their organization, values, and patterns of behavior, the societies of colonial British America were from the beginning far more European than many modern advocates of the doctrine of American exceptionalism have allowed. The second is that over time, as a result of the process of society-building that went on during the colonial era—a process variously referred to as Anglicization, Europeanization, or metropolitanization—those societies, at least in their older settled regions, were becoming more and more European in character until by the eve of the American Revolution they were much more like metropolitan Britain than they had ever been before.

But there are several problems with this position. First and most important, it is based upon a misinterpretation of the conclusions of social historians. To take only three examples, the discovery that the age of marriage did not differ radically from England to America does not speak to the contemporary contention that a far larger proportion of the free population in America married. The demonstration that there were considerable gradations of wealth in America does not address the contemporary argument that those gradations were far less extreme than in Europe. The finding that there were conspicuous levels of social dependency among the free populations of the colonies does not belie the contemporary point that, proportionately, those populations contained far fewer dependents than did any society in the Old World.

These and other similar findings do indeed show that many of the more crude and celebratory assessments by post–World War II exponents of American exceptionalism were wrong. Early modern America was not a place in which every free person belonged to the middle class. It was not a society without exploitation, social dependency, substantial differences in resources and power, or social conflict. It was not a place in which free people found it impossible to fail. It was not a place whose populations were consciously fleeing from all aspects of their Old World inheritance.

So far, however, modern social historians have not shown that contemporary participants in the intellectual construction of America were wrong in any of their principal contentions. The empirical base that gave vitality and credibility to contemporary contentions remains almost wholly intact. From what we now know from modern social history, the societies of colonial British and revolutionary America, in comparison with those of the Old World, did indeed, as contemporaries almost universally attested, have significantly higher proportions of property holders, higher rates of family formation, broader opportunities for achieving economic independence and personal empowerment, less poverty, fewer and less rigid social distinctions, and less powerful and less obtrusive political and religious establishments.

A second problem with the antiexceptionalist position is that it has distorted the logic of one of the principal analytic metaphors, specifically the metaphor of Anglicization or Europeanization, employed to conceptualize the process of social change in colonial British America. If over time the New World became more like the Old, if its resemblance to the Old World was greater at point B in the late eighteenth century than it had been at point A a century or a century and a half earlier, these developments did not mean that by the late eighteenth century that process was as yet far enough along to have transformed the New World into or made it identical to the Old, as the many pleas of those advocates for still further Europeanization during the closing years of the eighteenth century and for many decades thereafter emphatically attest.

If the consistent, pervasive, and as yet unrefuted case that early modern analysts made in behalf of American distinctiveness powerfully argues that early American historians ought to continue to take their testimony seriously, an exploration of evolving notions of American exceptionalism between 1492 and 1800 strongly suggests that modern historians of nineteenth- and twentieth-century America have framed their own discussions of the problem of American exceptionalism far too narrowly. If for early American historians the main issue in the discussion of the concept of American exceptionalism has been the broad question of how, in a great variety of ways, America was different from Europe, for historians of later periods of American history the discussion has largely revolved around the single question of whether America, like Europe, was riven with class conflict, whether the number and consciousness of propertyless workers and the strife generated by their conflicts with the possessing class were sufficient to warrant placing the United States in the mainstream of Western historical development as defined by Karl Marx and other modern social analysts.

The many people who contributed to the intellectual construction of America throughout the early modern period and thereby supplied the intellectual roots of the concept of American exceptionalism did not, however, define the question in these restricted terms. Their frame of reference was not modern social aspirations for an egalitarian one-class society without differences in wealth but the complex and highly stratified world of early modern Europe. Indeed, like their Old World contemporaries, they thought of society in terms not of the nineteenth-century concept of class but of the early modern concept of ranks. Their contention was not that America had a *classless*—that is, a middle-class—society, as some exceptionalist historians in the immediate post–World War II era came perilously close to claiming. Rather, they argued that, in contrast to the Old World, America had a *rankless* society in which all free people occupied the same social status in relationship to the law and enjoyed an equality of opportunity to strive for and earn respect.

Accordingly, these early analysts never suggested that within this one-rank society there were not significant gradations of wealth and considerable economic dependency among the free population. They did not contend that widespread economic opportunity had led to universal success or to a conflict-free society. On the contrary, the emphasis they placed on the importance of industry and activity to success implied the inevitability, even the desirability, of a stratified society with the successful—the meritorious—at the top and the unsuccessful—the failures—at the bottom. A situation in which both land and social dependents were the just and proper rewards of industry and merit seemed to them dramatically different from the situation in Europe, where emblems of rank and sureties of legal privilege were often the accoutrements of birth.

In short, contemporary analysts recognized that America had

among its free inhabitants both winners and losers—people of great wealth and no wealth, people with independence and people without it—yet by the existing standards of the Old World they still thought it highly exceptional. An understanding of all the ways in which they thought it exceptional will have to inform the scholarly debate for the modern as well as the early modern period before the question of American exceptionalism can be fully and meaningfully addressed.

The second major component in modern notions of American exceptionalism, the assumption of American national superiority, was a relatively late development during the early modern era. Virtually from the beginnings of settlement, analysts had heralded the colonies as refuges from tyranny and want. As the continuing apologies of people who lived in them and the criticisms of outside observers so thoroughly underlined, however, the emphasis upon the many exceptional qualities of these new early modern American worlds did not automatically suggest that they were in all respects superior worlds.

Only with the Revolution did contemporary observers begin to tout America as a social and political model and thereby, always implicitly and sometimes even explicitly, to claim for it superiority over the Old World. When as a result of their actions during the Revolution Americans started to feel better about themselves and their political societies, their country's interpreters increasingly began to express the hope that their achievements in the social and political realms might be exemplary, serving as a model for Europeans, the first step in a process that would transform the Old World into one resembling the New.

In the new order resulting from that transformation, both American observers and their Old World admirers hoped that in Europe, as in America, people would come to be not only receptive to but eager for change, to be oriented toward the present and the future rather than the past, and to be confident of the efficacy of human reason operating on—and generalizing from—experience to shape that present and that future. Henceforth, they hoped, instead of endeavoring to re-create some past golden age, people in the Old World would create, as those in the New World had already seemingly done, a wholly new world in the future—one in which the inadequacies of past and present worlds would at last be overcome.[6]

6. Durand Echeverria, *Mirage of the West: A History of the French Image of American Society to 1815* (Princeton, 1957), 151–52; Elisabeth Hansot, *Perfec-*

In this process the role of America was to be exemplary. In the sixteenth and seventeenth centuries, America had served as a place on which people in the Old World could project their hopes for recovering a lost world that was somehow simpler, better ordered, more benign, and more virtuous. During the eighteenth century, British North America, reconstituted as the United States after 1776, would become a concrete example encouraging people in the Old World to project their hopes for a better world into the future, and it would thereby make a significant contribution to the Enlightenment and its program of social and political reform.

Notwithstanding the implicit notion of superiority inherent in the emerging concept of America as a model for the rest of the world, as late as 1800 the concept of America as an exceptional entity still lacked that smug conceit of moral superiority that in the decades after World War II would give exceptionalism such deservedly ill fame. Some observers, especially those with millennialist aspirations, were starting to edge in that direction. A few were even beginning to articulate the idea of America—of the United States—as a redeemer nation and of Americans as a chosen people. But this idea remained subordinate to an emphasis upon images of openness, abundance, and individual empowerment of the sort that had been the primary features of American identification during the previous two centuries.

Both the old idea of America's distinctiveness and the new idea of its potential as a model for social and political change rested upon a systematic concentration upon the positive. By and large, the intellectual constructs of which those ideas formed the core ignored the darker side of American life. Rarely acknowledging the violence visited upon Amerindians by European intrusions upon their world, those constructs made little of the fact that the extensive property on which this allegedly model society was based had been expropriated from Amerindians, an enormous number of whom had either died or suffered cultural and physical dislocation in the process. Rarely emphasizing the violence inflicted upon blacks by the institution of chattel slavery and accompanying patterns of racial discrimination, the same constructs revealed little appreciation of the major extent to which the

---

tion and Progress: Two Modes of Utopian Thought (Cambridge, Mass., 1974), 95; Bertrand de Jouvenal, "Utopia for Practical Purposes," in *Utopias and Utopian Thought,* ed. Frank E. Manuel (Boston, 1966), 220; Mircea Eliade, "Paradise and Utopia: Mythical Geography and Eschatology," in ibid., 262–68.

liberty, prosperity, and expansiveness of America's free inhabitants had been purchased at the cost of keeping a large part of its population unfree. Giving little attention to the many social and legal restraints that excluded both Amerindians and blacks from sharing in the benefits enjoyed by Euroamericans, they displayed but slight awareness of the extent to which America had already become a caste society organized around racial categories. This systematic inattention to these "others" in the construction of an American identity and the racial prejudice that underlay that inattention would long continue to inhibit an appreciation of their important contributions in the definition of America.

In these ways, early modern images of America represented a palpable, if rarely acknowledged, deception of both the Old World and the New. Nevertheless, in its newfound role as a harbinger of the future progress to which humanity could aspire, America, as it had come to be conceived of and constructed by the late eighteenth century, finally acquired the respect of its own citizenry and helped Europe to transcend its ancient obsession with the past. By seeming to offer a blueprint for the future, America, with all its radical differences from the Old World, nourished on both sides of the Atlantic during the closing decades of the eighteenth century the confident and widely diffused, if ultimately illusory, notion that the future would be more favorable to humanity than the past.

Index

Abenakis, 64
Abenaki War, 78
Abolition movement, 154–56,
    186–89
Acosta, José de, 117; *Natural and
    Moral History of the Indies*, 22
Activity: ingredient in American
    character, 182–83
African Americans: demographic
    growth of, 80–81, 84–85; role in
    defining America, 93–95, 124,
    154–56, 186–89, 191, 208–9
America: symbolized, 2, 9, 132–33,
    144, 153, 190, 202–3; maps, 2, 14;
    promise of, 2, 25–30, 36, 53–55,
    121, 158–61, 162, 164–67, 174,
    195, 197; comparisons with
    Europe, 3–4, 7, 125–29, 204–5;
    European images of, 10–11, 173;
    novelties of, 11, 13; European
    failure to appreciate, 12–15;
    European interest in, 12–15, 131,
    201; definitions in European
    terms, 14–15, 17; as utopia, 25–
    29, 50–53, 55; as place to be acted
    upon, 29–30, 36; English expecta-
    tions of, 34–62 passim; impact
    on Europe, 48; as land of oppor-
    tunity, 61–62, 72, 134, 142–47,
    174–75, 182, 201–2; favorable
    conditions in, 68–78, 183; failures
    of, 89, 156–58, 164–66, 183; indi-
vidual achievements in, 89–92,
    117–20, 192–94; views of settle-
    ment in, 97, 147, 172, 176, 192;
    individualism in, 112–14; as new
    center of power, 123–24; superi-
    ority to Europe, 132; as model,
    136–41, 173, 194–97, 201, 207–8;
    as asylum, 140, 164, 187; as
    workshop or experimental cul-
    ture, 151–52, 167; favorable self-
    impressions, 162–64, 166–84; as
    exemplary, 201, 207–8; as exempt
    nation, 201–7
American exceptionalism: modern
    work on, 4–7, 201–9; contempo-
    rary concepts of, 45, 64, 88, 96,
    101, 114, 117, 122–23, 126, 130,
    142, 145, 150, 161, 167, 170, 177,
    197–99, 200–209
American Husbandry, 98, 99, 101,
    102, 104, 107, 111, 119, 122, 124
American Magazine, 92
American Philosophical Society, 198
American Revolution, 64, 95, 125,
    130, 131, 136–40, 147, 149, 154,
    155, 157, 173–75, 196, 200–201;
    and American character, 167–68,
    194
Amerindians, 34, 35, 40, 44–45,
    76, 89, 92–94, 102, 186, 192–93,
    208–9; European perceptions of,
    15–25, 28, 29, 30, 48; as savages,

16, 17, 21–22, 93, 117, 191; favorable impressions of, 17–20; as noble savages, 18–20; evangelization of, 20–22, 30, 35–37, 45, 61, 92; defense of, 22–24; extermination of, 32, 189; utopian commonwealth in Mexico, 51; as labor, 54; resistance by, 60, 65; influence on colonizers, 66–67; conflicts with, 78; enslavement of, 78; role in defining America, 92–95, 124, 186, 189–91, 208; costs of expansion for, 93–95, 124
Ames, Nathaniel, 123
Andrae, Johann Valentin, 46
Appleby, Joyce, 5
Archdale, John, 76

Bacon, Francis, 29, 46, 60
Bacon's Rebellion, 65
Baltimore, George Calvert, 1st Baron, 55
Bancroft, George, 3
Barlow, Joel, 168, 180
Bartram, John: view of house and garden, 102–3
Baudet, Henri, 25
Bell, Daniel, 5, 201
Beverley, Robert, 68; History of Virginia, 93
Blair, James, 105
Bolingbroke, Henry St. John, Viscount, 50
Boston, Mass.: view of, 88
Boyd, George: view of house and garden, 194
Brazil, 19
Buffon, Comte de, 128
Burke, Edmund, 101, 117, 119–20, 124
Bushango Tavern: view of, 176
Byrd, William, 80

Caesar, Julius, 17
Campanella, Tommaso, 46
Campbell, Mary B., 12

Carpenter's Hall (Philadelphia), 198
Character, American, 112–14, 145, 149–51, 162, 167–68, 180, 194; as active, 182–83
Charleston, S.C.: view of exchange in, 121
Charles II, 56
Coles, Paul, 9
College of New Jersey: view of, 127
College of William and Mary: view of, 83
Colman, John, 107
Columbian Magazine, 176, 184, 193, 197
Columbus, Christopher, 1–2, 8, 11, 12, 14, 15, 16, 21, 23, 25, 26, 45, 46, 200
Condorcet, Marquis de, 139–42, 144, 152, 156–58
Connecticut, 60, 156; colonial seal of, 43; black population in, 84
Constitution of 1787, 161; convention to draft, 177
Cooper, Sir Anthony Ashley, 56
Cooper, David, 154
Cooper, Peter, 86–87
Cortez, Hernan, 28, 30
Crèvecoeur, Hector St. John de, 104, 107, 109, 111, 114, 116, 118, 119, 122, 142, 145
Culpeper's Rebellion, 65
Culture: contrasts between European and other cultures, 8–10; superiority of European, 45–47; European patterns in America, 63, 117, 129, 184–86, 204–5; backwardness in colonies, 66–68, 128, 150–52, 156, 162, 183–84, 197; four-stage theory of, 117–19, 193

d'Ailly, Pierre: Imago Mundi, 26
Davis, David Brion, 154
Dawkins, Henry, 127
Day, Thomas, 197
De Bry, Theodore, 14, 19, 23, 31, 35

Declaration of Independence, 140, 157, 161

Defoe, Daniel, 69, 71

Delaware: population growth in, 79, 83; black population in, 84

Denton, Daniel, 69, 70, 77

De Pauw, Abbé Corneille, 128

Dickason, Olive Patricia, 20

Drake, Sir Francis, 37

Dwight, Theodore, 187, 188

Dwight, Timothy, 180

Education, 67–68, 186

Elias, Norbert: *The Civilizing Process*, 48

Elliott, J. H., 11, 12, 16, 18, 25

Emigration: as means of resolving English domestic problems, 39–43; of English lower classes, 72

England: expectations of America in, 34–62 passim; new order, 49–50; revolution of 1640s, 50; civil war, 56, 61; capture of Canada, 83

Equality, 3, 106–7, 128, 144, 177–82, 204

Erikson, Erik H., 106

Europe: comparisons with America, 3–4, 7, 125–29, 204–5; images of America in, 10–11, 123; failure to appreciate America, 12–15; interest in America, 12–15, 131, 201; definitions of America, 14–15, 17; perceptions of Amerindians, 15–25, 28, 29, 30, 48; culture of, 45–47; expansion of, 47; impact of America on, 48–50; and patterns of culture in America, 63, 117, 129, 184–86, 204–5; superiority of America to, 132

Exchange: building in Charleston, S.C., 121

Expansion: European, 47; American, 64–65, 78–89, 95–102, 106–7, 110, 192–93

Faneuil Hall, Boston, 120–21

Fenton, Edward, 37

Filmer, Sir Robert, 50

Fleming, John, 64

Four-stage theory of cultural development, 117–19, 193

Franklin, Benjamin, 89, 93, 98–99, 107, 118–19, 122, 123, 142

French Revolution, 195

Frobisher, Martin, 37

Furman, Richard, 196

Gallatin, Albert, 141, 151

Garasu, 19

Georgia, 90; expansion in, 79, 83; slavery in, 84

Gill, Moses: seat of, 181

Glorious Revolution, 65

Gordon, Peter, 59

Government, 76, 178, 204; American principle of, 135–36, 169–71

Greenblatt, Stephen, 12

Grenville, George, 90

Grotius, Hugo de, 117

Hakluyt, Richard: "Discourse of Western Planting," 36; views on America, 36–46, 53, 61, 117

Hakluyt, Richard (lawyer), 39, 40

Harrington, James, 50; *Oceania*, 56, 183

Harrison, Peter, 126

Hawke, John, 114

Hercules, 77

Hexter, J. H., 26

Hillsborough, Wills Hill, Viscount, 122

Hobbes, Thomas, 18, 117

Hodgen, Margaret T., 17, 18, 20

Holme, Thomas: design by, 57

Honour, Hugh, 32

Hulme, Peter, 44–45

Identity: American, 1, 3–4, 7, 96, 112–14, 145, 149–51, 162, 167–68, 180, 182–86, 194

Immigration: to colonies, 80, 84

Independence, individual: and creation of America, 75–78, 89, 109, 111, 134, 145–47, 150, 181, 182, 202

Industriousness: and creation of America, 73, 175–77, 180, 182, 191, 204

Ingersoll, Charles Jared, 177

Jamaica, 23

James II, 56

Jennings, Samuel, 157

Johnson, Samuel, 57

Kent, James, 169–70, 179, 183

King Philip's War, 65

Knox, William, 112

Lach, Donald F., 10

Las Casas, Bartolomé de, 22, 24

Law, 148, 157–58, 174

Leisler's Rebellion, 65

Leitch, Thomas, 121

Le Moyne, Jacques, 35

Le Roy, Louis, 11

Levin, Harry, 14

Liberty, 76, 128, 135–36, 140–42, 149, 151, 158–59, 163–64, 167, 171–74, 182–83, 193, 196–97; and slavery, 154–56, 188; symbolized, 157; and government, 168–69

Library Company of Philadelphia, 157, 198

Locke, John, 49, 56, 117; *Second Treatise of Government*, 52

Logan, James, 106

Louis XIV, 56

Mably, Abbé, 139

Magellan, Ferdinand, 14

Mandeville, Bernard, 49

Mandeville, Sir John, 10

Marriage age, 204

Martyr, Peter, 17

Marx, Karl, 206

Marx, Leo, 52–53

Maryland, 90; as new feudal society, 55–56; growth in, 83; slavery in, 84; state seal of, 164–65

Maryland Protestant Association, 65

Massachusetts, 60; black population growth in, 81

Mather, Cotton, 68

Mayhew, Jonathan, 92

Mazzei, Philip, 139, 142–43, 149, 154–56

Mein, John, 64

Mendieta, Geronimo de, 51

Mexico, 23–24; conquest of, 30; as utopia, 51

Montaigne, Michel Eyquem de, 25, 32

Montanus, Arnoldus, 40

More, Sir Thomas, 26–29, 32, 48, 50–51, 52

Mulberry Plantation, S.C.: view of, 186

Murrin, John, 6, 58

Nairne, Thomas, 75

Nassau Hall: view of, 127

New England, 46, 90, 101, 103; puritans, 63; degeneracy in, 68; expansion in, 79, 80

New Hampshire: growth in, 83

New Jersey, 90, 183; favorable depiction of, 68, 69; population growth in, 79, 83

Newport, R.I., 126; city hall, 113

New York, 90; code of arms, 44; favorable depiction of, 69; population growth in, 79, 83; black population growth in, 81, 84

Norris, John, 69, 70, 72, 73

North Carolina, 90, 183; unrest in, 65, 114; expansion in, 79, 83; slavery in, 84

Oglethorpe, James, 59

O'Gorman, Edmundo, 1, 125
Opportunity. *See* America: as land of opportunity

Paine, Thomas, 131–38, 140, 141, 142, 145, 164–66, 185; *Common Sense*, 132, 135, 163, 166; *The American Crisis*, 135; *The Rights of Man*, 135, 137; *Letter to Abbé Raynal*, 166
Parker, James, 44
Peake, James, 146
Peale, Charles Willson, 197
Penn, William, 56, 70, 72, 75
Pennsylvania, 60, 90, 102, 103, 183; social experimentation in, 56; favorable depiction of, 68, 69, 70, 72; population growth in, 79, 83; black population in, 84; state seal, 137
Peru, 23–24; conquest of, 30
Philadelphia, 177; design of, 57; views of, 86–87, 190
Philip II, 39
Pinckney, Charles, 177, 178, 182, 198
Pinkney, William, 187, 188
Pizarro, Francisco, 30
Plantations, colonies as, 39–44, 60
Plato, 161
Polo, Marco, 10
Population growth, 65–66, 79–81, 83–87, 100, 123; among blacks, 80–81, 84–85
Poresio, Francisco, 23
Portsmouth, N.H., 194
Portuguese: in Brazil, 19
Potter, Jim, 80
Pownall, Thomas, 138, 140, 143, 145–51, 155–60, 180
Price, Richard, 138–41, 143, 147, 150–52, 155–60
Promotional literature, 68–78, 88–89, 95
Prosperity, 102–6
Public expenditures, 100–101

Public realm, 112–14; small size in colonies, 72–73
Pufendorf, Samuel, 117
Purchas, Samuel, 46
Puritans, 63; creation of new society by, 55, 58

Quilt: depictions of America on, 97
Quiroga, Vasco de, 51

Raleigh, Sir Walter, 34, 35
Ramsay, David, 168, 170–71, 174, 178, 180, 183, 187, 189, 191–95
Rastell, John, 26
Raynal, Guillaume Thomas François, 139, 143, 150, 159
Rebellion, in colonies, 65
Redwood, Abraham, 126
Redwood Library (Newport, R.I.), 126
Reformation, Protestant, 49, 135
Renaissance, 13; discoveries, 2
Republicanism, 112
Rhode Island: black population in, 84
Ribault, Jean, 35, 37
Rice, David, 188
Robinson Crusoe, 125
Ronsard, Pierre, 18
Rowe, John H., 16
Rubruck, William of, 10
Ryan, Michael T., 11, 12, 16, 17

Sahagún, Bernardino de, 24
Savannah, Ga.: view of, 59
Scammell, Geoffrey, 20, 26
Scientific revolution, 46–47
Shakespeare, William, 52
Sheps, Arthur, 138
Slavery, 78, 93–94, 95, 111, 124, 128, 186–89, 208–9; attack on, 154–56
Slavin, Arthur J., 26
Smith, Adam, 93, 98–100, 106, 109–12, 117, 121, 123, 124, 142; *Wealth of Nations*, 90, 96

Smith, Robert, 127
Smith, Dr. William, 105
Social conditions, in America, 143, 151, 200
Social experimentation, in colonies, 54–61; failures of, 58–61; failure to solve England's problems, 61
Social mobility, in America, 102–4, 128, 134, 201–2
Society, in America: elites, 67, 107–9; differences from European, 107–10, 143; empowered free males in, 110–13; experimentation with, 151–52; stratification of, 185–86, 202, 206, 209
South Carolina, 90, 101, 102–3, 106, 183; unrest in, 65; favorable depiction of, 69, 70, 72, 73, 75, 76; conflict in, 78; expansion in, 79, 83; slavery in, 84
Spain: colonization of America by, 14, 22–24, 28–33, 34, 38, 40, 100
Spanish cruelty: legend of, 32, 35–36
Stamp Act Crisis, 163
Stiles, Ezra, 167, 170, 182, 183, 189, 193
Stradanus, Johanes, 9
Straet, Jan van der (Johanes Stradanus), 9
Suffrage, 183
Swift, Jonathan, 28, 50

Tacitus, 17, 181
Taxation, in colonies, 73, 100
Tempest, The, 52–54, 125
Tennent, William, 127
Thomas, Gabriel, 69, 70, 72
Thomas, Keith, 48
Tobacco plantation, 71, 74
Tobler, John, 91
Tocqueville, Alexis de, 4, 143
Todorov, Tzvetan, 12, 21, 24, 25
Towns, in colonies, 86–87, 101

Trenchard, John, 198
Tryon, William, 114
Tryon's Palace (New Bern, N.C.), 114–15
Tucker, St. George, 187–89
Tudors, 49
Turgot, M., 139–41, 155, 158
Turner, Frederick Jackson, 3
Tuscarora War, 65

Usselinx, William, 57
Utopia, 25, 26–27, 32, 58
Utopianism: and America, 26–29, 50–53, 55
Utrecht peace settlement, 78, 95

Van Meurs, Jacob, 40–41
Vespucci, Amerigo, 9, 14, 26
Villegaignon, Nicholas, 37
Virginia, 54, 60, 67, 68, 80, 82, 90, 101, 102, 103; use of Amerindian labor in, 54; expansion in, 79, 83; slavery in, 84, 154, 156
Virginia Company, 54
Vitoria, Francisco de, 22

Walker, Perez: mantle scene, 108
War: in colonies, 78, 81–83, 86
Wealth: America as source of, 30–33, 38–45, 61–62, 102–6, 142, 164; distribution of, 128, 177–82, 201–4, 206
Webster, Noah, 170
Whately, Thomas, 90
Whitaker, Benjamin, 106
Williams, Samuel, 163, 164, 173, 175, 178, 180, 182
Williamsburg, Va.: views of, 82
Winthrop, John, 55

Yamassee War, 65, 78

Zavala, Silvio, 51